W9-BRB-465

FEMINIST QUOTATIONS

FEMINIST QUOTATIONS

Voices of Rebels,

Reformers,

and Visionaries

COMPILED BY

Carol McPhee

Ann FitzGerald

Thomas Y. Crowell, Publishers
Established 1834
New York

Acknowledgments to publishers and authors for permission to reprint copyrighted materials will be found beginning on page 249.

FEMINIST QUOTATIONS: VOICES OF REBELS, REFORMERS, AND VISIONARIES. Copyright © 1979 by Carol McPhee and Ann FitzGerald. All rights reserved. Printed in the United States of America. No part of this book may be used or reproduced in any manner whatsoever without written permission except in the case of brief quotations embodied in critical articles and reviews. For information address Thomas Y. Crowell, Publishers, 521 Fifth Avenue, New York, N.Y. 10017. Published simultaneously in Canada by Fitzhenry & Whiteside Limited, Toronto.

FIRST EDITION

Designed by Stephanie Winkler

Library of Congress Cataloging in Publication Data

Main entry under title:
Feminist quotations.
   Includes indexes.
   1. Feminism—Quotations, maxims, etc. I. McPhee, Carol. II. FitzGerald, Ann.
HQ1154.F446   1979   301.41′2′08   78–3308
ISBN 0–690–01770–7

79 80 81 82 83 10 9 8 7 6 5 4 3 2 1

. . . so long as there stands yet in the
way any wrong so cankerous as reprisal for
free speech, so long must the woman-skald
of the future cry unwelcome truth in the
market-place.

ELIZABETH ROBBINS,
Ancilla's Share, 1924

Contents

Preface

In 1848, Emily Collins, a woman living in an isolated rural village, began to read the works of the feminists of her day. "When I . . . found," she wrote to the leaders of the movement, "that other women entertained the same thoughts that had been seething in my own brain, and realized that I stood not alone, how my heart bounded with joy!"

Times have not changed.

Today, feminists, recognizing that their own perceptions require validation, that their stores of courage and determination need replenishment, turn to the words of other women for support. They read. They listen to speeches. They attend meetings. They remember the sentences of other women—the apt quotations of feminist principle, the special insight, the weapon of wit— and they repeat them, to set the tone of a book, to underscore points in speeches, to help each other find relief in laughter.

Short quotations, we ourselves discovered, proved effective in the writing and speaking which our participation in the women's movement required. However, because most standard collections of quotations ignore feminist writers, we were often frustrated in our attempts to find the appropriate quotation for our purpose quickly. And so we began to make our own casual collection, copying out short prose statements whenever we encountered them as epigraphs in the works of contemporary writers. But, stimulating as these quotations were, they often appear with only attributions to the authors, a serious obstacle to those who wish to read the entire works from which they were excerpted. We also noticed a concentration on the famous leaders of the women's movement, while important thinkers whose works are not easily available were neglected.

So we decided to expand our casual collection into a reference book to provide a wide-ranging, accurate source of quotations for speakers, researchers, and those writing about the women's movement. And for all of us—for all women—we hoped to provide a book that would give feminists ready access to the perceptions of our sisters.

Feminist Quotations provides selections from the literature of the women's movement over a period of two hundred years, a list that includes eighteenth-century feminists such as Abigail Adams and Mary Wollstonecraft and modern writers such as Brownmiller, Friedan, Greer, and Rich. With one exception, these feminist, nonfiction prose quotations are excerpted from works originally published in English. The exception is Simone de Beauvoir's *The Second Sex* because of its powerful influence on the rebirth of the feminist movement in the 1960's. We have excluded feminist statements by such men as John Stuart Mill and Henry Blackwell because we believe they are adequately represented elsewhere.

In spite of these restrictions, nearly three hundred feminist writers and speakers are included in the collection. Some, like Stanton, Sanger, and Steinem, are frequently quoted by feminists. But to our great delight, our search led us to many voices unheard since their own day: to Lillie Devereux Blake who, in the late nineteenth century, hired a hall so she could reply, weekly, to the misogynist rector of New York's prestigious Trinity Church; to Lady Agnes Geraldine Fox-Pitt-Rivers Grove, who in 1908 wrote an urbane commentary, *The Human Woman;* and to Teresa Billington-Greig, who broke with English militants when they began to violate democratic principles.

Included here are the words of many unfamiliar American women who worked for women's rights during the long struggle from 1840 to 1921, the period covered in the six-volume *History of Woman Suffrage.* The wisdom of these women is preserved for us because the editors of the *History* believed that every woman's part in the movement, however occasional, should be recorded.

The title of the *History* is misleading, for it is far more than the annals of American women's struggle for the franchise. Susan B. Anthony, who organized the project, clipped news stories, saved minutes of every women's meeting that came her way, and gently nagged others to send materials they had saved. The *History* is a comprehensive collection of primary sources that detail eight decades of political activism, in towns and cities all over the nation, by women determined to break down all barriers to social, economic, and sexual equality with men. There we can read the major parts of Stanton's addresses to the New York State legislature, trying to persuade male politicians to modify laws governing married women's property; or a letter from Clara Nichols, of Pomo, California, who could not make the 3,000-mile trip to the Centennial Convention in Philadelphia but wanted her sisters to know what women in the mountains of Mendocino County were thinking.

Like the editors of the *History*, we wanted to include a great variety of contemporary spokeswomen and make available again important feminist statements from newsletters and periodicals that had short but vital lives in the 1960's and early 1970's. We do offer a great many modern quotations, but we regret that we had to eliminate some fine selections because we were unable to locate their authors for permission to quote extensively.

As we prepared the collection, we began to appreciate the variety of styles women during the last two hundred years have used to express themselves, from flat, practical Yankee speech to the precise, analytical, and often angry prose of modern academic women.

We enjoy the contrast between two great nineteenth-century speakers: Lucy Stone, who addresses her listeners in direct, honest sentences, and Angelina Grimké, who reflects, even in her letters, the emotional rhetoric of revival preachers. We also admire the spare sentences of the English suffragette Hannah Mitchell, as well as the powerful, cumulative sentences of our contemporary Susan Brownmiller. Occasionally, the sentences, for example, of Olive Schreiner or of Jane Addams seem excessively intricate; yet because these women express original and influential ideas, we feel we must include them. On the other hand, we had difficulty deciding which of the witty commentaries of their contemporary, Charlotte Perkins Gilman, to exclude.

With Susan B. Anthony we had two problems. First, we had to determine which of her sixty years of pithy, loving, and sometimes abrupt statements on civil rights, women's lives, and women's politics best represent her personality and the breadth of her intellectual involvement in the movement. Then we had to try to separate the crisp, deliberately colloquial dynamics of her words from statements which have been attributed to her only by legend. Unfortunately, we may not always have succeeded in distinguishing between Anthony's own words and the paraphrases of her biographer, Ida Husted Harper; the reports of convention secretaries; or the many speeches written for her by Elizabeth Cady Stanton, whose love for alliteration and subtle mockery suggests the source of authorship.

Of the nineteenth-century writers, Elizabeth Cady Stanton has become our favorite, not only because she writes pointedly on nearly every topic mentioned in our table of contents, but because she obviously enjoys the task of playing with words, passion, and wit as if they were three of her seven children. We find the moderns, sometimes bluntly phrased or outrageously expressed, so close to our own experience that we can have no favorites. By including more quotations from one modern writer than from another, we make no statement about our attitudes toward them, their importance in the women's movement, or their influence. Some writers may appear in only one or two sections because, like Margaret Sanger, they confine their analyses to quite specific areas of women's lives. Others appear frequently throughout the book, and still others are represented by just one quotation.

As we studied our collection, we found that feminist statements, no matter when uttered, fall into two major categories, which now constitute the major divisions of this book: "The Feminist As Critic" (Part I) and "The Feminist As Rebel and Visionary" (Part II). Within this division, we have organized the quotations into sections that reflect the fundamental interests of the women's movement: cultural attitudes, the various forms of male oppression, sex, marriage, motherhood, the aims of feminist political activity, self-determination, self-transcendence, and visions of the future. To give historical perspective to these themes, we have presented the quotations chronologically within each section.

This arrangement, besides demonstrating the range and diversity of the feminist movement, also reveals the constancy of themes in the long struggle. In voices that confront men with their history of domination and promises unkept, the grievances of past writers are discouragingly echoed in the words of contemporary feminists. Visions of the 1850's are still only visions. We believe it is a commentary on our society that women today cannot look back on their eighteenth- and nineteenth-century predecessors with that nostalgic respect people reserve for successful reformers. Unfortunately, even the earliest feminists still speak for the present.

We hope that we have made this book more than a practical reference, that anyone interested in social history will find the collection illuminating. We have also wanted to provide for the women of our time—particularly those who rebel and are isolated by rebellion—a consciousness of sisterhood with the women who have gone before, and a sense of reassurance and reaffirmation in the multitude of voices encouraging us to become a force in history.

We thank the many friends who have helped us in one or many phases of making this compilation. Their support, their skills, and their encouragement have been essential contributions. Special thanks must go to Elizabeth Ent, David Grant, Dan Krieger, Eva Logan, and Harriet McLoon; to Jule Ann McPhee, Barbara Spiegleman, and Smoak; to Mary Richards, Louise Moon, and Ann and Jeanne Wassam; to Jeanne and Tom Boyd; to Noelle, Beth, Claire, and Harvey Norton; and to the Taber family.

Carol McPhee
Ann FitzGerald

A Note to the Reader

Within its larger, two-part division (The Feminist As Critic and The Feminist As Rebel and Visionary), the quotations in this book are organized into chapters and subchapters by subjects. Each such section is arranged chronologically by the original dates of the quotations, so that the reader can get some overview of feminist thinking on that subject, sometimes from 1776 (the date of our earliest entry) to the present.

Because many of the quotations deal with more than one subject, we decided to classify each according to what we see as its major emphasis. We have supplied a subject index to direct readers to the secondary topics of quotations and to subjects that are not covered in the chapter and subchapter titles or that cut across them (as "the black woman" or "husbands"). The author index can be used to find all our selections from the works of particular feminists.

Peculiarities and apparent inconsistencies in some of the citations arise out of the sources themselves. For example, a newsletter or periodical of the late 1960's and the early 1970's may have been published at first in issues identified only by dates, but later with the more formal distinction of volume numbers.

One of our vital sources, *History of Woman Suffrage*, is such an unorthodox collection that some description of its organization will be helpful to an understanding of our citations for it. The six volumes of the *History* were published at irregular intervals: 1881, 1882, 1887, 1902, and the last two in 1922. The first three volumes were edited jointly by Elizabeth Cady Stanton, Susan B. Anthony, and Matilda Joslyn Gage; volume IV by Anthony and Ida Husted Harper; and the last two by Harper alone. Each volume has an introduction, in which the editors comment upon events of preceding years (in the first volume, those leading up to the convention at Seneca Falls in 1848), then proceeds chronologically through conventions, meetings, and gatherings of all sorts, recording their minutes, speeches, reports, resolutions, extemporaneous comments from the floor, and sometimes, lists of absolutely everybody who came and did or just came and sat. Interspersed with these materials are miscellaneous speeches and essays, reminiscences, letters, accounts of conversations, and even detailed reports of birthday parties for notables.

The materials are presented with much editorial inconsistency. Some pieces have titles, others do not; some women are identified only by their last names, or by their husbands' names. The contents of some of the volumes do not always reflect the chronology of the publication dates: When the editors came upon items that fell within the time span of an already published volume, they simply put them into the book then being prepared. These idiosyncrasies are reflected in the citations.

When a quotation from the *History* is attributed to a particular feminist, her name appears first in the citation, then the title of the speech or article (if the *History* supplies one), the date it was delivered or written, and the *History*'s title, volume number, and date. For such quotations we have not extended the citations by naming the editors of the volumes; only when a quotation is from an introduction or other unsigned editorial comment are the editors' names given.

PART I

The Feminist As Critic

I ask no favors for my sex. I surrender not our
claim to equality. All I ask of our brethren is
that they will take their feet from off our necks.
SARAH GRIMKÉ, *Letters on the Equality of the
Sexes*, 1838

1   Creatures of Men

Inferior Beings

. . . in the new code of laws, which I suppose it will be necessary for you to
make, I desire you would remember the ladies, and be more generous and favorable to them than [were] your ancestors. Do not put such unlimited power
into the hands of the husbands. Remember all men would be tyrants if they
could.

ABIGAIL ADAMS, to John Adams, 1776, *Familiar Letters of John Adams and
His Wife, Abigail Adams, During the Revolution*, ed. Charles Francis Adams, 1876

Considering the length of time that women have been dependent, is it surprising that some of them hug their chains, and fawn like the spaniel?

MARY WOLLSTONECRAFT, *A Vindication of the Rights of Woman*, 1792.

. . . how can a being be generous who has nothing of its own? or virtuous, who
is not free?

Ibid.

The being who patiently endures injustice, and silently bears insults, will soon
become unjust, or unable to discern right from wrong.

Ibid.

. . . supposing, no very improbable conjecture, that a being only taught to
please must still find her happiness in pleasing;—what an example of folly,
not to say vice, will she be to her innocent daughters!

Ibid.

Women are told from their infancy, and taught by the example of their mothers, that a little knowledge of human weakness, justly termed cunning, softness of temper, *outward* obedience, and a scrupulous attention to a puerile kind of propriety, will obtain for them the protection of man; and should they be beautiful, everything else is needless for at least twenty years of their lives.
Ibid.

If we surrender the right to *speak* to the public this year, we must surrender the right to petition next year and the right to *write* the year after. . . . What *then* can *woman* do for the slave when she is herself under the feet of man and shamed into *silence*?
ANGELINA GRIMKÉ, letter to Theodore Weld and John Greenleaf Whittier, 1837, *Letters of Theodore Weld, Angelina Grimké Weld, and Sarah Grimké, 1822–1844*, ed. Gilbert H. Barnes and Dwight L. Dumond, 1965

He [man] has done all he could to debase and enslave her mind; and now he looks triumphantly on the ruin he has wrought, and says, the being he has thus deeply injured is his inferior.
SARAH GRIMKÉ, Letter II, 1837, *Letters on the Equality of the Sexes*, 1838

"Her influence is the source of mighty power." This has ever been the flattering language of man ever since he laid aside the whip as a means to keep woman in subjection. He spares her body; but the war he has waged against her mind, her heart, and her soul, has been no less destructive to her as a moral being.
Ibid., Letter III, 1837

"Rule by obedience and by submission sway," or in other words, study to be a hypocrite, pretend to submit, but gain your point, has been the code of household morality which woman has been taught.
Ibid.

. . . women being educated, from earliest childhood, to regard themselves as inferior creatures, have not that self-respect which conscious equality would engender, and hence when their virtue is assailed, they yield to temptation with facility, under the idea that it rather exalts than debases them, to be connected with a superior being.
Ibid., Letter VIII, 1837

. . . I believe the laws which deprive married women of their rights and privileges, have a tendency to lessen them in their own estimation as moral and responsible beings . . .
Ibid., Letter XII, 1837

4

Deeply, deeply do I feel the degradation of being a woman—not the degradation of being what *God* made woman, but what *man* has made her.
> LYDIA MARIA CHILD, letter to Angelina Grimké, 1838, in Miriam Gurko, *The Ladies of Seneca Falls*, 1974

Man has gone but little way; now he is waiting to see whether Woman can keep step with him; but, instead of calling out, like a good brother, "You can do it, if you only think so," or impersonally, "Any one can do what he tries to do," he often discourages with school-boy brag: "Girls can't do that; girls can't play ball." But let any one defy their taunts, break through and be brave and secure, they rend the air with shouts.
> MARGARET FULLER, *Woman in the Nineteenth Century*, 1845

Woman by being thus subject to the control, and dependent on the will of man, loses her self-dependence; and no human being can be deprived of this without a sense of degradation. The law should sustain and protect all who come under its sway, and not create a state of dependence and depression in any human being.
> MARIANA JOHNSON, "Memorial to the Constitutional Convention of Ohio," 1850, *History of Woman Suffrage*, I, 1881

Man inflicts injury upon woman, unspeakable injury in placing her intellectual and moral nature in the background, and woman injures herself by submitting to be regarded only as a female.
> ABBY H. PRICE, address, *Proceedings of the Woman's Rights Convention, Held at Worcester, October 23 & 24, 1850, 1851*

Our republic has hitherto developed something akin to a savage lordliness in the other sex, in which he is to usurp all the privileges of freedom, and she is to take as much as she can get, after he is served.
> ELIZABETH OAKES SMITH, *Woman and Her Needs*, 1851

. . . even here, in this far-famed land of freedom . . . even here, woman. . . has yet to plead for her rights, nay for her life. For what is life without liberty, and what is liberty without equality of rights? And as for the pursuit of happiness, she is not allowed to choose any line of action that might promote it; she has only thankfully to accept what man in his magnanimity decides as best for her to do, and this is what he does not choose to do himself.
> ERNESTINE L. ROSE, Second National Convention, Friends of Woman Suffrage, 1851, *History of Woman Suffrage*, I, 1881

... for man does not yet feel, that what is unjust for himself, is also unjust for woman.

> ELIZABETH CADY STANTON, letter to Woman's Rights Convention, 1852, *Woman's Rights Tracts*, No. 10, n.d.

Poor human nature wants something to look down on. No privileged order ever did see the wrongs of its own victims . . .

> ELIZABETH CADY STANTON, American Equal Rights Association Convention, 1867, *History of Woman Suffrage*, II, 1882

The strong, natural characteristics of womanhood are repressed and ignored in dependence, for so long as man feeds woman she will try to please the giver and adapt herself to his condition.

> ELIZABETH CADY STANTON, "Address to the Woman Suffrage Convention," 1869, *History of Woman Suffrage*, II, 1882

... remember that the most ignorant men are ever the most hostile to the equality of women, as they have known them only in slavery and degradation.

> Ibid.

Women satisfied to endure, or see endured, such wrongs, exhibit the enervating effects of the false system under which they have lived. They manifest that servile condition that always attends subserviency.

> VIRGINIA PENNY, *Think and Act*, 1869

And here is the secret of the infinite sadness of women of genius; of their dissatisfaction with life, in exact proportion to their development. A woman who occupies the same realm of thought with man, who can explore with him the depths of science, comprehend the steps of progress through the long past and prophesy those of the momentous future, must ever be surprised and aggravated with his assumptions of headship and superiority, a superiority she never concedes, an authority she utterly repudiates. Words can not describe the indignation, the humiliation a proud woman feels for her sex in disfranchisement.

> E. C. STANTON, S. B. ANTHONY, M. J. GAGE, eds., *History of Woman Suffrage*, II, 1882

... it must be so delightful to be told that one is greater and grander than another simply because one has black eyes, or brown hair, or from the other physical accident of sex, not because one is really nobler, abler, or more capable. So we find men in all ages gladly accepting any reason, however slender;

any interpretation, however lame, that will enforce their authority over women.

LILLIE DEVEREUX BLAKE, *Women's Place Today*, 1883

The first event engraved on my memory was the birth of a sister when I was four years old. . . . I heard so many friends remark, "What a pity it is she's a girl!" . . . I did not understand at that time that girls were considered an inferior order of beings.

ELIZABETH CADY STANTON, *Eighty Years and More*, 1898

And thus it ever is: so long as woman labors to second man's endeavors and exalt his sex above her own, her virtues pass unquestioned; but when she dares to demand rights and privileges for herself, her motives, manners, dress, personal appearance, and character are subjects for ridicule and detraction.

Ibid.

Not woman, but the condition of woman, has always been a doorway of evil.

CHARLOTTE PERKINS GILMAN, *Women and Economics*, 1898

If woman alone had suffered under these mistaken traditions, if she could have borne the evil by herself, it would have been less pitiful, but her brother man, in the laws he created and ignorantly worshipped, has suffered with her. He has lost her highest help; he has crippled the intelligence he needed; he has belittled the very source of his own being and dwarfed the image of his Maker.

CLARA BARTON, First International Woman Suffrage Conference, 1902, *History of Woman Suffrage*, V, 1922

Who has not noticed that it is always the least virile and manly amongst the men who are so bent upon "keeping women in their proper place" (what they really want, of course, is to keep them out of it), and the least womanly amongst the women who are willing to abdicate their God-given right of human will in favour of an unlovely subservience to the mere brute strength of the male.

LADY GROVE, *The Human Woman*, 1908

Women are regarded, and too often regard themselves, as drones, or as mere accessories to the utility, the convenience, or the comfort of males.

Ibid.

... that many women are unconscious of the great force working against them does not prevent it from being a fact; and, if it be a fact, from its having a damaging influence on women in particular, and on the race in general.
Ibid.

No passing of legal enactments can set free a woman with a slave mind.
TERESA BILLINGTON-GREIG, *The Militant Suffrage Movement,* 1911

Doubtless every privileged class that ever existed has been firmly persuaded that the continuance of its privileges was necessary to the truest welfare of the community of which it formed a part.
GERTRUDE S. MARTIN, "The Education of Women and Sex Equality," *The Annals of the American Academy of Political and Social Science,* LVI, November 1914

There were tales of men who, deprived by circumstances of everything but their power over wife and child, found their greatest pleasure in the exercise of this power . . .
KATHARINE ANTHONY, *Mothers Who Must Earn,* 1914

The worser effect on both man and woman is found where woman's acceptance of insult, having grown mechanical, is eventually unconscious.
ELIZABETH ROBBINS, *Ancilla's Share,* 1924

A thousand voices cried . . . [woman] down—she hadn't enough children; she had too many; she was an ape; she was a dressed-up doll; she was a Puritan; she was an immoral minx; she was uneducated; they had taught her too much. Her pinched waist was formerly abused—now it was her slim and boyish body. Eminent surgeons committed themselves to the view that the boyish figure with its pliable rubber . . . corselets would be the ruin of the race, that race which had been superbly undegenerate through four centuries of armour-plate corset and eighteen-inch waists . . .
DORA RUSSELL, *Hypatia,* 1925

Their [women's] minds, their emotions, their creative impulses have been more savagely distorted through the years than the feet of Chinese women were distorted by custom-decreed bandages.
ALICE BEAL PARSONS, *Woman's Dilemma,* 1926

8

... when we remember further how much the tone of a man's health depends upon the conviction that it is all right ... we can easily see how the continually repeated suggestions made to women generally that they are inferior physically, the coddling themselves and being coddled, lying down after meals, taking seats that the stronger male gives them, have operated actually to induce inferiority.

Ibid.

Where there is no freedom there can be no morality. Women lived out their lives under a code imposed upon them by men, under conditions in which the feminine point of view was simply ignored as if it had no existence.

ALISON NEILANS, "Changes in Sex Morality," *Our Freedom and Its Results,* ed. Ray Strachey, 1936

The general contempt of women shown by women ... is commonly known. The fact that so many women intensely dislike ... purely feminine company cannot be accounted for solely on the ground that women "instinctively" prefer the company of the other sex. It is much more due to the fact that the accumulation of so many of their own despised kind is almost unbearable to them. It is as if they would see their own grimace reflected from a multiple distorting mirror.

VIOLA KLEIN, Ph.D., *The Feminine Character,* 1946

Man must work, and woman must exploit his labour. What else are they there for? And if the woman submits, she can be cursed for her exploitation; and if she rebels, she can be cursed for competing with the male: whatever she does will be wrong, and that is a great satisfaction.

DOROTHY SAYERS, "The Human-Not-Quite-Human," *Unpopular Opinions,* 1947

... women are past masters of the deference game. Deference attitudes are bits of behavior which ... announce that their possessor is someone who can be trusted to keep her place.

RUTH HERSCHBERGER, *Adam's Rib,* 1948

In every known human society, the male's need for achievement can be recognized. Men may cook, or weave or dress dolls or hunt hummingbirds, but if such activities are appropriate occupations of men, then the whole society, men and women alike, votes them as important. When the same occupations are performed by women, they are regarded as less important.

MARGARET MEAD, *Male and Female,* 1949

... maleness in America is not absolutely defined, it has to be kept and re-earned every day, and one essential element in the definition is beating women in every game that both sexes play, in every activity in which both sexes engage.

Ibid.

... dislike of virtues in women is typical of the patriarchal misogynist, who cannot tolerate qualities which weaken his sense of masculine superiority. The misogynist must be able to dislike women; the patriarch must be able to feel superior to them.

KATHARINE M. ROGERS, *The Troublesome Helpmate*, 1966

It is always true of an oppressed group that the mere fact of their existence means that to a certain extent they have accepted their inferior-colonial-secondary status. Taught self-hatred, they identify instead with the oppressor. Thus such [a] phenomenon as ... women responding with horror at the thought of a woman president.

ANNE KOEDT, "Women and the Radical Movement," *Notes from the First Year*, New York Radical Women, June 1968

No man plays a passive role in the oppression of females. The caste system could not function another day unless men vigorously acted out their oppressive roles, took their rewards for granted and stomped on women. Men not only support the caste system; they are terrified of losing any part of it.

ROXANNE DUNBAR AND LISA LEGHORN, "The Man's Problem," *No More Fun and Games*, November 1969

Women should perceive that the negative attitudes they hold toward their own femaleness are the creation of an anti-feminist society, just as the black shame at being black was the product of racism.

SHIRLEY CHISHOLM, *Unbought and Unbossed*, 1970

Thinking man orders his universe, builds a pyramid with himself placed automatically at the tip. All other living creatures are placed in a descending downward slope beneath him. For the philosopher man is a form of absolute, and woman must therefore be something less. ... The poor creature cannot help it, sighed the medieval schoolmen, she has no soul; you must make allowances, argued the men of reason, she was born without a rational faculty; how awful to be so deprived, said the analysts, sex is the fundamental urge and she was born without the wherewithal, no wonder she spends her days trying to mimic us.

EVA FIGES, *Patriarchal Attitudes*, 1970

The special tie women have with children is recognized by everyone. I submit, however, that the nature of this bond is no more than shared oppression.
> SHULAMITH FIRESTONE, *The Dialectic of Sex*, 1970

The smile is the child/woman equivalent of the shuffle; it indicates acquiescence of the victim to his own oppression.
> Ibid.

. . . no group is so oppressed as one which will not recognize its own oppression. Women's denial that they must deal with their oppression is a reflection of just how far they still have to go.
> Jo FREEMAN, "The Building of the Gilded Cage," Rep. Edith Green's Special Subcommittee on Education, 1970, *Discrimination Against Women*, U.S. Government Printing Office, 1971

Women learn in many ways to suppress their selfishness, and by doing so they suppress also their self-esteem. If most men hold women in contempt it is no greater than the contempt in which women hold themselves.
> SALLY KEMPTON, "Cutting Loose: A Private View of the Women's Uprising," *Esquire*, July 1970

. . . male chauvinism is an *attitude*—male supremacy is the objective *reality, the fact*.
> ROBIN MORGAN, "Goodbye to All That," *RAT, Subterranean News*, February 6, 1970

. . . New Masculinism . . . charges her . . . with a duty of finding the task the men around her need done from moment to moment. The nature of the task doesn't matter. She may shoot a gun or drive a truck or serve out a husband's unexpired term in the legislature—providing only that she does it in the name of somebody else and not for the greater glory of herself.
> CAROLINE BIRD, *Born Female*, rev. ed. 1971

Man's constant need to disparage woman, to humble her, to deny her equal rights, and to belittle her achievements—all are expressions of his innate envy and fear.
> ELIZABETH GOULD DAVIS, *The First Sex*, 1971

Women are reputed never to be disgusted. The sad fact is that they often are, but not with men; following the lead of men, they are most often disgusted with themselves.
> GERMAINE GREER, *The Female Eunuch*, 1971

11

Shying away from self-responsibility is common among women. Most of us go directly from our fathers to our husbands. There's more to the endearment, "baby," than meets the ear.

GABRIELLE BURTON, *I'm Running Away from Home, But I'm Not Allowed to Cross the Street,* 1972

The rituals of patriarchy *do* create false needs, such as the need to lean on father-figures instead of finding strength in the self, or the need for compulsive "self-sacrifice" because one is brainwashed into thinking that one is sinful and "unworthy."

MARY DALY, *Beyond God the Father,* 1973

Women by the time they are eighteen are so damaged, so beaten down, so tyrannized out of behaving in all the wonderful outspoken ways unfortunately characterized as masculine; a college committed to them has to take on the burden of repair—of remedial education, really.

NORA EPHRON, *Crazy Salad,* 1975

Sexism must be seen as the expression of a primal psychology of domination and repression forged in the one-sided emergence of the male in the struggle for survival. The life of sensuousness, celebration, leisure, free creativity, and exploration of feelings was allowed a small elite class, who stood on the backs of the toiling masses. Sexism was the first and basic model for this subjugation of one part of the race to bodily work, so that the other part could be free to create and enjoy.

ROSEMARY RADFORD RUETHER, *New Woman New Earth,* 1975

The excesses of women who seek to promote lesbianism as a political rather than a sexual choice ought not blind us to the value of the insights lesbian feminists are sharing . . . they can help heterosexual women to understand the extent to which fear of men's opinion and male power limits the search for self-knowledge.

PAULA WEIDEGER, *Menstruation and Menopause,* 1976

Like other dominated people, we have learned to manipulate and seduce, or to internalize men's will and make it ours, and men have sometimes characterized this as "power" in us; but it is nothing more than the child's or courtesan's "power" to wheedle and the dependent's "power" to disguise her feelings—even from herself—in order to obtain favors, or literally to survive.

ADRIENNE RICH, *Of Woman Born,* 1976

12

... our insistence on drawing up mental lists contrasting what is "masculine" with what is "feminine" diminishes not only individual women, but women as a class. It does so because male prestige is maintained by limiting female prestige—at the expense, ultimately, of the human wholeness of every individual.
    CASEY MILLER AND KATE SWIFT, *Words and Women*, 1977

Objects

She [woman] was created to be the toy of man, his rattle, and it must jingle in his ears whenever, dismissing reason, he chooses to be amused.
    MARY WOLLSTONECRAFT, *A Vindication of the Rights of Woman*, 1792

Liberty is the mother of virtue, and if women be, by their very constitution, slaves, and not allowed to breathe the sharp invigorating air of freedom, they must ever languish like exotics, and be reckoned beautiful flaws in nature.
    Ibid.

The cupidity of man soon led him to regard woman as property...
    SARAH GRIMKÉ, *Letters on the Equality of the Sexes*, 1838

Men ridicule every indication of disaffection on a woman's part, as if it must spring from an ill-organized mind or a diseased temper. We are a sort of puppet, to be placed, like Tom Thumb, upon a giant's palm, and act our fantastic part, either of smiles or tears, and they are to regard us with the same kind of tolerating, half-amused indulgence. Reformers are afraid to recognize our needs; they are afraid to allow human beings the free exercise of the faculties imparted by the Deity; they are afraid they might be abused; therefore they dole out bits of freedom to us as they would atoms of food to half-starved wretches.
    ELIZABETH OAKES SMITH, *Woman and Her Needs*, 1851

Her bondage, though it differs from that of the negro slave, frets and chafes her just the same. She too sighs and groans in her chains; and lives but in the hope of better things to come. She looks to heaven; whilst the more philosophical slave sets out for Canada.
    ELIZABETH CADY STANTON, letter to National Woman's Rights Convention, 1856, *History of Woman Suffrage*, I, 1881

By law, public sentiment, and religion—from the time of Moses down to the present day—woman has never been thought of other than a piece of property, to be disposed of at the will and pleasure of man...

> SUSAN B. ANTHONY, National Woman's Rights Convention, 1860, *History of Woman Suffrage*, I, 1881

In all history, sacred and profane, the woman is regarded and spoken of simply as the toy of man—made for his special use—to meet his most gross and sensuous desires. She is taken or put away, given or received, bought or sold.

> ELIZABETH CADY STANTON, National Woman's Rights Convention, 1860, *History of Woman Suffrage*, I, 1881

Mr. [Frederick] Douglass talks about the wrongs of the negro; but with all the outrages that he to-day suffers, he would not exchange his sex and take the place of Elizabeth Cady Stanton.

> SUSAN B. ANTHONY, American Equal Rights Association Convention, 1869, *History of Woman Suffrage*, II, 1882

... we women, from generation to generation, are drilled to be the apes of an artificial standard, made for us and imposed upon us by an outsider; a being who, in this attitude, becomes our natural enemy.

> JULIA WARD HOWE, American Woman Suffrage Association Convention, 1870, *History of Woman Suffrage*, II, 1882

By the law of every State in this Union to-day, the married woman has no right to the custody and control of her person. The wife belongs to her husband; and if she refuses obedience to his will, he may use moderate correction, and if she doesn't like his moderate correction, and attempts to leave his "bed and board," the husband may use moderate coercion to bring her back. The little word "moderate," you see, is the saving clause for the wife, and would doubtless be overstepped should her offended husband administer his correction with the "cat-o'-nine-tails," or accomplish his coercion with blood-hounds.

> SUSAN B. ANTHONY, "Address to the Citizens of New York State," 1873, *History of Woman Suffrage*, II, 1882

According to the standpoint of the observer, woman is a riddle to be solved, a conundrum to be guessed, a puzzle to be interpreted, a mystery to be explained, a problem to be studied, a paradox to be reconciled. She is a toy or a drudge, a mistress or a servant, a queen or a slave, as circumstances may decide. She is at once an irresponsible being, who must accept the destiny which comes to her... or she is responsible for everything, from Adam's eating of the apple in Paradise to the financial confusion which agitates us to-day.... I wish we could, as speedily as possible ... lay aside this nonsense ... and learn to regard woman as simply a human being ...

MARY F. EASTMAN, American Woman Suffrage Association Convention, 1878, *History of Woman Suffrage*, II, 1882

... in looking back over the many intervening years, we still wonder at the stolid incapacity of all men to understand that woman feels the invidious distinctions of sex exactly as the black man does those of color, or the white man the more transient distinctions of wealth, family, position, place, and power; that she feels as keenly as man the injustice of disfranchisement.

E. C. STANTON, S. B. ANTHONY, M. J. GAGE, eds., *History of Woman Suffrage*, II, 1882

It is impossible for one class to appreciate the wrongs of another. The coarser forms of slavery all can see and deplore, but the subjections of the spirit, few either comprehend or appreciate.

Ibid.

The labor of women in the house, certainly, enables men to produce more wealth than they otherwise could; and in this way women are economic factors in society. But so are horses.

CHARLOTTE PERKINS GILMAN, *Women and Economics*, 1898

It struck me as very remarkable that abolitionists, who felt so keenly the wrongs of the slave, should be so oblivious to the equal wrongs of their own mothers, wives, and sisters, when, according to the common law, both classes occupied a similar legal status.

ELIZABETH CADY STANTON, *Eighty Years and More*, 1898

The man of wealth or power defends his wife, daughter or sweetheart because she is his, just as he would defend his property. His own opinions, not her views, decide him concerning the things from which she should be protected. Should she ever need protection against "her protector," there is no one to give it ...

CATHARINE WAUGH McCULLOCH, National American Woman Suffrage Association Convention, 1900, *History of Woman Suffrage*, IV, 1902

The legislation we opposed [Contagious Diseases Acts] secured the enslavement of women and the increased immorality of men; and history and experience alike teach us that these two results are never separated.

JOSEPHINE E. BUTLER, *Personal Reminiscences of a Great Crusade*, 1911

15

The cry of women crushed under the yoke of legalised vice is not the cry of a statistician or a medical expert; it is simply a cry of pain, a cry for justice and for a return to God's laws in place of these brutally impure laws invented and imposed by man.
> Ibid.

Nowhere is woman treated according to the merit of her work, but rather as a sex. It is therefore almost inevitable that she should pay for her right to exist, to keep a position in whatever line, with sex favors.
> EMMA GOLDMAN, "The Traffic in Women," *Anarchism and Other Essays*, 1911

It is a conceded fact that woman is being reared as a sex commodity, and yet she is kept in absolute ignorance of the meaning and importance of sex.
> Ibid.

To the male . . . who depends mainly for his power for procuring the sex relation he desires, not on his power of winning and retaining personal affection, but on the purchasing power of his possessions as compared to the poverty of the females of his society, the personal loss would be seriously and at once felt, of any social change which gave to the woman a larger economic independence and therefore greater freedom of sexual choice.
> OLIVE SCHREINER, *Woman and Labour*, 1911

Ignorance is the first condition of enslavement, and ignorant women will always be the tools of the men who are the enemies of freedom.
> JULIA WARD HOWE, "The Moral Initiative as Belonging to Women," *Julia Ward Howe and the Woman Suffrage Movement*, ed. Florence Howe Hall, 1913

Woman has been content to mold herself to the shape desired by man wherever possible, and she has stifled her natural feelings and her own deep thoughts as they welled up.
> MARIE CARMICHAEL STOPES, *Married Love*, 1921

Both the wife and the prostitute were man's creatures . . . to be used for different purposes but equally to be used. It is hardly to be wondered at that man came to regard women as "the sex," and through his own management of their degradation came to feel and to express toward them a degree of contempt that cast considerable doubt on his own humanity.
> SUZANNE LA FOLLETTE, *Concerning Women*, 1926

16

There seems to be an unyielding opposition in many men's minds against treating the woman who gives herself promiscuously for money as a human being.

ALISON NEILANS, "Changes in Sex Morality," *Our Freedom and Its Results,* ed. Ray Strachey, 1936

Long before the Africans were enslaved and brought to our shores; long before the workman lost his independence; long before the Jew and the foreign-born were harried as inferiors, women were confined in the subordinate, the subservient niches of civilization.

SUSAN B. ANTHONY II, *Out of the Kitchen—Into the War,* 1943

The usury of the Jews and the extra-conjugal sexuality of the prostitutes were alike denounced by Church and State; but society could not get along without financial speculation and extramarital love; these functions were therefore assigned to wretched castes, segregated in ghettos or in restricted quarters.

SIMONE DE BEAUVOIR, *The Second Sex,* 1952

... actually, it is not by increasing her worth as a human being that she will gain value in men's eyes; it is rather by modeling herself upon their dreams. ... All girls, from the most servile to the haughtiest, learn in time that to please they must abdicate.

Ibid.

Common prostitution is a miserable occupation in which woman, exploited sexually and economically, subjected arbitrarily to the police, to a humiliating medical supervision, to the caprices of the customers, and doomed to microbes and disease, to misery, is truly abased to the level of a thing.

Ibid.

... adorned with the most modern artifices, beautified according to the newest techniques, she comes down from the remoteness of the ages, from Thebes, from Crete, from Chichén-Itzá; and she is also the totem set up deep in the African jungle; she is a helicopter and she is a bird; and there is this, the greatest wonder of all: under her tinted hair the forest murmur becomes a thought, and words issue from her breasts. Men stretch forth avid hands toward the marvel, but when they grasp it it is gone; the wife, the mistress, speak like everybody else through their mouths: their words are worth just what they are worth; their breasts also. ... One can appreciate the beauty of flowers, the charm of women, and appreciate them at their true value; if these treasures cost blood or misery, they must be sacrificed.

Ibid.

17

A woman who is herself only a sexual object, lives finally in a world of objects, unable to touch in others the individual identity she lacks herself.

BETTY FRIEDAN, *The Feminine Mystique*, 1963

So the female student feels like a citizen, like an individual among others in the body politic, in the civil society, in the world of the intellect. What she doesn't understand is that upon graduation she is stripped of her public life and relegated to the level of private property . . . she is doomed to become someone's secretary, or someone's nurse, or someone's wife, or someone's mistress. From now on if she has some contribution to make to society she is expected to make it privately through the man who owns some part of her.

BEVERLY JONES, "Radical Women as Students," 1968, *Masculine/Feminine*, ed. B. and T. Roszak, 1969

Intellectual development in a woman, or any kind of self-development, is of value to men only insofar as it is an addition to her value as a sexual object, like big breasts, only of course it is understood that big breasts are much more important to sexiness than a Ph.D.

TI-GRACE ATKINSON, "Juniata I: The Sacrificial Lamb," 1969, *Amazon Odyssey*, 1974

. . . the list [of female attributes] adds up to a typical minority-group stereotype—woman as nigger—if she knows her place (the home), she is really quite a lovable, loving creature, happy and childlike.

NAOMI WEISSTEIN, "Woman as Nigger," *Psychology Today*, October 1969

Women are told that they are welcome first and foremost as decoration for the male academic turf. Even in academe, women are sex objects.

ANN SUTHERLAND HARRIS, to Rep. Edith Green's Special Subcommittee on Education, 1970, *Discrimination Against Women*, U.S. Government Printing Office, 1971

Ambitious women are hazed, obstructed, and isolated in the same way as "uppity blacks," while the favors of the power structure are lavished on the "real woman" and the "good Negro." The tone in which women workers are praised for their tact, courtesy, loyalty, and tractability is a warning that the praise itself is a form of culture policing.

CAROLINE BIRD, *Born Female*, rev. ed., 1971

. . . the overblown breast is admired by modern men not as a daring sex symbol, as they like to think, but as a mother symbol.

ELIZABETH GOULD DAVIS, *The First Sex*, 1971

18

Implicit in the dream of rape is woman's true sense of herself, her true sub-conscious understanding of the actual position of value which she occupies in the life of the culture, her dread, long-felt conviction that she is not real to men. Her fantasies of rape are a culmination of the fact that she has always *been* raped. She is, preeminently, an object of lust; a creature upon whom the darker desires are realized; a source of release, of tension gathered and ten-sion exploded; a creature with whom the agony of passion and the morbid fear of sexuality are associated.

> VIVIAN GORNICK, "Woman as Outsider," *Woman in Sexist Society*, ed. Viv-ian Gornick and Barbara K. Moran, 1971

The universal sway of the feminine stereotype is the single most important factor in male and female woman-hatred. Until woman as she is can drive this plastic specter out of her own and her man's imagination she will contin-ue to apologize and disguise herself, while accepting her male's pot-belly, wattles, bad breath, farting, stubble, baldness and other ugliness without com-plaint.

> GERMAINE GREER, *The Female Eunuch*, 1971

Women who fancy that they manipulate the world by pussy power and gen-tle cajolery are fools. It is slavery to have to adopt such tactics.

> Ibid.

Women do literally sell their bodies—if not as prostitutes, then to the public-ity industries, modelling and so on—much as men and women sell their la-bour power. As a worker finds himself alienated in his own product, so (roughly speaking) a woman finds herself alienated in her own commercial-ized body.

> JULIET MITCHELL, *Woman's Estate*, 1971

Every woman in our society, like the few beautiful ones in the media, is a flesh peddler in the harem of this man's world.

> UNA STANNARD, "The Mask of Beauty," *Woman in Sexist Society*, ed. Viv-ian Gornick and Barbara K. Moran, 1971

I am WOMAN. Gaze into my ever-changing well of surprises. I am PTA mother in my brown wren dress, Saturday night swinger in my satin hot pants, home-maker in my perma-press housedress. The girl in me still peeks through my pleated skirt and knee socks; I am my husband's mistress in my black negli-gee. . . . If you or I get tired of "me," I have only to change my lipstick, flip my wig, buy a new dress.

> GABRIELLE BURTON, *I'm Running Away from Home, But I'm Not Allowed to Cross the Street*, 1972

19

Prostitutes are degraded and punished by society; it is their *humiliation* through their *bodies*—as much as their *bodies*—which is being purchased.
PHYLLIS CHESLER, *Women and Madness*, 1972

. . . many people have a subconscious idea that women are an altogether less complex species, more like, shall we say, rhododendrons, or beans, so that somewhere just around the corner is a simple answer on the lines of "they need plenty of phosphates," and that once this secret has been discovered life will be simpler. Women can be given what they want and they will then keep quiet, thus enabling the time and attention of real (i.e. male) people to be devoted to the important and difficult business of conducting their relations with other real people.
ELAINE MORGAN, *The Descent of Woman*, 1972

With so many bastions of his dominant status skidding out from under him, man hung on tight to the one symbol nobody could take away from him. He still, by God, had his penis. However cool and efficient and economically independent a female might be, if he ever had any tremor of doubt that he was worth three of her, he had only to remind himself that underneath that elegant exterior was a nude female . . .
Ibid.

["Sexual liberation"] has in fact been one more extension of the politics of rape, a New Morality of false liberation foisted upon women, who have been told to be free to be what women have always been, sex objects. The difference is simply that there is now social pressure for women to be available to any male at the beckon of a once-over, to be a nonprofessional whore.
MARY DALY, *Beyond God the Father*, 1973

Rape entered the law through the back door . . . as a property crime of man against man. Woman, of course, was viewed as the property.
SUSAN BROWNMILLER, *Against Our Will*, 1975

In war as in peace, the husbands of raped women place a major burden of blame for the awful event on their wives. The hallowed rights of property have been abused, and the property herself is held culpable.
Ibid.

The woman's body is the terrain on which patriarchy is erected.
ADRIENNE RICH, *Of Woman Born*, 1976

20

The Double Standard

Educating her for the Harem, but calling on her for the practices of the Portico, man expects from his odalisque the firmness of the stoic, and demands from his servant the exercise of those virtues which, placing the *élite* of his own sex at the head of its muster-roll, give immortality to the master. He tells her "that obscurity is *her* true glory, insignificance her distinction, ignorance her lot, and passive obedience the perfection of her nature"; yet he expects from her, as the daily and hourly habit of her existence, that conquest over the passions by the strength of reason, that triumph of moral energy over the senses and their appetites, and that endurance of personal privations and self-denials, which with him . . . are qualities of rare exception, the practices of most painful acquirement.

> LADY SYDNEY MORGAN, *Woman and Her Master*, 1840

We hold that whatever is essentially wrong for woman to do, can not be right for man. If deception and intrigue, the elements of political craft, be degrading to woman, can they be ennobling to man? If patience and forbearance adorn a woman, are they not equally essential to a manly character? If anger and turbulence disgrace woman, what can they add to the dignity of man?

> J. ELIZABETH JONES, "Address to the Women of Ohio," 1850, *History of Woman Suffrage*, I, 1881

Idleness, which is the root of all evil for men, is not particularly suited to be the root of all virtue for women.

> FRANCES POWER COBBE, "The Final Cause of Woman," *Woman's Work and Woman's Culture*, ed. Josephine E. Butler, 1869

. . . the injustice of society permits that to be right in man which would be considered very bad in woman. There is not in the Bible a code of morals for man and another for woman; but some men, self-indulgent to themselves and harsh in their judgment of women, have made one which, to some extent, regulates the general opinion of society. Custom blinds to the error of many things in civilized life.

> VIRGINIA PENNY, *Think and Act*, 1869

Now, why is it that man can hold woman to this high code of morals, like Caesar's wife—not only pure but above suspicion—and so surely and severely punish her for every departure, while she is so helpless, so powerless to check him in his license, or to extricate herself from his presence and control? His

21

power grows out of his right over her subsistence. Her lack of power grows out of her dependence on him for her food, her clothes, her shelter.

SUSAN B. ANTHONY, "Social Purity," 1875, Ida Husted Harper, *Life and Work of Susan B. Anthony*, II, 1898

Man deserves that we should consider his present unhappy condition. In all ages he has proved his reverence for woman by embodying every virtue in female form, and has left none for himself.

LILLIE DEVEREUX BLAKE, "The Rights of Men," National Woman Suffrage Association Convention, 1887, *History of Woman Suffrage*, IV, 1902

We are to be taught that "love, joy, peace, long-suffering, gentleness, goodness, faith, meekness" (especially meekness), "and temperance" are the ideals of life "for women only." Men, we presume, with that characteristic bearing of the burdens of life, have forsworn all these delectable qualities (or most of them), because they and the exercise of a vote cannot go together. Anyhow, not in women.

LADY GROVE, *The Human Woman*, 1908

. . . already in municipal elections it has been shown that more is expected in the way of competence in a female candidate than a male. . . . A man's qualifications for the public unpaid posts to which he is aspiring are more or less taken for granted, whereas a woman is required to give some guarantee of fitness for what she is undertaking.

Ibid.

Masculine ethics, colored by masculine instincts, always dominated by sex, has at once recognized the value of chastity in the woman, which is right; punished its absence unfairly, which is wrong; and then reversed the whole matter when applied to men, which is ridiculous.

CHARLOTTE PERKINS GILMAN, "Charlotte Perkins Gilman's Dynamic Social Philosophy," *Current Literature*, July 1911

A feebler and more frivolous type [of woman] has been more congenial to them [the common world of men], and while expecting and exacting from us a stricter morality than that required of their own sex, they have been at no small pains to obstruct in us the sources of moral inspiration, and to make us feel that to please them is our highest duty and our greatest honor.

JULIA WARD HOWE, "The Moral Initiative as Belonging to Women," *Julia Ward Howe and the Woman Suffrage Movement*, ed. Florence Howe Hall, 1913

I find something of this element in the feeling of men toward women. "You are our subordinates, bound to serve and obey, and you should therefore have certain inestimable qualities which we do not feel obliged to possess. You *should* be better than we."
    Ibid.

With a strange inconsistency, women were held to a stricter account than were men in matters of personal morality. Extra restraint was imposed upon them from without, form and ceremony hedged them in on every side. But now the civilized world is learning that the only availing moral restraint comes from within.
    JULIA WARD HOWE, "Speech on Equal Rights," *Julia Ward Howe and the Woman Suffrage Movement*, ed. Florence Howe Hall, 1913

The local recreational organizations seem to accept this segregation of the sexes as fundamental and proceed accordingly. Mothers' meetings are diligently organized by social workers, but the father is left to go to the saloon.
    KATHARINE ANTHONY, *Mothers Who Must Earn*, 1914

He comes to her unblushing for aid to maintain a social order, and in particular those masculine monopolies, which were established in contempt of her. He is not ashamed, not yet, to entreat women by their personal self-denial and by every conceivable form of organised effort to constitute themselves the financial backbone as well as the pack-horse of the vast system of public charities, many of which are necessitated largely by the exclusion of woman's view from public affairs.
    ELIZABETH ROBBINS, *Ancilla's Share*, 1924

An extraordinary inconsistency appears in the fact that since Christian thought has chiefly connected morality with chastity, woman came to be regarded as the repository of morality, and as such to be considered on a higher moral plane than man. But it was really her economic and social inferiority that made her the repository of morality. She must embody the ideal of sexual restraint that her husband often found it inconvenient or onerous to attain for himself; and any unfaithfulness to this ideal on her part inflicted upon him a mysterious injury called "dishonour." He might indulge his own polygamous leanings with impunity, but his failure to make effective his sexual monopoly of his wife made him liable to contempt and ridicule.
    SUZANNE LA FOLLETTE, *Concerning Women*, 1926

It would be impossible to imagine a more profoundly corrupting influence than the dual ideal of sexuality and chastity that has been held up before womankind.
Ibid.

A double standard of wages is tallied with a double standard of morals.
SUSAN B. ANTHONY II, *Out of the Kitchen—Into the War*, 1943

Woman knows that the masculine code is not hers, that man takes for granted she will not observe it since he urges her to abortion, adultery, wrongdoing, betrayals, and lies, which he condemns officially.
SIMONE DE BEAUVOIR, *The Second Sex*, 1952

The idiocy of a code of law which considered women so weak and irresponsible that they should not take part in public affairs and could not handle property but at the same time placed on the allegedly weaker sex the onus of resisting the advances of the stronger and the responsibility of bringing up illegitimate children practically unaided, seems well-nigh incredible.
CONSTANCE ROVER, *Love, Morals and the Feminists*, 1970

... if they [men] refuse to protect, they have no
right whatever to govern.
    MARY ANN RADCLIFFE, *The Female Advocate,*
    1799

2   The Ruling Class

Violence

As you go down in the scale of manhood, the idea strengthens at every step, that woman was created for no higher purpose than to gratify the lust of man. Every daily paper heralds some rape on flying, hunted girls; and the pitying eyes of angels see the holocaust of womanhood no journal ever notes. . . . I trace the slender threads that link these hideous, overt acts to creeds and codes that make an aristocracy of sex.
    ELIZABETH CADY STANTON, editorial, *The Revolution,* 1869, *History of Woman Suffrage,* II, 1882

It is sometimes claimed that men are the "natural protectors" of women. Are they? Who is it that women fear on lonely roads at night, the members of their own sex or of that sex that claim to be their natural protectors? Any observer of the world knows, that while men may be very good protectors for the women of their own families, they are often very poor protectors for the women of other men's families.
    LILLIE DEVEREUX BLAKE, *Women's Place Today,* 1883

... witness the records of the courts with the wife-beaters and slayers, the rapists, the seducers, the husbands who have deserted their families, the schemers who have defrauded widows and orphans—witness all these and then say if all men are the natural protectors of women.
    S. B. ANTHONY, I. H. HARPER, eds., *History of Woman Suffrage,* IV, 1902

Out of doors is unsafe because women are not there. If women were there, everywhere, in the world which belongs to them as much as to men, then everywhere would be safe. We try to make the women safe in the home, and keep them there; to make the world safe for women and children has not occurred to us.

CHARLOTTE PERKINS GILMAN, *The Home,* 1903

Long years ago, men threw stones and filth at women who asked for enfranchisement. Gradually public opinion killed out this hooliganism. Then came the militants, and, by smashing windows and arson and general terrorism, revived the ape in men, so that, for some years past, all women are once more in danger of violence from men.

H. M. SWANWICK, *The Future of the Women's Movement,* 1913

[Patriotism] was sadly curtailed by the usual male limitations. Sweet and proper they called it that a man should die for his country—always death in the foreground, always fighting as the chief service.

CHARLOTTE PERKINS GILMAN, *His Religion and Hers,* 1923

With the extolling of woman's purity, men have purported to put woman on a pedestal. What they have done is to take the defense of her honor out of her own hands, discourage her muscular reflexes, and virtually encourage various members of their sex to wage war on the purity that woman holds dear.

RUTH HERSCHBERGER, *Adam's Rib,* 1948

. . . in a totally collectivized society, women might become men's equals, or superiors, *even in physical force*. Not only the psychological state, but also the somatic state of women is a "function" of the social order, and in the present order of things, physical force is a symptom, not a cause, of masculine superiority.

ELISABETH MANN BORGESE, *Ascent of Woman,* 1963

It is a vain delusion that rape is the expression of uncontrollable desire or some kind of compulsive response to overwhelming attraction. . . . The act is one of murderous aggression, spawned in self-loathing and enacted upon the hated other.

GERMAINE GREER, *The Female Eunuch,* 1971

Whatever the motivation, male sexuality and violence in our culture seem to be inseparable. James Bond alternately whips out his revolver and his cock, and though there is no known connection between the skills of gun-fighting and love-making, pacifism seems suspiciously effeminate.

SUSAN GRIFFIN, "Rape: The All-American Crime," *Ramparts,* 10, September 1971

Indeed, the existence of rape in any form is beneficial to the ruling class of white males. For rape is a kind of terrorism which severely limits the freedom of women and makes women dependent on men.
>Ibid.

Women will not be free as long as walking down the street, with eyes straight ahead, stomach contracted, is like running the gauntlet.
>ANN SHELDON, "Rape: A Solution," *Women: A Journal of Liberation*, III, circa 1972

Rape is an act of group against group: male against female. . . . it is also an act of male against male, in which the latter is attacked by the pollution of his property. Rape is expressive of group-think, and group-think is at the core of racial prejudice whose logical conclusion and final solution is genocide.
>MARY DALY, *Beyond God the Father*, 1973

A black man walking through certain white neighborhoods or a white man walking through certain black neighborhoods can understand the fear of unprovoked attack. It is the same fear a woman has when she walks down the street at night—any street, even her own. Women are always in someone else's territory.
>ANDRA MEDEA AND KATHLEEN THOMPSON, *Against Rape*, 1974

. . . rape is perhaps the foremost male fantasy in our society.
>Ibid.

Recognizing that rapists are in no significant sense different from other men does not make the act less horrible. Rather, it brings into question the society in which ordinary men *can* be rapists.
>Ibid.

Rape is a dull, blunt, ugly act committed by punk kids, their cousins and older brothers, not by charming, witty, unscrupulous, heroic, sensual rakes, or by timid souls deprived of a "normal" sexual outlet, or by *super-menschen* possessed of uncontrollable lust. And yet, on the shoulders of these unthinking, predictable, insensitive, violence-prone young men there rests an age-old burden that amounts to an historic mission: the perpetuation of male domination over women by force.
>SUSAN BROWNMILLER, *Against Our Will*, 1975

Women have been raped by men, most often by gangs of men, for many of the same reasons that blacks were lynched by gangs of whites: as group punishment for being uppity, for getting out of line, for failing to recognize "one's place," for assuming sexual freedoms, or for behavior no more provocative than walking down the wrong road at night in the wrong part of town and presenting a convenient, isolated target for group hatred and rage.
Ibid.

The Laws

I can not say that I think you very generous to the Ladies, for whilst you are proclaiming peace and good will to men, Emancipating all Nations, you insist upon retaining an absolute power over Wives. But you must remember that Arbitrary power is like most other things which are very hard, very liable to be broken . . .
ABIGAIL ADAMS, to John Adams, 1776, *Familiar Letters of John Adams and His Wife, Abigail Adams, During the Revolution,* ed. Charles Francis Adams, 1876

Woman . . . is a cipher in the nation; or, if not actually so in representative governments, she is only counted, like the slaves of the South, to swell the number of law-makers who form decrees for her government, with little reference to her benefit, except so far as her good may promote their own.
SARAH GRIMKÉ, *Letters on the Equality of the Sexes,* 1838

If, in the first era of society, woman was the victim of man's physical superiority, she is still, in the last, the subject of laws, in the enactment of which she has had no voice—amenable to the penalties of a code, from which she derives but little protection. While man, in his first crude attempts at jurisprudence, has surrounded the sex with restraints and disabilities, he has left its natural rights unguarded, and its liberty unacknowledged.
LADY SYDNEY MORGAN, *Woman and Her Master,* 1840

Equality before the law, and the right of the governed to choose their governors, are established maxims of reformed political science; but in the countries most advanced, these doctrines and their actual benefits are as yet enjoyed exclusively by the sex that in the battle-field and the public forum has wrenched them from the old time tyrannies. They are yet denied to Woman, because she has not yet *so* asserted or won them for herself; for political justice pivots itself upon the barbarous principle that "Who would be free, *themselves* must strike the blow."

> PAULINA WRIGHT DAVIS, address, *Proceedings of the Woman's Rights Convention, Held at Worcester, October 23 & 24, 1850*, 1851

The earth has never yet seen a truly great and virtuous nation, for woman has never yet stood the equal with man.

> ELIZABETH CADY STANTON, letter, *Proceedings of the Woman's Rights Convention, Held at Worcester, October 23 & 24, 1850*, 1851

A woman who has a good husband glides easily along under his protection, while those who have bad husbands, of which, alas! there are too many, are not aware of the depths of their degradation until they suddenly and unexpectedly find themselves, through the influence of the law, totally destitute, condemned to hopeless poverty and servitude, with an ungrateful tyrant for a master.

> MARY UPTON FERRIN, address to Judiciary Committee of the Massachusetts Legislature, 1850, *History of Woman Suffrage*, I, 1881

Well, I do not pretend to know exactly what woman's rights are; but I do know that I have groaned for forty years, yea, for fifty years, under a sense of woman's wrongs.

> MEHITABLE HASKELL, Second National Convention, Friends of Woman Suffrage, 1851, *History of Woman Suffrage*, I, 1881

A sister has well remarked that we do not believe that man is the cause of all our wrongs. We do not fight men—we fight bad principles.

> ERNESTINE L. ROSE, Fourth National Woman's Rights Convention, 1853, *History of Woman Suffrage*, I, 1881

Would to God you could know the burning indignation that fills woman's soul when she turns over the pages of your statute books, and sees there how like feudal barons you freemen hold your women.

> ELIZABETH CADY STANTON, "Address to the Legislature of the State of New York," 1854, *History of Woman Suffrage*, I, 1881

I have no country and no hope of a country! On all this broad continent there is no mountain so high, no valley so deep, that I can take my child by the hand and say "It is mine." The stars and stripes may float above me, but I cannot appeal to the flag to protect my equal right to my baby as its father is protected in his right.

> Lucy Stone, circa 1859, quoted by her husband in "The Women's Campaign of 1896," *The Woman's Column*, IX, September 26, 1896

You who have read the history of nations, from Moses down to our last election, where have you ever seen one class looking after the interests of another? Any of you can readily see the defects in other governments, and pronounce sentence against those who have sacrificed the masses to themselves; but when we come to our own case, we are blinded by custom and self-interest. Some of you who have no capital can see the injustice which the laborer suffers; some of you who have no slaves can see the cruelty of his oppression; but who of you appreciate the galling humiliation, the refinements of degradation, to which women (the mothers, wives, sisters, and daughters of freemen) are subject, in this the last half of the nineteenth century? How many of you have ever read even the laws concerning them that now disgrace your statute-books? In cruelty and tyranny, they are not surpassed by any slaveholding code in the Southern States . . .

> Elizabeth Cady Stanton, "Address to the Legislature of the State of New York," 1860, *History of Woman Suffrage*, I, 1881

They [laws] make a married woman a beggar all her life, although she may have a rich husband, and a most pitiable one, if he is poor.

> Mariam H. Fish, letter to Susan B. Anthony, 1863, *History of Woman Suffrage*, II, 1882

It is all very well for the privileged order to look down complacently and tell us, "This is the negro's hour; do not clog his way; do not embarrass the Republican party with any new issue; be generous and magnanimous; the negro once safe, the woman comes next." Now, if our prayer involved a new set of measures, or a new train of thought, it would be cruel to tax "white male citizens" with even two simple questions at a time; but the disfranchised all make the same demand, and the same logic and justice that secures suffrage to one class gives it to all.

> Elizabeth Cady Stanton, letter to the *Standard*, 1865, *History of Woman Suffrage*, II, 1882

Your laws degrade, rather than exalt woman! your customs cripple, rather than free; your system of taxation is alike ungenerous and unjust.

> Elizabeth Cady Stanton, "Address to New York State Constitutional Convention," 1867, *History of Woman Suffrage*, II, 1882

What an unspeakable privilege to have that precious jewel—the human soul—in a setting of *white manhood*, that thus it can pass through the prison, the asylum, the alms-house, the muddy waters of the Erie canal, and come forth undimmed to appear at the ballot-box at the earliest opportunity, there to bury its crimes, its poverty, its moral and physical deformities, all beneath the rights, privileges, and immunities of a citizen of the State.

> Ibid.

There is a great stir about colored men getting their rights, but not a word about the colored women; and if colored men get their rights, and not colored women theirs, you see the colored men will be masters over the women, and it will be just as bad as it was before.

> SOJOURNER TRUTH, American Equal Rights Association Convention, 1867, *History of Woman Suffrage*, II, 1882

I have had opportunities of seeing and knowing the condition of both sexes, and will bear my testimony, that the black women are, and always have been, in a far worse condition than the men.

> PHOEBE COUZINS, American Equal Rights Association Convention, 1869, *History of Woman Suffrage*, II, 1882

To keep a foothold in society woman must be as near like man as possible, reflect his ideas, opinions, virtues, motives, prejudices, and vices. She must respect his statutes, though they strip her of every inalienable right, and conflict with that higher law written by the finger of God on her own soul. . . . She must accept things as they are and make the best of them. To mourn over the miseries of others, the poverty of the poor, their hardships in jails, prisons, asylums, the horrors of war, cruelty, and brutality in every form, all this would be mere sentimentalizing. To protest against the intrigue, bribery, and corruption of public life, to desire that her sons might follow some business that did not involve lying, cheating, and a hard, grinding selfishness, would be arrant nonsense.

> ELIZABETH CADY STANTON, Woman Suffrage Convention, 1869, *History of Woman Suffrage*, II, 1882

If we look over the history of jury trial, we find in all ages, and nations, the greatest stress laid on every man being judged by his equals. . . . If nobles cannot judge peasants, or peasants nobles, how can man judge woman?

> ELIZABETH CADY STANTON, periodical *The Revolution*, circa 1870, in Alma Lutz, *Created Equal*, 1940

31

The fifth commandment, "Honor thy father and thy mother," can not be obeyed while boys are taught by our laws and constitutions to hold all women in contempt.

> ISABELLA BEECHER HOOKER, to Congressional Committee of the District of Columbia, 1870, *History of Woman Suffrage*, II, 1882

Women never realize their inability to effect a reform until they attempt it, and then they find how closely interwoven with politics are all such matters, and how entirely without political power are they themselves ...

> SUSAN B. ANTHONY, Women's Temperance Crusaders, 1874, in Ida Husted Harper, *Life and Work of Susan B. Anthony*, vol. I, 1898

Had they ["our revolutionary fathers"] thrust the British yoke from the necks of their wives and daughters as indignantly as they thrust it from their own, the legal subjection of the women of to-day would not stand out as it now does—the reproach of our republican government.

> MRS. C. I. H. NICHOLS, letter to National Woman Suffrage Association Convention, 1876, *History of Woman Suffrage*, III, 1887

Under authority and this false promise of "protection," self-reliance, the first incentive to freedom, has not only been lost, but the aversion of mankind for responsibility has been fostered by the few.... Obedience and self-sacrifice—the virtues prescribed for subordinate classes, and which naturally grow out of their condition—are alike opposed to the theory of individual rights and self-government.

> E. C. STANTON, S. B. ANTHONY, M. J. GAGE, eds., *History of Woman Suffrage*, I, 1881

The more complete the despotism, the more smoothly all things move on the surface.

> Ibid.

To prate of indirect influence is absurd. The women of this nation are in it just as a party of Americans would be in Russia were they passing the winter there. They would not be responsible for the evils they saw about them; they would have no power to change anything. With no right of suffrage and no official positions, what responsibility can attach to that class who thus live as strangers in their own land, and are in truth women without a country?

> LILLIE DEVEREUX BLAKE, *Women's Place Today*, 1883

A dear and noble friend, one who aided our work most efficiently in the early days, said to me, "Why do you say the 'emancipation of women?' " I replied, "Because women are political slaves!"

> SUSAN B. ANTHONY, National Woman Suffrage Association Convention, 1884, *History of Woman Suffrage*, IV, 1902

The coat of arms of the State of New York represents Liberty and Justice supporting a shield on which is seen the sun rising over the hills that guard the Hudson. How are justice and liberty depicted? As a police judge and an independent voter? Oh no; as two noble and lovely women! What an absurdity in a State where there is neither liberty nor justice for any woman!

> LILLIE DEVEREUX BLAKE, National Woman Suffrage Association Convention, 1884, *History of Woman Suffrage*, IV, 1902

The war was over. The rights of the black man, for whom the women had worked and waited, were secured, but under the new amendment, by which his race had been made free, the white women of the United States were more securely held in political slavery [by the addition of the word "male" to the 14th Amendment].

> HARRIET H. ROBINSON, "Massachusetts," Chapter XXXI, *History of Woman Suffrage*, III, 1887

Experience has fully proved that sympathy as a civil agent is vague and powerless until caught and chained in logical propositions and coined into law.

> ELIZABETH CADY STANTON, International Council of Women, 1888, *History of Woman Suffrage*, IV, 1902

There is not one impulse of gratitude in my soul for any of the fragmentary privileges which by slow degrees we have wrung out of our oppressors during the last half century, nor will there be so long as woman is robbed of all the essential rights of citizenship.

> ELIZABETH CADY STANTON, letter to National Woman Suffrage Association Convention, 1889, *History of Woman Suffrage*, IV, 1902

My reply to the argument of our opponents that "if women vote they must also fight," is this: All men have not earned their right to the ballot by the bullet; and, if only those who fight should vote, there are many sickly men, many weak little men, many deformed men, and many strong and able-bodied but cowardly men, who should at once be disfranchised.

> AMELIA BLOOMER, undated article, in D. C. Bloomer, *Life and Writings of Amelia Bloomer*, 1895

Woman needs the elective franchise to destroy the prevalent idea of female inferiority.

> AMELIA BLOOMER, "Woman's Right to the Ballot," undated, in D. C. Bloomer, *Life and Writings of Amelia Bloomer*, 1895

... if we introduce one particle of our belated and illogical political and legal subjection of women to men into any savage or half-civilized community, we shall spoil the domestic virtues that community already possesses, and we shall not ... inoculate them with the virtues of civilized domestic life.

> ANNA GARLIN SPENCER, "Duty to the Women of Our New Possessions," National American Woman Suffrage Association Convention, 1899, *History of Woman Suffrage*, IV, 1902

Most of the departments in a modern city can be traced to woman's traditional activity, but in spite of this, so soon as these old affairs were turned over to the care of the city, they slipped from woman's hands, apparently because they then became matters for collective action and implied the use of the franchise.

> JANE ADDAMS, *Newer Ideals of Peace*, 1907

... the evils which are pointed out in our commonwealth today are not the evils of a democracy, but of an amorphous something which is afraid to be a democracy.

> FRANCES SQUIRE POTTER, "Women and the Vote," National American Woman Suffrage Association Convention, 1908, *History of Woman Suffrage*, V, 1922

The only man who can be in any way excused for wanting to withhold freedom from women is the man who is himself a slave.

> ANNA HOWARD SHAW, National American Woman Suffrage Convention, 1909, *History of Woman Suffrage*, V, 1922

Whether it is in an industrial dispute, in the legislature, or in the courts, that woman is struggling for what she considers her rights, it is always political weapons which in the last resort are turned against her, and she stands helpless, for she has no political weapon wherewith she may defend herself ...

> ALICE HENRY, "Women and the Trade-Union Movement in the United States," *Proceedings of the Academy of Political Science*, I, 1910

Life is full of hidden remedial powers which society has not yet utilized, but perhaps nowhere is the waste more flagrant than in the matured deductions and judgments of the women, who are constantly forced to share the social injustices which they have no recognized power to alter.

JANE ADDAMS, *A New Conscience and an Ancient Evil*, 1912

You may tell us that our place is in the home. There are 8,000,000 of us in these United States who must go out of it to earn our daily bread and we come to tell you that while we are working in the mills, the mines, the factories and the mercantile houses we have not the protection that we should have. You have been making laws for us and the laws you have made have not been good for us. Year after year working women have gone to the Legislature in every State and have tried to tell their story of need. . . . They have gone believing in the strength of the big brother, believing that the big brother could do for them what they should, as citizens, do for themselves. They have seen time after time the power of the big interests come behind the big brother and say to him, "If you grant the request of these working women you die politically."

LEONORA O'REILLY, address to joint session of the Senate Judiciary Committee and Senate Committee on Woman Suffrage, 1912, *History of Woman Suffrage*, V, 1922

In true Christianity there is no moral distinction of sex, neither male nor female. But in the political life even of free America, the man opens the door for himself and shuts it against his wife, opens the door for his son, and shuts it upon his daughter. And this, I say, is demoralizing.

JULIA WARD HOWE, "The Moral Initiative as Belonging to Women," *Julia Ward Howe and the Woman Suffrage Movement*, ed. Florence Howe Hall, 1913

The religion which makes me a moral agent equally with my father and brother, gives me my right and title to the citizenship which I am here to assert. I ought to share equally with them its privileges and its duties. No man can have more at stake in the community than I have.

JULIA WARD HOWE, "Boston, A Little Island of Darkness," *Julia Ward Howe and the Woman Suffrage Movement*, ed. Florence Howe Hall, 1913

Our industrial epoch has corroded our morals and hardened our hearts as surely as slavery injured its contemporaries, and far more subtly. There is grave reason to fear that it may have unfitted us for the oncoming state of civilization.

FLORENCE KELLEY, *Modern Industry in Relation to the Family, Health, Education, Morality*, 1914

The fact is that the nation is either dead or asleep. In my opinion there is undoubted evidence that the nation is dead, because women have knocked in vain at the door of administrators, archbishops, and even the King himself. The Government have closed all doors to us. And remember this—a state of death in a nation . . . leads to one thing, and that is dissolution . . .

>   MARY RICHARDSON, address to court, quoted in Emmelline Pankhurst, *My Own Story*, 1914

If men would divest themselves for one moment of the thought that women are related to them and other men, if they would think of women as they think of each other, as distinct human beings, with all the rights and privileges and desires and hopes and aspirations of human beings, then I doubt very much whether any man fundamentally sound and logical in his attitude toward great moral and political questions could ever again utter a democratic principle without recognizing its application to the womanhood of the nation.

>   ANNA HOWARD SHAW, "Equal Suffrage—A Problem of Political Justice," *The Annals of the American Academy of Political and Social Science*, LVI, November 1914

[American women] are so patriotic that every blessed woman in the country was writing Washington, or her organization was writing for her, asking the Government what she could do for the war and of course the Government did not know; it has not yet the least idea of what women can do.

>   ANNA HOWARD SHAW, National American Woman Suffrage Association Convention, 1917, *History of Woman Suffrage*, V, 1922

We believe that men cannot be truly free so long as women are held in political subjection.

>   MILLICENT GARRETT FAWCETT, *The Women's Victory—and After*, 1920

Woman was and is condemned to a system under which the lawful rapes exceed the unlawful ones a million to one.

>   MARGARET SANGER, *Woman and the New Race*, 1920

We intended to know why, if democracy were so precious as to demand the nation's blood and treasure for its achievement abroad, its execution at home was so undesirable.

>   DORIS STEVENS, *Jailed for Freedom*, 1920

In Arizona they [suffragists] saw a complete *volte face* on the part of the
Council ... from a strong favorable majority to an insidious opposition that
filibustered the suffrage bill of 1899 into innocuous desuetude; they heard the
popping of corks and the clinking of wine glasses that accompanied the barter
and sale of senatorial votes to the proprietors of the prosperous saloons of the
State ...

> CARRIE CHAPMAN CATT AND NETTIE ROGERS SHULER, *Woman Suffrage and
> Politics*, 1923

The crime of war is bad enough: this butchery of hope and promise and human lives is one so black that the heart and mind of every woman who has
borne a child should revolt against it until it is tolerated no more.

> DORA RUSSELL, *Hypatia*, 1925

I know of no stronger argument for the social philosophy of the anarchist; for
there is no more striking proof of the incapacity of human beings to be their
brothers' keepers than man's failure, through sheer levity, over thousands of
years to govern woman either for his good or her own.

> SUZANNE LA FOLLETTE, *Concerning Women*, 1926

Women have served all these centuries as looking-glasses possessing the magic
and delicious power of reflecting the figure of man at twice its natural size.
Without that power probably the earth would still be swamp and jungle. The
glories of all our wars would be unknown. We should still be scratching the
outlines of deer on the remains of mutton bones and bartering flints for
sheepskins or whatever simple ornament took our unsophisticated taste. Su-
perman and Fingers of Destiny would never have existed. The Czar and the
Kaiser would never have worn their crowns or lost them. Whatever may be
their use in civilised societies, mirrors are essential to all violent and heroic action.

> VIRGINIA WOOLF, *A Room of One's Own*, 1929

Women *are* the community, just as much as men are, and there is no reason to
suppose that injustice put upon one part of the community, for the benefit of
another part of it, is of any advantage to the whole.

> RAY STRACHEY, "Changes in Employment," *Our Freedom and Its Results*,
> ed. Ray Strachey, 1936

Legally, of course, our husbands are in the position of benevolent monarchs. They have the power to take our wages and our property and even our children; but usually they refrain from exercising the privilege. . . . I prefer living in a democracy to a monarchy, however benevolent it may be.
SUSAN B. ANTHONY II, *Out of the Kitchen—Into the War*, 1943

[Man] was afraid and his ego was deflated, so he said he had "reason," which is just a Godlike Phallus. All the instruments man ever created, like levers, pistons, etc., are just substitute phalluses. Finally man invented the atomic bomb, the biggest phallus in history . . .
ELIZABETH HAWES, *Anything But Love*, 1948

Too often the great decisions are originated and given form in bodies made up wholly of men, or so completely dominated by them that whatever of special value women have to offer is shunted aside without expression.
ELEANOR ROOSEVELT, last speech in United Nations, 1952, in Joseph P. Lash, *Eleanor: The Years Alone*, 1972

Of my two "handicaps," being female put many more obstacles in my path than being black.
SHIRLEY CHISHOLM, *Unbought and Unbossed*, 1970

Discriminating against women in politics is particularly unjust, because no political organization I have seen could function without women. They do the work that the men won't do. . . . They would still be exploiting my abilities if I had not rebelled. Increasingly, other women are reaching the same conclusion.
Ibid.

. . . the most disenfranchised and exploited minority in this country is still its women.
Ibid.

America as a nation is both racist and anti-feminist.
SHIRLEY CHISHOLM, "The 51% Minority," Conference on Women's Employment, 1970, *The American Sisterhood*, ed. Wendy Martin, 1972

Policy, even that affecting very directly the lives of millions of women, is made mostly by men. In a man's view of the world, he earns the money; it is his duty to love and honor his mother, to support his wife and children, and to provide for his widow and orphans. In this rather simple view of today's

38

world, a woman is a mother, a wife, or a widow. Laws made and interpreted in this country almost exclusively by men for 180 years have locked these views into the statutory and case law of the country.

MARTHA GRIFFITHS, "Women and Legislation," *Voices of the New Feminism,* ed. Mary Lou Thompson, 1970

Only men wrote the Constitution; women were expressly excluded in intent and content.

WILMA SCOTT HEIDE, to U.S. Senate Subcommittee on Constitutional Amendments, 1970, *Equal Rights,* U.S. Government Printing Office, 1970

. . . discrimination because of one's sex is just as degrading, dehumanizing, immoral, unjust, indefensible, infuriating and capable of producing societal turmoil as discrimination because of one's race.

PAULI MURRAY, to Rep. Edith Green's Special Subcommittee on Education, 1970, *Discrimination Against Women,* U.S. Government Printing Office, 1971

The law, it seems, has done little but perpetuate the myth of the helpless female best kept on her pedestal. In truth, however, that pedestal is a cage bound by a constricting social system and hemmed in by layers of archaic and anti-feminist laws.

FAITH SEIDENBERG, "The Submissive Majority: Modern Trends in the Law Concerning Women's Rights," *Cornell Law Review,* LV, January 1970

Since woman's greatest misfortune has been that she was looked upon as either angel or devil, her true salvation lies in being placed on earth; namely, in being considered human, and therefore subject to all human follies and mistakes.

EMMA GOLDMAN, "Woman Suffrage," *Anarchism and Other Essays*, 1911

3 Figures of Fantasy

The *"True"* Woman

. . . all women are to be levelled, by meekness and docility, into one character of yielding softness and gentle compliance.

MARY WOLLSTONECRAFT, *A Vindication of the Rights of Woman*, 1792

. . . to attract the notice and win the attentions of men, by their external charms, is the chief business of fashionable girls. They seldom think that men will be allured by intellectual acquirements, because they find, that where any mental superiority exists, a woman is generally shunned and regarded as stepping out of her "appropriate sphere," which, in their view, is to dress, to dance, to set out to the best possible advantage her person, to read the novels which inundate the press, and which do more to destroy her character as a rational creature, than any thing else.

SARAH GRIMKÉ, Letter VIII, 1837, *Letters on the Equality of the Sexes*, 1838

Let it not be said, wherever there is energy or creative genius, "She has a masculine mind."

MARGARET FULLER, *Woman in the Nineteenth Century*, 1845

Are we willing to be denied every post of honor and every lucrative employment—to be reckoned as the *inferior sex*, and but half paid for what we do—to feel that we are a proscribed caste, in all our aspirations for excellence and great and noble exertion, and to receive in return the fulsome, and sickening

40

flattery of perverted taste—to be complimented about our shrinking delicacy, our feminine weakness, our beautiful dependence!

> ABBY H. PRICE, address, *Proceedings of the Woman's Rights Convention, Held at Worcester, October 23 & 24, 1850,* 1851

They may endure every hardship, labor in the most menial employment, expose themselves to the gaze of licentious men upon the theatrical stage, become paupers or public prostitutes, and nobody cares; they are within their "sphere." But let them come forth like true women, pleading in the name of God and humanity that their wrongs may be redressed, and their rights restored, and they are at once condemned. They have outstepped their sphere and become "mannish."

> AMELIA BLOOMER, letter in *The Lily,* 1851, in D. C. Bloomer, *Life and Writings of Amelia Bloomer,* 1895

No! there is no reason against woman's elevation, but there are deep-rooted, hoary-headed prejudices. The main cause of them is, a pernicious falsehood propagated against her being, namely, that she is inferior by her nature. Inferior in what? What has man ever done, that woman, under the same advantages, could not do?

> ERNESTINE L. ROSE, Second National Convention, Friends of Woman Suffrage, 1851, *History of Woman Suffrage,* I, 1881

The fear that a woman may deviate the slightest from conventionalism in any way, has become a nervous disease with the public. Indeed, so little is she trusted as a creation, that one would think she were made marvellously beautiful, and endowed with gifts of thought and emotion only for the purpose of endangering her safety—a sort of spiritual locomotive with no check wheel . . .

> ELIZABETH OAKES SMITH, *Woman and Her Needs,* 1851

Let her assert the laws of her being, let her say she is capable of more than this narrow sphere, that she grieves and frets in the cage, and the fault is grievous. She is ill-tempered, ambitious, unwomanly—as though womanhood had but one signification.

> Ibid.

The majority believe that their wives and mothers are household chattels; believe that they were expressly created for no other purposes than those of maternity in their highest aspect; in their next for purposes of passion. . . . [that] they are compounds of tears, hysterics, frettings, scoldings, complainings; made up of craftiness and imbecilities, to be wheedled, and

41

coaxed, and coerced like unmanageable children. *The idea of a true, noble womanhood is yet to be created.*

> ELIZABETH OAKES SMITH, *The Una*, 1853, *History of Woman Suffrage*, I, 1881

When men stand upon the public platform and deliver elaborate essays on women and their right of suffrage, they talk about their weakness, their devotion to fashion and idleness. What else have they given women to do?

> FRANCES D. GAGE, American Equal Rights Association Convention, 1867, *History of Woman Suffrage*, II, 1882

. . . we must not fall into the absurdity of supposing that all women can be adapted to one single type, or that we can talk about "Woman" (always to be written with a capital W) as if the same characteristics were to be found in every individual species, like "the Lioness" and "the Pea-hen."

> FRANCES POWER COBBE, "The Final Cause of Woman," *Woman's Work and Woman's Culture*, ed. Josephine E. Butler, 1869

Some men tell us we must be patient and persuasive; that we must be womanly. My friends, what is man's idea of womanliness? It is to have a manner which pleases him—quiet, deferential, submissive, approaching him as a subject does a master. He wants no self-assertion on our part, no defiance, no vehement arraignment of him as a robber and a criminal . . . while every right achieved by the oppressed has been wrung from tyrants by force; while the darkest page on human history is the outrages on women—shall men still tell us to be patient, persuasive, womanly?

> ELIZABETH CADY STANTON, National American Woman Suffrage Association Convention, 1890, *History of Woman Suffrage*, IV, 1902

It was feared then, as now, that women would become tyrannical and unbearable if they were allowed too much independence.

> JULIA LATHROP, "Woman Suffrage and Child Welfare," National American Woman Suffrage Convention, 1912, *History of Woman Suffrage*, V, 1922

. . . the natural woman, like Rousseau's natural man, is a creature about which we really know very little.

> ALICE BEAL PARSONS, *Woman's Dilemma*, 1926

General statements are still made about women which no moderately intelligent person would permit himself to make about men; the assumption that women are all the same, and that they are all really rather silly and helpless, still continually betrays itself.

> MARY AGNES HAMILTON, "Changes in Social Life," *Our Freedom and Its Results,* ed. Ray Strachey, 1936

A man likes to feel that he has "dependents." . . . He looks in the glass and sees himself as perhaps others see him—physically negligible, mentally ill-equipped, poor, unimportant, unsuccessful. He looks in the mirror he keeps in his mind, and sees his wife clinging to his arm and the children clustered round her skirts; all looking up to him, as that giver of all good gifts, the wage-earner. The picture is very alluring.

> ELEANOR RATHBONE, M. P., "Changes in Public Life," *Our Freedom and Its Results,* ed. Ray Strachey, 1936

. . . rule number one for all American women: You are to be seen and felt, but not heard.

> ELIZABETH HAWES, *Anything But Love,* 1948

. . . a premium was early put on woman's remaining a mystery. It simplifies everything—if no woman knows what she wants, and if it is impossible for a mere man to understand what women want, the nuisance of discussion can be set aside.

> RUTH HERSCHBERGER, *Adam's Rib,* 1948

One is not born, but rather becomes, a woman.

> SIMONE DE BEAUVOIR, *The Second Sex,* 1952

Woman is thus slave, queen, flower, hind, stained-glass window, wanton, servant, courtesan, muse, companion, mother, sister, child, according to the fugitive dreams, the imperious commands, of her lover.

> Ibid.

The feminine mystique says that the highest value and the only commitment for women is the fulfillment of their own femininity. . . . It says this femininity is so mysterious and intuitive and close to the creation and origin of life that man-made science may never be able to understand it.

> BETTY FRIEDAN, *The Feminine Mystique,* 1963

The mistake, says the mystique, the root of women's troubles in the past, is that women envied men, women tried to be like men, instead of accepting their own nature, which can find fulfillment only in sexual passivity, male domination, and nurturing, maternal love.
Ibid.

The new theorists of the self, who are men, have usually evaded the question of self-realization for a woman. Bemused themselves by the feminine mystique, they assume that there must be some strange "difference" which permits a woman to find self-realization by living through her husband and children, while men must grow to theirs.
Ibid.

Lesbian is the word, the label, the condition that holds women in line. When a woman hears this word tossed her way, she knows she is stepping out of line.
ELLEN BEDOZ, RITA MAE BROWN, et al., "The Woman-Identified Woman," © 1970, Radical Lesbians, in *The American Sisterhood*, ed. Wendy Martin, 1972

One distressing thing is the way men react to women who assert their equality: their ultimate weapon is to call them unfeminine. They think she is anti-male; they even whisper that she's probably a lesbian.
SHIRLEY CHISHOLM, *Unbought and Unbossed*, 1970

Any woman who fails to achieve orgasm on occasion, who discovers that she does not love her husband as much as she feels she ought, or who finds that she does not want to start a family or is not as involved with her children as society tells her she should be, is liable to worry about whether she is in some way rejecting her own femininity.
EVA FIGES, *Patriarchal Attitudes*, 1970

The fear of sacrificing femininity at the altar of success has kept thousands of girls "in their place."
LETTY COTTIN POGREBIN, *How to Make It in a Man's World*, 1970

Another nonprofit service that women dominate is the adjustment of complaints. They have an easier time holding customers to the rules because a woman isn't expected to have the authority to break regulations.
CAROLINE BIRD, *Born Female*, rev. ed., 1971

44

The perfect woman should be soft, charitable, passive, supportive of others—mainly her husband, then her children—and never self-centered.

JO ANN FUCHS, "The Woman of the Wealthy: A Value for All," *Women: A Journal of Liberation*, II, circa 1971

I am not real to him. I am not real to my civilization. I am not real to the culture that has spawned me and made use of me. I am only a collection of myths. I am an existential stand-in. The idea of me is real—the temptress, the goddess, the child, the mother—but *I* am not real. The mythic proportions of woman are recognizable and real; it is only the human dimensions that are patently false and will be denied to the death, our death.

VIVIAN GORNICK, "Woman as Outsider," *Woman in Sexist Society,* ed. Vivian Gornick and Barbara K. Moran, 1971

Passivity itself prevents a woman from ever considering her own potential for self-defense and forces her to look to men for protection. The woman is taught fear, but this time fear of the other; and yet her only relief from this fear is to seek out the other.

SUSAN GRIFFIN, "Rape: The All-American Crime," *Ramparts*, 10, September 1971

[The Black woman] has been forced to accept the images of what the larger society says a woman should be but at the same time accept the fact that in spite of how she strives to approximate these models, she can never reach the pedestal upon which white women have been put.

JOYCE A. LADNER, *Tomorrow's Tomorrow: The Black Woman*, 1971

Like woman herself, the family appears as a natural object, but is actually a cultural creation.

JULIET MITCHELL, *Woman's Estate*, 1971

On the one hand she must allow herself to be an object in order to get a man, on the other she will look down on herself for doing so. Unless she takes a cynical view of her use of her femininity, she is bound to suffer from a sense of inferiority. Perhaps the division between femininity and self creates the famous mystique of woman!

CHARLOTTE WOLFF, M.D., *Love Between Women*, 1971

Because of the male bias which has shaped our mentality for so many years, not only do women who exercise power receive no reward for it in the form of prestige or deference, but they are actually punished. They are "henpeck-

ing" their husbands. They are "castrating bitches," or worse. They are unwomanly, unnatural, deviant, and hence execrable. Unless, that is—and this is
the heart of the matter—they are clever enough, as they usually are, to hide
their light under a bushel, and to convince everyone, including their husbands, how brightly the masculine light shines.

JESSIE BERNARD, *The Future of Marriage,* 1972

As women, most of our lives with men are dramatic and theatrical affairs. We
"play" at being women; we dress up like Mommy—for Daddy's sake; we're
always on stage, working at being some other woman—a "beautiful" woman,
a "happy" woman, a well-paid-for woman.

PHYLLIS CHESLER, *Women and Madness,* 1972

Female emotional "talents" must be viewed in terms of the overall price exacted by sexism. It is illogical and dangerous to romanticize traits that one
purchases with one's freedom and dignity—even if they are "nice" traits;
even if they make one's slavery more bearable; even if they charm and soothe
the oppressor's rage and sorrow, staying his hand, or leave-taking, for one
more day.

Ibid.

Much of our submissive, conciliatory, compassionate, and seductive behaviors
have been cultivated in order to avoid either the fact or the onus of rape.

Ibid.

... the ... theory—that women are "closer to nature" and therefore subhu-
man ... has been one of the main justifications behind the subjugation of
women for centuries. And it's also the same theory that has had women
burned as witches and thrown into insane asylums!

LINDA JENNESS, "An Answer to Norman Mailer's 'Prisoner of Sex,' " *Feminism and Socialism,* ed. Linda Jenness, 1972

Lesbian-baiting is, of course, a favorite masculine ploy in putting down feminists.

DEL MARTIN AND PHYLLIS LYON, *Lesbian/Woman,* 1972

This fantasy world of sex which veils our experience is the world of sex as seen
through male eyes. It is a world whose eroticism is defined in terms of female
powerlessness, dependency, and submission.

LINDA PHELPS, "Female Sexual Alienation," *Women: A Journal of Liberation,* III, circa 1972

In this country, if you're any one of those things—poor, black, fat, female, middle-aged, on welfare—you count less as a human being. If you're *all* those things, you don't count at all. Except as a statistic.

JOHNNIE TILLMON, "Welfare Is a Women's Issue," *Ms.*, Spring 1972

Of course I don't want to lose my husband. But if our relationship depends on my constantly striving to fit a particular image so I won't lose my man, it isn't worth it.

CHARLOTTE HOLT CLINEBELL, *Meet Me in the Middle*, 1973

Too many of us as women have been irresponsible and frivolous, and too content with our lot. None of the traditional images of women—passive sweet child, holy mother, seductive temptress, or manipulative witch—demands enough of us as human beings.

Ibid.

As long as we accept the stereotypes that are presented to us in everything from pulp detective stories to Oscar-winning films—that women are naturally passive, childlike, and vulnerable, and that men are naturally aggressive, brutal, and uncontrollable—the rape situation will not change. Men will see the act of rape as a way of proving themselves; women will see rape as an inevitable threat.

ANDRA MEDEA AND KATHLEEN THOMPSON, *Against Rape*, 1974

Even though I was outwardly a girl and had many of the trappings generally associated with girldom . . . I spent the early years of my adolescence absolutely certain that I might at any point gum it up. I did not feel at all like a girl. I was boyish. I was athletic, ambitious, outspoken, competitive, noisy, rambunctious.

NORA EPHRON, *Crazy Salad*, 1975

If she refuses to talk like a lady, she is ridiculed and subjected to criticism as unfeminine; if she does learn, she is ridiculed as unable to think clearly, unable to take part in a serious discussion: in some sense, as less than fully human.

ROBIN LAKOFF, *Language and Woman's Place*, 1975

The romantic agenda always suggests that the "noble savages" should remain in their soulful primitivity, so they can nourish what the dominant group has lost. This may give women, blacks, peasants, or Indians a better image, but it leaves them basically where they have always been.

ROSEMARY RADFORD RUETHER, *New Woman New Earth*, 1975

The concern with ecology could repeat the mistakes of nineteenth-century romanticism. . . . Women will again be asked to be the "natural" wood-nymph and earth mother and to create places of escape from the destructive patterns of the dominant culture. Women will be told that their "highest calling" is to service this type of male need for sex, rest, emotionality, and escape from reality in a simulated grassy flower Eden.

Ibid.

. . . we realized that one of our central fantasies was our wish to find a man who could . . . make us feel alive and affirm our existence. It was as if we were made of clay and man would mold us, shape us, and bring us to life. This was the material of our childhood dreams: "Someday my prince will come." We were always disappointed when men did not accomplish this impossible task for us. And we began to see our passive, helpless ways of handing power over to others as crippling to us.

BOSTON WOMEN'S HEALTH BOOK COLLECTIVE, *Our Bodies, Ourselves*, 2d ed., 1976

The irrational fear of lesbianism is used not only to divide us from other women but also to keep all women isolated from each other, to keep women from becoming close friends. It also serves to keep women "in their place": any woman who acts assertive or holds a "man's" job may be labeled a dyke.

Ibid.

But we have also experienced, more intuitively and unconsciously, men's fantasies of our power, fantasies rooted far back in infancy, and in some mythogenetic zone of history. Whatever their origins, for most women these male fantasies, because so obliquely expressed, have been obscured from view. What we did see, for centuries, was the hatred of overt strength in women, the definition of strong independent women as freaks of nature, as unsexed, frigid, castrating, perverted, dangerous; the fear of the maternal woman as "controlling," the preference for dependent, malleable, "feminine" women.

ADRIENNE RICH, *Of Woman Born*, 1976

A woman is not born to suffer (or overcome suffering through moral perfection) any more than she is born unclean. While there is plenty of evidence that women have remarkable capacities to endure pain, there is no evidence that we are born masochists or saints. Female masochism appears to be one more male fantasy rationalizing male inattention to women's needs . . .

PAULA WEIDEGER, *Menstruation and Menopause*, 1976

48

The "Evil" Woman

Men have written for us, thought for us, legislated for us; and they have constructed from their own consciousness an effigy of a woman, to which we are expected to conform. It is not a Woman that they see; God forbid that it should be; it is one of those monsters of neither sex, that sometimes outrage the pangs of maternity, but which expire at the birth; whereas the distorted image to which men wish us to conform, lives to bewilder, to mislead, and to cause discord and belittlement where the Creator designed the highest dignity, the most complete harmony.

ELIZABETH OAKES SMITH, *Woman and Her Needs*, 1851

Frances D. Gage said that allusion had been made . . . to the popular sentiment, that men are what their mothers made them. She repelled this sentiment as an indignity to her sex. What mother, she asked, ever taught her son to drink rum, gamble, swear, smoke, and chew tobacco? The truth was, that the boy was virtually taught to regard his mother as inferior, and that it was not manly to follow her instructions.

Records of the Woman's Rights Convention, 1852, *History of Woman Suffrage*, I, 1881

Just imagine an inhabitant of another planet entertaining himself some pleasant evening in searching over our great national compact, our Declaration of Independence, our Constitutions, or some of our statute-books; what would he think of those "women and negroes" that must be so fenced in, so guarded against? Why, he would certainly suppose we were monsters, like those fabulous giants or Brobdingnagians of olden times, so dangerous to civilized man, from our size, ferocity, and power.

ELIZABETH CADY STANTON, "Address to the Legislature of the State of New York," 1860, *History of Woman Suffrage*, I, 1881

If a man commits suicide, it is forthwith charged to unpleasant domestic relations. If another, in a fit of insanity, takes himself out of the world his wife's extravagance is the cause. So, too, "the extravagance of the wife" is offered as an excuse for the reckless spendthrift and defaulter. If a man deserts his wife and family and goes after strange women, the wife is in some way to blame for it; and if he gratifies his lust by the ruin of innocent girls, there are enough of his fellows to come to his defense by implicating his wife as the guilty cause of his ruin. And so on to the end of the chapter, the same old story:

"The woman whom Thou gavest me did it." What a pitiful sneaking plea to come from the self-styled "lords of creation," the boasted superiors of woman!

> AMELIA BLOOMER, "Is It Right for Women to Lecture?" in D. C. Bloomer, *Life and Writings of Amelia Bloomer*, 1895

Could the dark secrets of insane asylums be brought to light we should be shocked to know the great number of rebellious wives, sisters, and daughters who are thus sacrificed to false customs and barbarous laws made by men for women.

> ELIZABETH CADY STANTON, *Eighty Years and More*, 1898

. . . it is one of the ugliest sides of this ugly traffic [prostitution] that the men who buy the women seem to hate and despise them so, and they then proceed to generalise about all women on the data of the hated and despised ones.

> H. M. SWANWICK, *The Future of the Women's Movement*, 1913

Because I am I, an odd piece of Egotism who could not make the riffle of living according to the precepts and standards society demands of itself, I find myself locked up with others of my kind in a "hospital" for the insane. There is nothing wrong with me—except I was born at least two thousand years too late. Ladies of Amazonian proportions and Berserker propensities have passed quite out of vogue and have no place in this too damned civilized world.

> LARA JEFFERSON, *These Are My Sisters*, 1947

The insult, the real reflection on our culture's definition of the role of women, is that as a nation we only noticed that something was wrong with women when we saw its effects on their sons.

> BETTY FRIEDAN, *The Feminine Mystique*, 1963

. . . the modern attacks on Mom seem to be the currently fashionable way in which fears always latent are to be expressed. The menace which earlier centuries attached to the devouring whore, ours attaches to the devouring mother.

> KATHARINE M. ROGERS, *The Troublesome Helpmate*, 1966

The frequency with which derangement follows loss of virtue [in nineteenth-century women's fiction] suggests the exquisite sensibility of woman, and the possibility that, in the women's magazines at least, her intellect was geared to her hymen, not her brain.

> BARBARA WELTER, "The Cult of True Womanhood: 1820–1860," *American Quarterly*, XVIII, Summer 1966

Woman as a source of danger, as a repository of externalized evil, is an image that runs through patriarchal history. She is witch, demoness, scarlet woman, schemer, and her power in the minds of men usually increases in inverse proportion to her actual power in the world of reality.

EVA FIGES, *Patriarchal Attitudes,* 1970

Cretins, albinos, and mongoloids must be treated with respect by the television scriptwriter—but not so the American woman. She may be portrayed with impunity as stupid, grasping, selfish, fiendish, scatterbrained, unreliable, ignorant, irritating, and ridiculous—and no one says a word. Women are supposed to take it all like good sports—or like outsiders whose feelings are of no account.

ELIZABETH GOULD DAVIS, *The First Sex,* 1971

It is, of course, quite true that men, too, have grievances. There has certainly been no lack of recognition of them, since men have been complaining of their lot from time immemorial, and, a good deal of the time, not only blaming it on women but also convincing women of their culpability.

JESSIE BERNARD, *The Future of Marriage,* 1972

Neither genuinely mad women, nor women who are hospitalized for conditioned female behavior, are powerful revolutionaries.... Their behavior is "mad" because it represents a socially powerless individual's attempt to unite body and feeling.

PHYLLIS CHESLER, *Women and Madness,* 1972

... because ascetic spirituality defined sin as the disordering of the flesh to the spirit ... the equation of woman with body also made her peculiarly the symbol of sin.

ROSEMARY RADFORD RUETHER, *Liberation Theology,* 1972

The myth of the Fall ... amounts to a cosmic false naming. It misnames the mystery of evil, casting it into the distorted mold of the myth of feminine evil. In this way images and conceptualizations about evil are thrown out of focus and its deepest dimensions are not really confronted.

MARY DALY, *Beyond God the Father,* 1973

The existence of "good" women—according to male standards of being unmolested private property—has required the existence of "bad" women, who have been scapegoats for male sexual guilt.

Ibid.

Women, though encouraged to imitate the sacrificial love of Jesus, and thus willingly accept the victim's role, remain essentially identified with Eve and evil. Salvation comes only through the male.
Ibid.

Historically, medicine ratified the dangers of women by describing women as the source of venereal disease. Today, we are more likely to be viewed as mental health hazards—emasculating men and destructively dominating children.
BARBARA EHRENREICH AND DEIRDRE ENGLISH, *Complaints and Disorders,* 1973

The fall was from some primeval division into two sexes. I think any bioanalytically oriented person knows we were originally one sex.
JILL JOHNSTON, *Lesbian Nation,* 1973

Simultaneously the "Devil's Gateway" and the Virgin Mother, the hated and the adored, woman becomes, in Western mythology, a chimera without substance.
ROSEMARY RADFORD RUETHER, Preface, *Religion and Sexism,* 1974

. . . for the message they gave was to live a life of fear, and to it they appended the dire warning that the woman who did not follow the rules must be held responsible for her own violation.
SUSAN BROWNMILLER, *Against Our Will,* 1975

. . . through centuries of suckling men emotionally at our breasts we have also been told that we were polluted, devouring, domineering, masochistic, harpies, bitches, dykes, and whores.
ADRIENNE RICH, *Of Woman Born,* 1976

While Western religions have traditionally portrayed the spiritual nature of human beings and their relation to God in male terms, sexuality is portrayed as female, the embodiment of sin, forever distracting men from godliness: sons of God but daughters of Eve.
CASEY MILLER AND KATE SWIFT, *Words and Women,* 1977

We are taught that man most loves and admires
the domestic type of woman. This is one of the
roaring jokes of history. The breakers of hearts,
the queens of romance, the goddesses of a thousand devotees, have not been cooks.

CHARLOTTE PERKINS GILMAN, *The Home,* 1903

4   The Aristocracy of Sex

Romance and Chivalry

I doubt whether pity and love are so near akin as poets feign, for I have seldom seen much compassion excited by the helplessness of females, unless they
were fair.

MARY WOLLSTONECRAFT, *A Vindication of the Rights of Woman,* 1792

No woman, who understands her dignity as a moral, intellectual, and accountable being, cares aught for any attention or any protection, vouchsafed
by "the promptings of chivalry, and the poetry of romantic gallantry."

ANGELINA GRIMKÉ, Letter XI, *Letters to Catherine E. Beecher,* 1837

Ah! how many of my sex feel in the dominion, thus unrighteously exercised
over them, under the gentle appellation of *protection,* that what they have
leaned upon has proved a broken reed at best, and oft a spear.

SARAH GRIMKÉ, Letter III, 1837, *Letters on the Equality of the Sexes,* 1838

I confess, considering the high claim men in this country make to great politeness and deference to women, it does seem a little extraordinary that we
should be urged to work for the brethren. I should suppose it would be more
in character with "the generous promptings of chivalry, and the poetry of romantic gallantry". . . for them to form societies to educate their sisters, seeing
our inferior capacities require more cultivation to bring them into use, and
qualify us to be helpsmeet for them.

Ibid., Letter XV, 1837

How has a little wit, a little genius, been celebrated in a Woman!
MARGARET FULLER, *Woman in the Nineteenth Century*, 1845

There may be real though very foolish tenderness in the motive which refuses to open to woman the trades and professions that she could cultivate and practice with equal profit and credit to herself. The chivalry that worships womanhood is not mean, though it at the same time enslaves the objects of its overfond care.
PAULINA WRIGHT DAVIS, address, *Proceedings of the Woman's Rights Convention, Held at Worcester, October 23 & 24, 1850*, 1851

... for disguise it as man and women may, this perpetual adulation, this fostering of our pettiness, our vanity, our love of luxury, is but the mode of holding us in the pupilage of sex—recognizing only our relation in one aspect of life, and ignoring all other claims.
ELIZABETH OAKES SMITH, *Woman and Her Needs*, 1851

"Dat man ober dar say dat womin needs to be helped into carriages, and lifted ober ditches, and to hab de best place everywhar. Nobody eber helps me into carriages, or ober mud-puddles, or gibs me any best place!" And raising herself to her full height, and her voice to a pitch like rolling thunder, she asked, "And a'n't I a woman? Look at me! Look at my arm! (and she bared her right arm to the shoulder, showing her tremendous muscular power). I have ploughed, and planted, and gathered into barns, and no man could head me! And a'n't I a woman? I could work as much and eat as much as a man— when I could get it—and bear de lash as well! And a'n't I a woman?"
SOJOURNER TRUTH, 1851, in Frances D. Gage, "Reminiscences," *History of Woman Suffrage*, I, 1881

Divines may preach thanksgiving sermons on the poetry of the arm-chair and the cradle; but when they lay down their newspapers, or leave their beds a cold night to attend to the wants of either, I shall begin to look for the golden age of chivalry once more.
ELIZABETH CADY STANTON, letter to Gerrit Smith, 1855, *History of Woman Suffrage*, I, 1881

... a man in love will jump to pick up a glove or a bouquet for a silly girl of sixteen, whilst at home he will permit his aged mother to carry pails of water and armfuls of wood, or his wife to lug a twenty-pound baby, hour after hour, without ever offering to relieve her.
Ibid.

We are told woman has all the rights she wants; and even women, I am ashamed to say, tell us so. They mistake the politeness of men for rights— seats while men stand in this hall tonight, and their adulations; but these are mere courtesies. We want rights.

> LUCY STONE, Woman's Rights Convention, 1855, *History of Woman Suffrage*, I, 1881

We, as a class, are tired of one kind of protection, that which leaves us everything to do, to dare, and to suffer, and strips us of all means for its accomplishment.

> ELIZABETH CADY STANTON, "Address to the Legislature of the State of New York," 1860, *History of Woman Suffrage*, I, 1881

I shall have little hope for woman, till *she* learns to feel that to die for love is not so much a pitiful as a disgraceful thing . . .

> CAROLINE WELLS DALL, *The College, The Market, and the Court*, 1861

The [novel] . . . has thus far done infinite harm, by drawing false distinctions between the masculine and feminine elements of human nature, and perpetuating, through the influence of genius often *intensifying*, the educational power of a false theory of love.

> Ibid.

To the young lady whose lover has been for months declaring himself "her slave" there must be something of a shock when she finds, a few weeks after marriage, that he has a very distinct idea that he is rightfully the master; and, as she looks on her new visiting card, bearing the words "Mr. and Mrs. So and So," the name his alone, and the Mr. placed before the Mrs., showing that he is regarded as really the superior, perhaps she realizes that she is in truth "merged" in her husband.

> LILLIE DEVEREUX BLAKE, *Women's Place Today*, 1883

It is better to have the power of self-protection than to depend on any man, whether he be the governor in his chair of state, or the hunted outlaw wandering through the night, hungry and cold and with murder in his heart. We are tired of the pretence that we have special privileges, and the reality that we have none. Of the fiction that we are queens, and the fact that we are subjects; of the symbolism that exalts our sex but is only a meaningless mockery! We demand that these shadows shall take substance!

> LILLIE DEVEREUX BLAKE, National Woman Suffrage Association Convention, 1884, *History of Woman Suffrage*, IV, 1902

We are told that men protect us; that they are generous, even chivalric in their protection. Gentlemen, if your protectors were women, and they took all your property and your children, and paid you half as much for your work, though as well or better done than your own, would you think much of the chivalry which permitted you to sit in street-cars and picked up your pocket-handkerchief?

> MARY B. CLAY, to House Judiciary Committee, 1884, *History of Woman Suffrage*, IV, 1902

The talk of sheltering woman from the fierce storms of life is the sheerest mockery, for they beat on her from every point of the compass, just as they do on man, and with more fatal results, for he has been trained to protect himself, to resist, to conquer . . .

> ELIZABETH CADY STANTON, "The Solitude of Self," to Senate Committee on Woman Suffrage, 1892, *History of Woman Suffrage*, IV, 1902

The love of protecting too often degenerates into downright tyranny.

> ELIZABETH CADY STANTON, *Eighty Years and More*, 1898

The man needs the wife and has her—needs the world and has it. The woman needs the husband—and has him; needs the world—and there is the husband instead. He stands between her and the world, with the best of intentions, doubtless; but a poor substitute for full human life.

> CHARLOTTE PERKINS GILMAN, *The Home*, 1903

. . . if you will give us justice we feel that it will mean a great deal more than chivalry ever did.

> HELEN LORING GRENFELL, to House Judiciary Committee, 1904, *History of Woman Suffrage*, V, 1922

Women are frequently invited to bewail the death of chivalry. What chivalry meant, in these days, was the protection by individual men of their own women against the depredations of other men.

> H. M. SWANWICK, *The Future of the Women's Movement*, 1913

The pedestal platitude appeals less and less to the intelligence of southern women, who are learning in increasing numbers that the assertion that they are too good, too noble, too pure to vote, in reality brands them as incompetents.

> PATTIE RUFFNER JACOBS, National American Woman Suffrage Association Convention, 1915, *History of Woman Suffrage*, V, 1922

The mass of legislation and regulation designed to protect women from the fatigues and hazards of industry would seem . . . to have been animated more by chivalry than by scientific knowledge; and while chivalry may be all very well in its place, it can hardly be expected to solve the industrial problem of women.

SUZANNE LA FOLLETTE, *Concerning Women*, 1926

. . . chivalry is not compulsory, while prostitution is.
Ibid.

. . . the truth is that since the beginning, the whole feminine world has been in a conspiracy to shield and protect men. Only in fables of chivalry is woman the sheltered sex. Visit any American home and you will find grandmothers, mothers, wives, sisters, aunts, daughters and female servants consecrated to one great purpose—guarding the male members of the family from the vicissitudes of everyday life.

FLORENCE GUY SEABURY, in *Laughing Their Way*, ed. Martha Bensley Bruère and Mary Ritter Beard, 1934

Gone are the silly old days when Grandfather gruffly said that no daughter of his should ever work. Grandfather was perhaps just a little selfish in proclaiming this idea. Men are apt to be. Grandfather no doubt had an idea that if women went to work he might be relegated to the home and the women would take over everything.

ELIZABETH HAWES, *Anything But Love*, 1948

Women do not often recognize that courtship is a phase in which the preferences of women are ritualistically catered to: the wooing is a preliminary concession to those pressure contacts women love—gentleness, tenderness, kissing, caressing. With marriage comes a startling change of events, the woman's preferences being set aside in favor of the duties of marriage. . . . The man has heroically fulfilled the role of suitor, onerous though it may have been, and now considers it his right to indulge in his own preferred types of pressure contact, learned on the playing field.

RUTH HERSCHBERGER, *Adam's Rib*, 1948

Go ahead and *love!* we say to women. But don't get so excited about it!
Ibid.

Protectiveness has often muffled the sound of doors closing against women. . . .

> BETTY FRIEDAN, *The Feminine Mystique*, 1963

And love. As long as we're on sacred cows, let's finish them. What is love but the payoff for the consent to oppression? What is love but need? What is love but fear? In a just society, would we need love?

> TI-GRACE ATKINSON, "Vaginal Orgasm as a Mass Hysterical Survival Response," 1968, *Amazon Odyssey*, 1974

"Love" is the woman's pitiful deluded attempt to attain the human.

> TI-GRACE ATKINSON, "Radical Feminism and Love," 1969, *Amazon Odyssey*, 1974

Chivalry, then, makes equals unequal. . . . The less respect a woman gets as a person, the more she values the gestures of "respect" she can command as a woman.

> DANA DENSMORE, "Chivalry—The Iron Hand in the Velvet Glove," *No More Fun and Games*, November 1969

. . . love is the only circumstance in which the female is pardoned for sexual activity.

> KATE MILLETT, *Sexual Politics*, 1970

ROMANTIC LOVE [is] a putup job utilized to trap women into giving up their identities.

> CAROLINE BIRD, *Born Female*, rev. ed., 1971

Sensuality

The sensualist, indeed, has been the most dangerous of tyrants, and women have been duped by their lovers, as princes by their ministers, whilst dreaming that they reigned over them.

> MARY WOLLSTONECRAFT, *A Vindication of the Rights of Woman*, 1792

Modesty must be equally cultivated by both sexes, or it will remain a sickly hothouse plant, whilst the affectation of it, the fig leaf borrowed by wantonness, may give a zest to voluptuous enjoyments.

> Ibid.

Men have, indeed, been for more than a hundred years, rating women for countenancing vice. But, at the same time, they have carefully hid from them its nature, so that the preference often shown by women for bad men arises rather from a confused idea that they are bold and adventurous, acquainted with regions which women are forbidden to explore, and the curiosity that ensues, than a corrupt heart in the woman. As to marriage, it has been inculcated on women, for centuries, that men, have not only stronger passions than they, but of a sort that it would be shameful for them to share or even understand . . .

MARGARET FULLER, *Woman in the Nineteenth Century*, 1845

Can there be anything more outrageous than the idea that a healthy, grown woman, full of life and passion, must deny nature's demand, must subdue her most intense craving, undermine her health and break her spirit, must stunt her vision, abstain from the depth and glory of sex experience until a "good" man comes along to take her unto himself as a wife?

EMMA GOLDMAN, "Marriage and Love," *Anarchism and Other Essays*, 1911

. . . it is only when the egoistic man fears that the unmated woman may be active and content, that his sensitive vanity is up in arms, and he is dismayed at the notion of a woman, of her free choice, forgoing man. He is content there should be millions of spinsters, if only they are unhappy.

H. M. SWANWICK, *The Future of the Women's Movement*, 1913

Women are moved by sexual impulses towards particular men, not towards men as a whole, and men will never understand women so long as they do not recognise this.

Ibid.

[The husband's] idea of marriage is too often that of providing a home for a female who would in turn provide for his physical needs, including sexual satisfaction. Such a husband usually excludes such satisfaction from the category of the wife's needs, physical or spiritual.

MARGARET SANGER, *Woman and the New Race*, 1920

Chastity being the virtue that man exacted from the woman who was his property, moral and immoral came to mean no more than chaste or loose in sexual matters.

MARY AGNES HAMILTON, "Changes in Social Life," *Our Freedom and Its Results*, ed. Ray Strachey, 1936

Before marriage sex relations are anti-social. After marriage they are useful and ennobling.

ELIZABETH HAWES, *Anything but Love*, 1948

Is it true that women's bodies are naturally less tidy than men's? Is it correct that the secretions of the female are more objectionable than the analogous secretions of the male? While advertisements, it can be expected, exploit the ignorance and puritanism of the public, physicians themselves sometimes reveal a subtle conviction that women's glands are a little less civilized than men's.

RUTH HERSCHBERGER, *Adam's Rib*, 1948

Just as he wants her to be at once warm and cool in bed, he requires her to be wholly his and yet no burden; he wishes her to establish him in a fixed place on earth and to leave him free, to assume the monotonous daily round and not to bore him, to be always at hand and never importunate; he wants to have her all to himself and not to belong to her; to live as one of a couple and to remain alone.

SIMONE DE BEAUVOIR, *The Second Sex*, 1952

Sex is the only frontier open to women who have always lived within the confines of the feminine mystique. In the past fifteen years, the sexual frontier has been forced to expand perhaps beyond the limits of possibility, to fill the time available, to fill the vacuum created by denial of larger goals and purposes for American women.

BETTY FRIEDAN, *The Feminine Mystique*, 1963

The charge that woman is more lustful than man, perhaps the most prominent in the whole arsenal of misogyny, can be traced to three . . . underlying motives: a sexual ascetic is likely to project his own lustful feelings upon women; an ambivalent lover will accuse his mistress of unfaithfulness or sexual insatiability . . . ; and a patriarch is apt to worry constantly that the wife he owns may rebel against his sovereignty by giving her body to other men.

KATHARINE M. ROGERS, *The Troublesome Helpmate*, 1966

Masculine society has insisted on seeing in sexuality that same sense of conflict and competition that it has imposed upon its relation to the planet as a whole. From the bedroom to the board room to the international conference table, separateness, differentiation, opposition, exclusion, antithesis have been the cause and goal of the male politics of power.

BETTY ROSZAK, "The Human Condition," *Masculine/Feminine*, ed. B. and T. Roszak, 1969

It is an ironic fact that man, having tried to confine woman more and more to the bedroom, should then complain that woman is always trying to drag him back to bed. What else is the poor soul supposed to do, to avoid dying of sheer boredom?

EVA FIGES, *Patriarchal Attitudes*, 1970

. . . in addition to being sexually deprived, these women [diagnosed as "frigid"] were told to blame themselves when they deserved no blame. Looking for a cure to a problem that has none can lead a woman on an endless path of self-hatred and insecurity. For she is told by her analyst that not even in her one role allowed in a male society—the role of woman—is she successful. She is put on the defensive, with phony data as evidence that she better try to be even more feminine, think more feminine, and reject her envy of men. That is, shuffle even harder, baby.

ANNE KOEDT, "The Myth of the Vaginal Orgasm," *Voices from Women's Liberation*, ed. Leslie B. Tanner, 1970

For two thousand years the male "brotherhood" . . . [has] testified to what extent men are socialized to separate love and sex and to fear the former and condemn the latter—in women.

PHYLLIS CHESLER, *Women and Madness*, 1972

. . . if ever you want a really good laugh, I would recommend reading up some of the incredibly involved and convoluted arguments of a male evolutionist trying to explain why woman, alone of all the primates, equipped herself with a hymen, which appears on the face of it to have no other purpose than to keep him out.

ELAINE MORGAN, *The Descent of Woman*, 1972

From an early age, we are alienated from ourselves as sexual beings by a male society's ambivalent definition of our sexuality; we are sexy but we are pure; we are insatiable but we are frigid; we have beautiful bodies but we must shave and anoint them.

LINDA PHELPS, "Female Sexual Alienation," *Women: A Journal of Liberation*, III, circa 1972

Men would think it was ridiculous if psychiatrists went around saying that many of them don't really need orgasms. They should be content just to be affectionate and share love, etc., etc. Yet unfortunately, many men still hope or believe that this male supremacist myth about women is true.

BARBARA SEAMAN, *Free and Female*, 1972

Isn't it remarkable that when you insist on controlling your own time, you are being rude, but when a man insists on taking up your own time, he is being friendly?
    ANDRA MEDEA AND KATHLEEN THOMPSON, *Against Rape*, 1974

... the fear and hatred of our bodies has often crippled our brains.
    ADRIENNE RICH, *Of Woman Born*, 1976

Uterine Myths

We ask ourselves in some bewilderment, if women commit deeds of violence only when their monthly period induces an emotional instability, when do men commit their six times as many deeds of violence?
    ALICE BEAL PARSONS, *Woman's Dilemma*, 1926

It is difficult to figure out the exact statistical year when the average American woman may be expected to go to pieces. Most of the Authorities indicate this crack-up has something to do with the menopause, which is apt to come between 40 and 50.

However, no woman in the USA can be unaware of the fact that she is supposed to begin by the age of 33 to work herself up into a state of complete jitters. This condition is merely supposed to reach its climax when menopause occurs. It can go on for years previous.
    ELIZABETH HAWES, *Anything But Love*, 1948

A woman's importance is her reproductive function: the "mother" is the most politically, socially, and economically catered to woman in our society. God help her when she's passed her fertile years; not only does she cease being a mother, but there is reluctance to define her as even a woman.
    TI-GRACE ATKINSON, "Juniata I: The Sacrificial Lambs," 1969, *Amazon Odyssey*, 1974

There is no bar mitzvah for menopause.
    PAULINE BART, "Depression in Middle-Aged Women," *Woman in Sexist Society*, ed. Vivian Gornick and Barbara K. Moran, 1971

The only way of accounting for the evolutionary emergence of the menopause in women is by the assumption that the tribe as a whole, and not merely the individual, derived some benefit from the presence of those females who although sterile lived to a ripe and healthy old age. In some way or other,

62

and in a way that applied to no other species that we know of, grannies were good for them.
> ELAINE MORGAN, *The Descent of Woman*, 1972

For a woman, her menstrual cycle is only a very minor part of her identity, and at worst an annoyance, whereas from reading men's comments about this biological process, one might be led to believe that woman's destiny is conditioned by a debilitating loss of blood and the need for constant transfusions.
> CLARA MARIA HENNING, "Canon Law and the Battle of the Sexes," *Religion and Sexism*, ed. R. R. Ruether, 1974

Menstrual blood was thought to be attractive to devils and unclean spirits, and a menstruating woman would by her presence sour milk and kill the grass she walked upon, according to popular belief.
> ELEANOR COMMO MCLAUGHLIN, "Equality of Souls, Inequality of Sexes: Woman in Medieval Theology," *Religion and Sexism*, ed. R. R. Ruether, 1974

Our youth-oriented culture tends to present menopause as a descent into "uncool" middle and old age. In a society which equates our sexuality with our ability to have children, menopause is wrongly thought to mean the end ... of our sexual pleasure....
> BOSTON WOMEN'S HEALTH BOOK COLLECTIVE, *Our Bodies, Ourselves*, 2d ed. 1976

... menstrual politics has dominated social and economic relations between the sexes since the beginning of time. In all their struggles for equality—the suffrage movement, the labor movement, the struggle for ERA—women have been obliged to fight against an enemy who will not contend with them in the halls of Congress or the courts of law. The enemy is within every woman, but it is not her menstruation. Rather, it is the habit of mind regarding menstruation into which she has been led by centuries of male domination. She has been taught that menstruation is disabling, and so she has been disabled.
> JANICE DELANEY, MARY JANE LUPTON, AND EMILY TOTH, *The Curse: A Cultural History of Menstruation*, 1976

Thus far neither doctor nor patient respects the experiences of menstruation and menopause. While Western women do not walk about in the drapery of Purdah, the veils of secrecy, shame, and disrespect similarly constrict the female personality. The unknown and hidden aspects of woman's life are some-

63

times described as the riddle of female identity and sometimes derided as the soiled evidence of corruption.

PAULA WEIDEGER, *Menstruation and Menopause*, 1976

The most damning euphemism attached to menstruation reflects the belief that the monthly flow of blood is the curse God laid upon woman for her sin in Eden.

Ibid.

Most women become sexually invisible after menopause, not because of any mysterious or well-known physical upheaval but because the culture expects them to.

Ibid.

The government treats menstrual paraphernalia as a luxury and taxes it.

Ibid.

Reproduction

Men exhibit some common sense in breeding all animals except those of their own species.

EMILY COLLINS, "Reminiscences," circa 1848, *History of Woman Suffrage*, I, 1881

Alas! Alas! who can measure the mountains of sorrow and suffering endured in unwelcome motherhood in the abodes of ignorance, poverty, and vice, where terror-stricken women and children are the victims of strong men frenzied with passion and intoxicating drink?

ELIZABETH CADY STANTON, *Eighty Years and More*, 1898

Society is so beautifully sentimental on the subject of murder. Abortion is looked upon as murder. But do those who make our Christian laws ever hesitate to kill children born or unborn when there is a sufficient profit in the act?

DOROTHY KELLY, "Prevention and the Law," *The Woman Rebel*, I, April 1914

Marriage laws abrogate the freedom of woman by enforcing upon her a continuous sexual slavery and a compulsory motherhood.

MARGARET SANGER, "Marriage," *The Woman Rebel*, I, April 1914

The woman who goes to the abortionist's table is not a criminal but a martyr—a martyr to the bitter, unthinkable conditions brought about by the blindness of society at large.

MARGARET SANGER, *Woman and the New Race,* 1920

In an ideal society, no doubt, birth control would become the concern of the man as well as the woman. The hard, inescapable fact which we encounter today is that man has not only refused any such responsibility, but has individually and collectively sought to prevent woman from obtaining knowledge by which she could assume this responsibility for herself.

Ibid.

I read recently in an article by G. K. Chesterton, that sex without gestation and parturition is like blowing the trumpets and waving the flags without doing any of the fighting. From a woman such words, though displaying inexperience, might come with dignity; from a man they are an unforgivable, intolerable insult. What is man's part in sex but a perpetual waving of flags and blowing of trumpets and avoidance of the fighting?

DORA RUSSELL, *Hypatia,* 1925

Instead of joining in the universal condemnation of illegitimacy, it seems more reasonable to question the ethics of a society which permits it to exist. Certainly no social usage could be more degrading to women as mothers of the race than that which makes it a sin to bear a child; and nothing could be more grotesquely unjust than a code of morals, reinforced by laws, which relieves men from responsibility for irregular sexual acts, and for the same acts drives women to abortion, infanticide, prostitution and self-destruction.

SUZANNE LA FOLLETTE, *Concerning Women,* 1926

If one is willing to have children, Rhythm is probably the best method of contraception.

ELIZABETH HAWES, *Anything But Love,* 1948

"Ah, what a thrill to feel the first faint flutter of life as the tiny one moves about. How amusing it is to feel his impatient kicks through the tight abdominal wall." All male physicians agree on this.

Ibid.

65

To label family planning and legal abortion programs "genocide" is male rhetoric, for male ears. It falls flat to female listeners, and to thoughtful male ones.

SHIRLEY CHISHOLM, *Unbought and Unbossed*, 1970

No matter what men think, abortion is a fact of life. Women will have them; they always have and always will. Are they going to have good ones or bad ones? Will the good ones be reserved for the rich while poor women have to go to quacks?

Ibid.

The idea that bearing children is the primary reason for a woman's existence has always been very widespread and is still with us. One could almost say that it is a fundamental tenet of the male mind.

EVA FIGES, *Patriarchal Attitudes*, 1970

Men will change the laws on abortion even if women do nothing. . . . And they'll do it for the wrong reasons, for population control instead of for the dignity of women. All I'm working for is enough time so that women will know what it means to control their own bodies and make their own decisions before the government goes the other way and puts birth control pills in the drinking water.

LANA PHELAN, quoted by Mary Reinholz, "Storming the All Electric Doll House," *Los Angeles Times, West* magazine, June 7, 1970

If we are to come to grips with the problem of population growth it is vital that women have alternate life styles other than extensive child bearing. There is little reason for a woman to limit her family if the only realistic alternative is a job far below her capabilities, coupled with extensive educational and occupational discrimination.

BERNICE SANDLER, to Rep. Edith Green's Special Subcommittee on Education, 1970, *Discrimination Against Women*, U.S. Government Printing Office, 1971

Men have borne up well while forcing women to bear down in unwelcome labor and to bow down in lifetime subservience to the unwanted fruits of sex.

NATALIE SHAINESS, M.D., "Abortion Is No Man's Business," *Psychology Today*, May 1970

When legalized abortion is suggested the anti-abortionist immediately cried, "infanticide!" Yet his shrill voice is silent in the face of war.... Our society accepts war—a ritualized, institutionalized form of murder—and yet protests the removal of an unsentient cluster of cells.

Ibid.

Some women see abortion as a necessary measure for themselves but no one sees it as the fulfillment of her greatest dreams.

MARY DALY, *Beyond God the Father*, 1973

Abortion is violence: a deep, desperate violence inflicted by a woman upon, first of all, herself. It is the offspring, and will continue to be the accuser, of a more pervasive and prevalent violence, the violence of rapism.

ADRIENNE RICH, *Of Woman Born*, 1976

Motherhood

To be a good mother—a woman must have sense, and that independence of mind which few women possess who are taught to depend entirely on their husbands.

MARY WOLLSTONECRAFT, *A Vindication of the Rights of Woman*, 1792

While different men have different duties, different functions, different spheres, ranging from the heights of Parnassus to the bowels of the earth, why legislate all women into a nutshell? Because a man is a father, must he needs be nothing else? Are lawyers, merchants, tailors, cobblers, bootblacks less skilled in their specialties because they vote? Because some women are mothers, shall all women concentrate every thought in that direction? and can those who are mothers be nothing else? Have not those who are training up sons and daughters an interest beyond the home, in the great outer world, where they are soon to act their part?

ELIZABETH CADY STANTON, reply to Horace Greeley's report on the New York State Constitutional Convention, *New York Independent*, 1867, *History of Woman Suffrage*, II, 1882

It is, in fact, often taken for granted, that though for women who have only themselves to think of, it may be a good thing to have some intellectual resources, for *mothers* there is nothing like good sound ignorance.

EMILY DAVIES, LL.D., "Some Account of a Proposed New College for Women," Annual Meeting of the National Association for the Promotion of Social

Science, 1868, *Thoughts on Some Questions Relating to Women, 1860–1908*, 1910

The woman who has given birth to a son has fulfilled her "mission." The celibate woman,—be she holy as St. Theresa, useful as Miss Nightingale, gifted as Miss Cornwallis,—has entirely missed it.

This doctrine, of course, belongs properly to ages of barbarism, when the material always took precedence of the spiritual . . .

FRANCES POWER COBBE, "The Final Cause of Woman," *Woman's Work and Woman's Culture*, ed. Josephine E. Butler, 1869

The woman is uniformly sacrificed to the wife and mother.

E. C. STANTON, S. B. ANTHONY, M. J. GAGE, eds., *History of Woman Suffrage*, I, 1881

There would be more sense in insisting on man's limitations because he can not be a mother, than on woman's because she can be.

ELIZABETH CADY STANTON, National Woman Suffrage Association Convention, 1885, *History of Woman Suffrage*, IV, 1902

I have no sympathy with the old idea that children owe parents a debt of gratitude for the simple fact of existence, generally conferred without thought and merely for their own pleasure. How seldom we hear of any high or holy preparation for the office of parenthood! Here, in the most momentous act of life, all is left to chance.

ELIZABETH CADY STANTON, *Eighty Years and More*, 1898

On one occasion, after addressing the legislature, some of the ladies, in congratulating me, inquired, in a deprecating tone, "What do you do with your children?" "Ladies," I said, "it takes me no longer to speak, than you to listen; what have you done with your children the two hours you have been sitting here?"

Ibid.

The mother—poor invaded soul—finds even the bathroom door no bar to hammering little hands.

CHARLOTTE PERKINS GILMAN, *The Home*, 1903.

If there were an instinct inherent in human mothers sufficient to care rightly for their children, then all human mothers would care rightly for their children. Do they?

Ibid.

Our voices thrill and tremble with pathos and veneration as we speak of "the mothers of great men—" mother of Abraham Lincoln! Mother of George Washington! and so on. Had Wilkes Booth no mother? Was Benedict Arnold an orphan?

Ibid.

The conditions of home life are not those best suited to the right growth of children. Infant discipline is one long struggle to coerce the growing creature into some sort of submission to the repressions, the exactions, the arbitrary conventions of the home.

Ibid.

... our longer period of infancy and its overlapping continuity, a possible series of babies lasting twenty years or so, demanded a permanent home; and so long as the mother had sole charge of this progressive infant party she must needs be there to attend to her maternal duties.

Ibid.

In supplying the men for the carnage of a battlefield, women have not merely lost actually more blood, and gone through a more acute anguish and weariness, in the long months of bearing and in the final agony of child-birth, than has been experienced by the men who cover it; but in the long months and years of rearing that follow, the women of the race go through a long, patiently endured strain which no knapsacked soldier on his longest march has ever more than equalled...

OLIVE SCHREINER, *Woman and Labour*, 1911

... when her biographer says of an Italian woman poet, "during some years her Muse was intermitted," we do not wonder at the fact when he casually mentions her ten children.

ANNA GARLIN SPENCER, *Woman's Share in Social Culture*, 1912

Men write books and poems about the beauty and sacredness of motherhood, but if one looks round the world one lives in, one finds that men are, for the most part, not charmed by the motherly qualities in women, and that the

69

women upon whom men have in the past lavished titles and jewels and wealth are not the motherly type at all.

H. M. SWANWICK, *The Future of the Women's Movement*, 1913

If one of the necessities for genius is intense egotism (because no great work can be done without intense concentration, and this is impossible if the attention is perpetually switched off in order to do other people's bidding), there is something to be said for the notion that genius will interfere with motherhood.

Ibid.

Woman's role has been that of an incubator and little more.

MARGARET SANGER, *Woman and the New Race*, 1920

It is a curious fact that a civilization devoted to mother-worship, that publicly professes a worship of mother and child, should close its eyes to the appalling waste of human life and human energy resulting from those dire consequences of leaving the whole problem of child-bearing to·chance and blind instinct.

MARGARET SANGER, *The Pivot of Civilization*, 1922

... when one listens to the good old saws about the glory of motherhood, one may be interested to know the conditions under which it is proposed to call it glorious; and when domesticity is held up to admiration as woman's natural vocation, one wonders whether the sponsor of domesticity is willing to put his argument to the test by leaving her free to choose that vocation or not, as she will, or whether his praise is a mere preface to the demand that she be forced into this natural vocation by the method of denying her an alternative.

SUZANNE LA FOLLETTE, *Concerning Women*, 1926

Diluvial irruptions of sentimentalism are continually spewed over nobility and self-sacrifice in the rôle of motherhood; yet men have taken care in the past to deny them guardianship of their own children.

Ibid.

According to recent scientific findings, it comes to this: man is secretly conscious of a biological inferiority, since he cannot bear children. Therefore, he must be continually propped up by those who do bear them, in order to feel a sure-enough place in the universe.

FLORENCE GUY SEABURY, in *Laughing Their Way*, ed. Martha Bensley Bruère and Mary Ritter Beard, 1934

How can the mother who believes she herself doesn't matter rear her children *for* anything? The only bearable theory is that we bring our children up to adulthood because we believe in adulthood—in its satisfactions and in the possibilities it offers for infinite growth and development.

DELLA CYRUS, "Why Mothers Fail," *Atlantic Monthly,* 179, March 1947

You naturally loved and idolized your mother in childhood, love and idolize her now in your early teens, and will love and idolize her in your old age. You must do this either because she submits all your quarrels with her to the arbitration of your mutual love or because she is a wicked tyrant. It doesn't matter.

The main question is, do you get the kind of service you should out of her, or don't you? Is your mother attending to your every need and to the housework?

ELIZABETH HAWES, *Anything But Love,* 1948

That the child is the supreme aim of woman is a statement having precisely the value of an advertising slogan.

SIMONE DE BEAUVOIR, *The Second Sex,* 1952

The child then senses that his mother is halfway between authority and helplessness. He can run to his father if his mother tries anything unjust; but if his father beats him there is little his mother can offer except tea and sympathy.

SHULAMITH FIRESTONE, *The Dialectic of Sex,* 1970

Society is pleased to honor the men who leave their jobs to serve in the armed forces. Their jobs are guaranteed for their return. . . . They are paid for their services in times of war, and honored if they give their lives in the course of that service. There are no memorials to the millions of women who have died in childbirth, and when a working woman becomes pregnant, she must take leave of absence. Often she will lose her job and accumulated seniority.

ANN SUTHERLAND HARRIS, to Rep. Edith Green's Special Subcommittee on Education, 1970, *Discrimination Against Women,* U.S. Government Printing Office, 1971

We commit a grievous error by trying to push every woman to produce and raise children, regardless of her personal desires or inclinations. Then we compound our error by considering the whole process immune from training. Mere biology gets one into it, and often hope and luck are the only things that get one through it.

GABRIELLE BURTON, *I'm Running Away from Home, But I'm Not Allowed to Cross the Street,* 1972

Women in modern Judeo-Christian societies are motherless children.
PHYLLIS CHESLER, *Women and Madness*, 1972

Women, although similar to each other in many ways, are more isolated from each other *in terms of groups* than men are. Women are not consolidated into either public or powerful groups. Women as mothers are "grouped" with their children (who grow up and leave them), and only temporarily and superficially with other women: for example, in parks, at women's auxiliary functions, and at heterosexual parties. Such women only keep each other company as they fulfill what they feel are "freely" chosen private lives rather than necessary public labor.
Ibid.

The only requirement in capitalist society for taking on the responsibility of caring for infants and children is the distinction of having a uterus. Under this system, children are at the complete mercy of whatever parents they happen to be born to, regardless of their ability (or desire) to raise them.
RUTHANN MILLER, "A Reply to Dr. Spock on Child Care," *Feminism and Socialism*, ed. Linda Jenness, 1972

The guilt that creates and perpetuates a national atonement rite like Mother's Day is spawned in childhood.
CHARLOTTE HOLT CLINEBELL, *Meet Me in the Middle*, 1973

Each generation of women has been sacrificed to its own children. History has been the holocaust of women.
ROSEMARY RADFORD RUETHER, *New Woman New Earth*, 1975

I remember early the sense of conflict, of a battleground none of us had chosen, of being an observer who, like it or not, was also an actor in an endless contest of wills. This was what it meant to me to have three children under the age of seven.
ADRIENNE RICH, *Of Woman Born*, 1976

The mother-child relationship is the essential human relationship. In the creation of the patriarchal family, violence is done to this fundamental human unit.
Ibid.

The systems men have created are homogeneous systems, which exclude and degrade women or deny our existence; and the most frequent rationalization for our exclusion from those systems is that we are or ought to be mothers.
    Ibid.

"Childless" women have been burned as witches, persecuted as lesbians, have been refused the right to adopt children because they were unmarried. They have been seen as embodiments of the great threat to male hegemony: the woman who is not tied to the family, who is disloyal to the law of heterosexual pairing and bearing.
    Ibid.

Marriage, to women as to men, must be a luxu-
ry, not a necessity; an incident of life, not all of
it.
SUSAN B. ANTHONY, "Social Purity," 1875, in Ida
Husted Harper, *Life and Work of Susan B.
Anthony,* vol. II, 1898

5   The Business of Marriage

Woman's Vocation

This habitual cruelty is first taught at school, where it is one of the rare sports
of the boys to torment the miserable brutes that fall in their way. The transition, as they grow up, from barbarity to brutes to domestic tyranny over
wives, children, and servants, is very easy.
MARY WOLLSTONECRAFT, *A Vindication of the Rights of Woman,* 1792

I believe men more frequently marry for love, than women; because they
have a freer choice. I am afraid to conjecture how large a proportion of wom-
en marry because they think they shall not have a better chance, and dread
being dependent.
LYDIA MARIA CHILD, *The Mother's Book,* 1831

Parents, I appeal to you: are you willing to train your daughters with reference only to marriage? Are you willing they should be the prey of that sickly
sentimentality, that effeminate weakness, which is produced by making that
one idea the focus of life?
PAULINA WRIGHT DAVIS, address, *Proceedings of the Woman's Rights Convention, Held at Worcester, October 23 & 24, 1850,* 1851

But it will be said that the husband provides for the wife, or in other words,
he feeds, clothes, and shelters her! I wish I had the power to make every one
before me fully realize the degradation contained in that idea. Yes! he *keeps*
her, and so he does a favorite horse; by law they are both considered his
property. Both may, when the cruelty of the owner compels them to, run

74

away, be brought back by the strong arm of the law, and according to a still extant law of England, both may be led by the halter to the market-place, and sold.

ERNESTINE L. ROSE, Second National Convention, Friends of Woman Suffrage, 1851, *History of Woman Suffrage*, I, 1881

Every married man, and every married woman, knows, either from experience or observation, that it is not an unfrequent thing for a man to refuse his wife the supply of money necessary to uphold her position in society, *if she fail to become in all things the subservient creature she is expected to be in the marriage relation.*

ELIZABETH OAKES SMITH, *Woman and Her Needs*, 1851

The marriage relation is certainly, at some time in the life of individuals, the natural and harmonious state; but as it now stands, it is a bondage more than a life-giving sacrament. The parties are unequal; the affinities essential to a joyful and peaceful relation are often wanting; the wife is not the help-meet for the man, but the appendage, the housekeeper, the female, of the establishment . . .

Ibid.

To follow the empty round of fashion, to retail gossip and scandal, to be an ornament in the parlor or a mere drudge in the kitchen, to live as an appendage to any human being, does not fill up nor satisfy the capacities of a soul awakened to a sense of its true wants, and the far-reaching and mighty interests which cluster around its existence.

ANN PRESTON, Woman's Rights Convention, 1852, *History of Woman Suffrage*, I, 1881

"Golden rules for wives"—"duty of wives"—how sick we are at the sight of such paragraphs! Why don't our wise editors give us now and then some "golden rules" for husbands, by way of variety?

AMELIA BLOOMER, editorial in *The Lily*, circa 1855–1860, in D. C. Bloomer, *Life and Writings of Amelia Bloomer*, 1895

Marriage has ever been a one-sided matter, resting most unequally upon the sexes. By it, man gains all—woman loses all; tyrant law and lust reign supreme with him—meek submission and ready obedience alone befit her. Woman has never been consulted; her wish has never been taken into consideration as regards the terms of the marriage compact.

SUSAN B. ANTHONY, Woman's Rights Convention, 1860, *History of Woman Suffrage*, I, 1881

75

At the present day women are cheap; their value in the great world's market has sunk to a very low ebb. Their attitude, speaking generally, is that of cringing for a piece of bread. What dignity can there be in the attitude of women in general, and toward men in particular, when marriage is held (and often necessarily so, being the sole means of maintenance) to be the one end of a woman's life, when it is degraded to the level of a feminine profession . . . ; when the insipidity or the material necessities of so many women's lives make them ready to accept almost any man who may offer himself.

> JOSEPHINE E. BUTLER, Introduction, *Woman's Work and Woman's Culture*, 1869.

A habit of submission and constraint, united with solitude, strengthens our passions and increases our evil propensities.

> VIRGINIA PENNY, *Think and Act*, 1869

Many a woman is tempted by her low wages to marry for a home.

> Ibid.

. . . I object to the teachings of the Church on this question [marriage]. Its interpretation of the Bible, making man the head of the woman, and its forms of marriage, by which she is given away as an article of merchandise, and made to vow obedience as a slave to a master, are all alike degrading to my sex. . . . Second, the position of the State on this question is quite as objectionable as that of the Church. . . . There is not a man in this nation, who, knowing what the laws are, but would repudiate for himself a relation that would so wholly merge his individual existence in that of another human being.

> ELIZABETH CADY STANTON, "The Man Marriage," periodical *The Revolution*, circa 1869, in Alma Lutz, *Created Equal*, 1940

There is an old saying that "a rose by any other name would smell as sweet," and I submit if the deprivation by law of the ownership of one's own person, wages, property, children, the denial of the right as an individual, to sue and be sued, and to testify in the courts, is not a condition of servitude most bitter and absolute, though under the sacred name of marriage?

> SUSAN B. ANTHONY, "Address to the Citizens of New York State," 1873, *History of Woman Suffrage*, II, 1882

A family unity which is only bound together with a table-cloth is of questionable value.

> CHARLOTTE PERKINS GILMAN, *Women and Economics*, 1898

This belief prevailed, to a great extent, in regard to a woman who attempted any vocation outside of domestic service, that by so doing she became at once and forever unfitted for the duties of wife and mother. Of all the old prejudices that cling to the hem of woman's garments and persistently impede her progress, none holds faster than this. The idea that she owes service to man instead of to herself, and that it is her highest duty to aid his development rather than her own, will be the last to die.

SUSAN B. ANTHONY, "The Position of Women in the Political Life of the United States," *Women in Politics*, ed. Countess of Aberdeen, 1900

Home to the man first means mother, as it does to all creatures, but later, and with renewed intensity, it means his own private harem—be it never so monogamous—the secret place where he keeps his most precious possession.

CHARLOTTE PERKINS GILMAN, *The Home*, 1903

Every natural tendency to self-indulgence is steadily increased by the life service of an entire wife.

Ibid.

At any rate, while it is true that some marriages are based on love, and while it is equally true that in some cases love continues in married life, I maintain that it does so regardless of marriage, and not because of it.

EMMA GOLDMAN, "Marriage and Love," *Anarchism and Other Essays*, 1911

If the world is ever to give birth to true companionship and oneness, not marriage, but love will be the parent.

Ibid.

The institution of marriage makes a parasite of woman, an absolute dependent. It *incapacitates* her for life's struggle, *annihilates* her social consciousness, paralyzes her imagination, and then imposes its gracious protection, which is in reality a snare, a travesty on human character.

Ibid.

... far too often, marriage puts an end to woman's intellectual life. Marriage can never reach its full stature until women possess as much intellectual freedom and freedom of opportunity within it as do their partners.

MARIE CARMICHAEL STOPES, *Married Love*, 1921

... nothing renders the subject more helpless against the dominance of the State than marriage.

> SUZZANE LA FOLLETTE, *Concerning Women*, 1926

Curiously enough, this idea of the essential holiness and consequent indissolubility of the marriage-bond has coexisted in Christian society with the most cold-blooded practice of marrying for convenience, for money, for social prestige, for place and power, for everything that ignores or negates the spiritual element in sexual union.

> Ibid

For man, marriage is regarded as a state; for woman, as a vocation. For man, it is a means of ordering his life and perpetuating his name; for woman it is considered a proper and fitting aim of existence.

> Ibid.

Here we have an occupation [housewife and mother] in which a far greater number of persons is engaged than in any other whatever—an occupation which is essential to the very existence of society; for its poorer members peculiarly onerous, since they have no time off and no holidays; and in so far as the maternity part of it is concerned, peculiarly dangerous. Yet it is so little recognized by society that those engaged in it are described in the census as "unoccupied."

> ELEANOR F. RATHBONE, M.P., "Changes in Public Life," *Our Freedom and Its Results*, ed. Ray Strachey, 1936

When pettiness is found in women of the working class—and it does exist there, of course—it is for the same reason that prompts middle- and upper-class women. That reason is the traditional women's position of economic dependence, and the fact that our means of earning a livelihood has been restricted in the main to marrying.

> SUSAN B. ANTHONY II, *Out of the Kitchen—Into the War*, 1943

Perhaps if I had really understood my own nature, as I came to do later, I should not have married, for I soon realized that married life, as men understand it, calls for a degree of self-abnegation which was impossible for me. I needed solitude, time for study, and the opportunity for a wider life.

> HANNAH MITCHELL, *The Hard Way Up*, 1946, published 1968

Most of us who were married found that "Votes for Women" were of less interest to our husbands than their own dinners. They simply could not understand why we made such a fuss about it.
Ibid.

As long as women are forced to be homemakers in order to be mothers, we are compelled to hold fast to our one inadequate ideal for women—the home-maker-mother ideal.
DELLA CYRUS, "Why Mothers Fail," *Atlantic Monthly,* 179, March 1947

If economic necessity forces you to be productive outside your home after marriage, you will be taught how to pretend you aren't doing it. If you show any symptoms before marriage of going after a career for any reason other than that of facilitating your search for a man, you are peculiar and eccentric. If you go about saying you want and like to be a Worker you'll be considered dangerous.
ELIZABETH HAWES, *Anything But Love,* 1948

After marriage, all things change. And one of them better be you.
Ibid.

Anything can be made to work if you just want it to enough. We are a nation of boosters, and the Rotarian spirit pervades marriage as well as real estate.
RUTH HERSCHBERGER, *Adam's Rib,* 1948

The perfect marriage is like the gold the ancient alchemists were hotly in pursuit of. It didn't matter how often the chemical constituents failed them: something must have been wrong with the recipe.
Ibid.

It has been said that marriage diminishes man, which is often true; but almost always it annihilates woman.
SIMONE DE BEAUVOIR, *The Second Sex,* 1952

Did anyone ever tell Toscanini, or Bach, that he had to choose between music and family, between art and a normal life?
ELISABETH MANN BORGESE, *Ascent of Woman,* 1963

They [American women] were admired, envied, pitied, theorized over until they were sick of it, offered drastic solutions or silly choices that no one could take seriously. They got all kinds of advice . . . on how to adjust to their role as housewives. No other road to fullfillment was offered to American women in the middle of the twentieth century. Most adjusted to their role and suffered or ignored the problem that has no name. It can be less painful for a woman, not to hear the strange, dissatisfied voice stirring within her.

 BETTY FRIEDAN, *The Feminine Mystique*, 1963

Togetherness was a poor substitute for equality; the glorification of women's role was a poor substitute for free participation in the world as an individual.
 Ibid.

No society can consider that the disadvantages of women have been overcome so long as the pursuit of a career exacts a personal deprivation of marriage and parenthood, or the pursuit of happiness in marriage and family life robs a woman of fulfillment in meaningful work.

 ALICE ROSSI, "Women in Science, Why So Few?" *Science*, 148, May 1965

Self-sacrifice is the leitmotiv of most of the marital games played by women . . .
 GERMAINE GREER, *The Female Eunuch*, 1971

There are two marriages, then, in every marital union, his and hers. And his . . . is better than hers.
 JESSIE BERNARD, *The Future of Marriage*, 1972

For it is the husband's role—not necessarily his own wishes, desires, or demands—that proves to be the key to the marriage and requires the wife to be more accommodating.
 Ibid.

Women at marriage move from the status of female to that of neuter being.
 Ibid.

We therefore "deform" the minds of girls, as traditional Chinese used to deform their feet, in order to shape them for happiness in marriage. It may therefore be that married women say they are happy because they are sick rather than sick because they are married.
 Ibid.

80

Both psychotherapy and white or middle-class marriage isolate women from each other; both emphasize individual rather than collective solutions to woman's unhappiness; both are based on a woman's helplessness and dependence on a stronger male authority figure . . .

PHYLLIS CHESLER, *Women and Madness*, 1972

There was a time . . . when I was less threatened by those female colleagues of my husband who were *not* married than by those who were. If they weren't married, at least they weren't successful as women. Or so I decided.

CHARLOTTE HOLT CLINEBELL, *Meet Me in the Middle*, 1973

Why does a career, for many middle-aged women, seem like the only choice? I think for the same reason that wifing and motherhood often seems the only choice for younger women. Those are the accepted values of society.

Ibid.

Homemaking

How far the wife was intended to be the slave to her husband, I know not; but certain we are, she was designed to be his friend, his companion, and united part; or according to the gentlemen's phrase, his *better part;* and yet how often do we see her sinking under the burden of a household load, whilst the unfeeling husband is lavishing away the substance which ought to be the comfort and support of a family?

MARY ANN RADCLIFFE, *The Female Advocate*, 1799

The right punishment for those men who denounce schemes for the "Higher Education of Women," and ordain that women should only learn to cook and sew and nurse babies, should be to spend the whole term of their natural lives in such homes as are made by the female incapables formed on such principles.

FRANCES POWER COBBE, "The Final Cause of Woman," *Woman's Work and Woman's Culture*, ed. Josephine E. Butler, 1869

There is a class of women, (as well as men,) that insist upon it a woman's province is at home—whether she has a home or not.

VIRGINIA PENNY, *Think and Act*, 1869.

The isolated household is responsible for a large share of woman's ignorance and degradation. A mind always in contact with children and servants, whose aspirations and ambitions rise no higher than the roof that shelters it, is necessarily dwarfed in its proportions.

> E. C. STANTON, S. B. ANTHONY, M. J. GAGE, eds., *History of Woman Suffrage*, I, 1881

I suffered with mental hunger, which, like an empty stomach, is very depressing. I had ... no stimulating companionship. ... I now [1847] fully understood the practical difficulties most women had to contend with in the isolated household, and the impossibility of woman's best development if in contact, the chief part of her life, with servants and children. ... The general discontent I felt with woman's portion as wife, mother, housekeeper, physician, and spiritual guide, the chaotic conditions into which everything fell without her constant supervision, and the wearied, anxious look of the majority of women impressed me with a strong feeling that some active measures should be taken to remedy the wrongs of society in general, and of women in particular.

> ELIZABETH CADY STANTON, *Eighty Years and More*, 1898.

The home is a human institution. All human institutions are open to improvement.

> CHARLOTTE PERKINS GILMAN, *The Home*, 1903

The little industrial group of the home—from two to five or ten—is very near the bottom of the line of economic progress. It costs men more money, women more work, both more time and strength than need be by more than half. A method of living that wastes half the time and strength of the world is not economical.

> Ibid.

The effect of the home ... upon marriage is a vitally interesting study. Two people, happily mated, sympathetic physically and mentally, having many common interests and aspirations, proceed after marrying to enter upon the business of "keeping house," or "home-making." This business is not marriage, it is not parentage, it is not child-culture. It is the running of the commissary and dormitory departments of life, with elaborate lavatory processes.

> Ibid.

The currents of home-life are so many, so diverse, so contradictory, that they are only maintained by using the woman as a sort of universal solvent; and this position of holding many diverse elements in solution is not compatible

with the orderly crystallisation of any of them, or with much peace of mind
to the unhappy solvent.
    Ibid.

The home, in its very nature, is intended to shield from danger; it is in origin
a hiding place, a shelter for the defenseless. Staying in it is in no way condu-
cive to the growth of courage.
    Ibid.

Justice was born outside the home and a long way from it; and it has never
even been adopted there.
    Ibid.

The home is the cradle of all the virtues, but we are in a stage of social development where we need virtues beyond the cradle size.
    Ibid.

How does staying in one's own house all one's life affect the mind? We cannot
ask this question of a man, for no man has ever done it except a congenital invalid.
    Ibid.

The first tendency of the incessant home life is to exaggerate personality. The
home is necessarily a hotbed of personal feeling. There love grows intense and
often morbid; there a little irritation frets and wears in the constant pressure
like a stone in one's shoe.
    Ibid.

Minds are not vats to be filled eternally with more and ever more supplies. It
is *use,* large, free, sufficient use that the mind requires, not mere information.
Our college girls have vast supplies of knowledge; how can they use it in the
home? Could a college boy apply his education appropriately to "keeping
house"—and, if not, how can the girl? Full use of one's best faculties—this is
health and happiness for both man and woman.
    Ibid.

The best proof of man's dissatisfaction with the home is found in his universal
absence from it.
    Ibid.

... given the possession of the intensest joy a mother is capable of feeling in her relation towards her children, her husband, and her home, and given the fulfillment of her duties towards all three to the most conscientious heights attainable, it is not enough to occupy a fully-equipped, intellectual, healthy human female, any more than it would be enough for a fully-equipped, intellectual, healthy human father, whose delight in his children, his wife, and his home is often no less great than the mother's.

LADY GROVE, *The Human Woman*, 1908

The home of to-day is commonly far from perfect. From its evil traditions of women's subjection and inferiority come some of the worst of our social and economic evils. The suffragette who is content with the home as it is, built upon the subjection of the woman and continued by the infringement of the rights of the child, is not a true rebel but the victim of superficial emotion.

TERESA BILLINGTON-GREIG, *The Militant Suffrage Movement, 1911*

Psychological tests have shown us that women vary as greatly in their inclinations and capacities as men. In being forced against their inclinations to perform by economically wasteful methods those particular processes of dishwashing, cooking, sweeping, bed-making and mending which now represent about all that is left of the much more complicated duties once belonging to the housewife, individual women may be seriously warped out of their natural bents.

ALICE BEAL PARSONS, *Woman's Dilemma*, 1926

On the whole housekeeping itself, as it is still done, is unskilled and non-specialized. The housewife must perforce be jack-of-all-trades in order to cook, clean, sew, wash, iron, shop, care for children and perform the other tasks commonly associated with housewifehood. She cannot afford to specialize as a cook because she has the washing to do; she cannot become an expert laundress because there is the shopping and meal planning; she cannot become a nutritionist or dietician because she has to care for her children, too. In short, the essence of housekeeping is its infinite variety of little jobs.

SUSAN B. ANTHONY II, *Out of the Kitchen—Into the War*, 1943

At eight years old my weekly task was to darn all the stockings for the household, and I think my first reactions to feminism began at this time when I was forced to darn my brothers' stockings while they read or played cards or dominoes.

HANNAH MITCHELL, *The Hard Way Up*, 1946, published 1968

Even my Sunday leisure was gone [after marriage to a young socialist] for I soon found that a lot of the Socialist talk about freedom was only talk and these Socialist young men expected Sunday dinners and huge teas with home-made cakes, potted meat and pies, exactly like their reactionary fellows.
    Ibid.

No wonder it is so difficult to interest married women in social reform. The modern demand for a forty-hour week seems like a joke to the wife and mother who is lucky if hers is only a seventy-hour week.
    Ibid.

. . . strange to say, even when men are willing for their wives to take on public work, they never seem to understand that this cannot always be done between mealtimes.
    Ibid.

Home is full of good, but life is difficult in it. The trouble is caused, not by the home, but by what goes on in it.
    ELIZABETH HAWES, *Anything But Love*, 1948

The picture of the happy housewife doing creative work at home—painting, sculpting, writing—is one of the semi-delusions of the feminine mystique. There are men and women who can do it; but when a man works at home, his wife keeps the children strictly out of the way, or else.
    BETTY FRIEDAN, *The Feminine Mystique*, 1963

Men often claim that it is women who want to be married, and this is usually said as some sort of justification and with the implication that if it had been up to Him, and at this point you're treated to a deprecating leer, there wouldn't be any marriage. As with so much that men say, there is a great deal of truth in this. If it were up to men there probably wouldn't be marriage—witness the New Left—and it is also true that it is women who usually insist on the legal contract. What is not mentioned, however, is that men want and demand, one way or another, all the services from women that the legal marriage contract is payment for, and like any free enterpriser, if he can get these services for nothing, so much the more profit for him.
    TI-GRACE ATKINSON, "Juniata I: The Sacrificial Lamb," 1969, *Amazon Odyssey*, 1974

The most wasteful "brain drain" in America today is the drain in the kitchen sink.

ELIZABETH GOULD DAVIS, *The First Sex*, 1971

For many women, sitting down to a machine, be it a typewriter or a power sewing machine, is a rest after the unremitting employment of all their physical strength and energy in service of a young family.

GERMAINE GREER, *The Female Eunuch*, 1971

Loneliness is never more cruel than when it is felt in close propinquity with someone who has ceased to communicate. Many a housewife staring at the back of her husband's newspaper or listening to his breathing in bed is lonelier than any spinster in a rented room.

Ibid.

The full-time housewife still bears this significance: "There's no need for *my* wife to work," "I wouldn't let my wife work . . ."

JULIET MITCHELL, *Women's Estate*, 1971

The "freedom" of the housewife is her isolation.

Ibid.

The family is a stronghold of what capitalism needs to preserve but actually destroys: private property and individualism. The housewife-mother is the guardian and representative of these. She is a backward, conservative force—and this is what her oppression means. She is forced to be the stone in the stream.

Ibid.

The fostering of a child's loyalty to the individual family unit is paralleled by the inculcation of patriotism, chauvinism, and religion. The family plays the central role in implanting in infants and children the character structure without which no one could accept the hierarchical, exploitative, and alienating social relations intrinsic to capitalism.

"Towards a Mass Feminist Movement," Resolution, National Convention of the Socialist Workers Party, 1971, *Feminism and Socialism*, ed. Linda Jenness, 1972

Dismissing the housewife syndrome, as some unsympathetic observers do, is like telling a man dying of malnutrition that he's lucky he isn't dying of cancer.

JESSIE BERNARD, *The Future of Marriage*, 1972

The "morality" of the family system justifies authority, discipline, obedience, possessiveness, inequality, jealousy, sexual repression, competition, and rivalry.

DIANNE FEELEY, "The Family," *Feminism and Socialism*, ed. Linda Jenness, 1972

I have a very clear, keen memory of myself the day after I was married: I was sweeping a floor.

ADRIENNE RICH, *Of Woman Born*, 1976

Men monopolize not only the most advantageous employments, and such as exclude wom-
en from the exercise of them, by the publicity
of their nature, or the extensive knowledge they
require, but even many of those, which are consistent with the female character. Another
heavy discouragement to the industry of wom-
en, is the inequality of the reward of their labour, compared with that of men, an unjustice
which pervades every species of employment
performed by both sexes.

PRISCILLA WAKEFIELD, *Reflections on the
Present Condition of the Female Sex,* 1798

6   The Economy's Pawn

The Unpaid Homemaker

I even know of one woman, not by any means low in the scale of position,
who proposed to do the labor of one of her servants, provided her penurious
husband would pay her, a wife, the price of service.

ELIZABETH OAKES SMITH, *Woman and Her Needs,* 1851

Wives, by their labor and economy, in domestic matters, really earn, on an
average, as much as their husbands.

VIRGINIA PENNY, *Think and Act,* 1869

The census does not include the services of the mother and daughter among
the *paid* vocations, though, as is well known, in many instances they do all the
housework of the family. They get no wages, and therefore do not appear
among the "useful classes." They are not earners, but savers of money. A
money-*saver* is not a recognized factor, either in political economy or in the
State census.

HARRIET H. ROBINSON, "Massachusetts," circa 1876, *History of Woman Suffrage,* III, 1887

Woman has been the great unpaid laborer of the world . . . she is not paid according to the value of the work done, but according to sex.

> E. C. STANTON, S. B. ANTHONY, M. J. GAGE, eds., *History of Woman Suffrage*, I, 1881

Even where a woman does all the work of a family, rising early and late taking rest, cooking and washing, cleaning and mending, and performing all sorts of housework, her husband will talk of "supporting" her, and never seem to think that he owes her any wages for her labor.

> LILLIE DEVEREUX BLAKE, *Women's Place Today*, 1883

Unpaid work never commands respect; it is the paid worker who has brought to the public mind conviction of woman's worth.

> HARRIOT STANTON BLATCH, "Woman as an Economic Factor," National American Woman Suffrage Association Convention, 1898, *History of Woman Suffrage*, IV, 1902

How can we expect women to rise at once to an organised demand for equal pay for equal work, when heretofore they have been perforce content with doing all the work of which they were capable for no pay at all. The habit of working for nothing, alone, because one must, does not develop a far-seeing, self-respecting, co-operative independence! I speak of those women who work at home, unpaid, unrecognised, but still labourers, and who contribute to the world the habit of submissive industry, asking nothing for itself, and caring nothing for its neighbours.

> CHARLOTTE PERKINS GILMAN, "Equal Pay for Equal Work," *Women in Industrial Life*, ed. Countess of Aberdeen, 1900

We seek by talking and writing, by poetising and sermonising, and playing on every tender sentiment and devout aspiration, to convince the housewife that there is something particularly exalted and beautiful, as well as useful, in her occupation. This shows our deep-rooted error of sex-distinction in industry. We consider the work of the woman in the house as essentially feminine, and fail to see that, as work, it is exactly like any other kind of human activity, having the same limitations and the same possibilities.

> CHARLOTTE PERKINS GILMAN, *The Home*, 1903

Women in industry are the victims of traditional prejudices: . . . the idea that woman's place is in the home, that women workers have no dependents, that they work for pin-money and therefore do not need a living wage, that upon them alone depends the future health of the race.

> SUZANNE LA FOLLETTE, *Concerning Women*, 1926

What had our mothers been doing then that they had no wealth to leave us? Powdering their noses? Looking in at shop windows?... Mary's mother ... may have been a wastrel in her spare time (she had thirteen children by a minister of the church), but if so her gay and dissipated life had left too few traces of its pleasures on her face.

VIRGINIA WOOLF, *A Room of One's Own*, 1929

This transfer from paid to unpaid work is the great governing circumstance in the life and condition of women. It is called "ceasing to be employed on marriage."

MARY AGNES HAMILTON, *Women at Work*, 1941

In a society in which money determines value, women are a group who work outside the money economy. Their work is not worth money, is therefore valueless, is therefore not even real work. And women themselves, who do this valueless work, can hardly be expected to be worth as much as men, who work for money.

MARGARET BENSTON, "The Political Economy of Women's Liberation," *Monthly Review*, September 1969

At present, the support of a family is a hidden tax on the wage earner—his wage buys the labor power of two people.

Ibid.

A working woman has to operate a home in a world that assumes that a homemaker's time is worth less than the wages of the lowest-paid worker for money.

CAROLINE BIRD, *Born Female*, rev. ed., 1971

A woman should be able to *choose* whether to work outside her home or in it, to choose whether she wants to care for her own children all the time or part-time. And the people who work in child care centers have to be paid decent wages or our kids won't get decent care.

JOHNNIE TILLMON, "Welfare Is a Women's Issue," *Ms.*, Spring 1972

The image of the mother in the home, however unrealistic, has haunted and reproached the lives of wage-earning mothers. But it has also become, and for men as well as women, a dangerous archetype: the Mother, source of angelic love and forgiveness in a world increasingly ruthless and impersonal;... the

symbol and residue of moral values and tenderness in a world of wars, brutal competition, and contempt for human weakness.
ADRIENNE RICH, *Of Woman Born*, 1976

The Untrained

The few employments open to women, so far from being liberal, are menial; and when a superior education enables them to take charge of children as governesses, they are not treated like the tutors of sons . . .
MARY WOLLSTONECRAFT, A *Vindication of the Rights of Woman*, 1792

. . . that women from their education and the present state of civilized life are in the same condition [as savages], cannot . . . be controverted. To laugh at them then, or satirize the follies of a being who is never to be allowed to act freely from the light of her own reason, is as absurd as cruel; for that they who are taught blindly to obey authority will endeavour cunningly to elude it, is most natural and certain.
Ibid.

There is a vulgar persuasion, that the ignorance of women, by favoring their subordination, ensures their utility. 'Tis the same argument employed by the ruling few against the subject many in aristocracies; by the rich against the poor in democracies; by the learned professions against the people in all countries.
FRANCES WRIGHT, *Course of Popular Lectures*, 1829

In most families, it is considered a matter of far more consequence to call a girl off from making a pie, or a pudding, than to interrupt her whilst engaged in her studies. This mode of training necessarily exalts, in their view, the animal above the intellectual and spiritual nature, and teaches women to regard themselves as a kind of machinery, necessary to keep the domestic engine in order, but of little value as the *intelligent* companions of men.
SARAH GRIMKÉ, Letter VIII, 1837, *Letters on the Equality of the Sexes*, 1838

Sex, like rank, wealth, beauty, or talent, is but an accident of birth. As you would not educate a soul to be an aristocrat, so do not to be a woman.
MARGARET FULLER, *Woman in the Nineteenth Century*, 1845

I consider the great wrongs she [woman] has endured as but legitimate fruits of the false education she has received. By education I mean not mere book learning, but the whole moral, intellectual, physical, domestic, and civil education: these have been almost entirely neglected, and only the ornamental cultivated. She has never been taught to think or act for herself.

> AMELIA BLOOMER, letter in *The Lily*, 1851, in D. C. Bloomer, *Life and Writings of Amelia Bloomer*, 1895

While their sons as they come to manhood are given some kind of occupation that will afford not only healthy exercise of the body and mind but also the means of an honorable independence, the daughters are kept at home in inactivity and indolence, with no higher object in life than to dress, dance, read novels, gossip, flirt and "set their caps" for husbands.

> AMELIA BLOOMER, article for *Western Home Visitor*, circa 1854, in D. C. Bloomer, *Life and Writings of Amelia Bloomer*, 1895

... the census does not tell how many of these two and a half millions [of women] are working for starvation wages, nor how many of them have declined from a position of respectability to which they were born to one in any class or rank, however low, in which they may have a chance of earning a piece of bread. Nor does the census include among these breadwinners the armies of women, counted by thousands in all our towns and cities, who are forced downwards to the paths of hell, by the pressure from above, through the shutting up of avenues to a livelihood by means of trade monopolies among men, and through the absence of any instruction or apprenticeship to qualify them for employment.

> JOSEPHINE E. BUTLER, Introduction, *Woman's Work and Woman's Culture*, 1869

[Men] say God never intended woman to reason, they shut their college doors against her so that she can not study that manly accomplishment, and then they blame her for taking a short cut [intuition] to the same conclusion they reach in their roundabout lumbering processes of ratiocination.

> ELIZABETH CADY STANTON, letter to *The Revolution*, 1869, *History of Woman Suffrage*, II, 1882.

The practical exclusion of girls from the highest educational advantages offered to this class is in very many cases equivalent to a sentence of lifelong pauperism and dependence.

> ELIZABETH C. WOLSTENHOLME, "The Education of Girls, Its Present and Its Future," *Woman's Work and Woman's Culture*, ed. Josephine E. Butler, 1869

The injustice to women consists in appropriating to men all the artificial and acquired advantages of education and training. . . . But equality of education must precede equality of industrial training.

    Ibid.

He has kept the woman ignorant of all the technologies of the world. Fatal renewal of the Hebrew myth, he has eaten of the tree of knowledge, has kept the fruit for himself.

    JULIA WARD HOWE, American Woman Suffrage Association Convention, 1870, *History of Woman Suffrage*, II, 1882

Previous to 1825, girls could attend only the primary schools of Boston. Through the influence of Rev. John Pierpont, the first high-school for girls was opened in that city. There was a great outcry against this innovation; and, because of the excitement on the subject, and the *great number of girls* who applied for admission, the scheme was abandoned.

    HARRIET H. ROBINSON, "Massashusetts," circa 1876, *History of Woman Suffrage*, III, 1887

[The woman of the 1830's] could do nothing with . . . [knowledge], even if she could get it. So she made a *fetich* of some male relative, and gave him the mental food for which she herself was starving, and devoted all her energies towards helping him to become what she felt, under better conditions, she herself might have been.

    Ibid.

Only think what would be the effect on a set of young men who should be reared like girls, kept mostly in the house, forbidden to romp lest they should be "tom-boys," . . . instructed only in the lighter accomplishments, . . . taught that beauty was their highest gift, and marriage the object of life. What sort of creatures would these young men be at twenty? I think we may really found a claim for woman's superiority on the fact that, in spite of this monstrous process of destruction, our girls are as bright as they are.

    LILLIE DEVEREUX BLAKE, *Women's Place Today*, 1883

Boys and girls are expected, also, to behave differently to each other, and to people in general,—a behavior to be briefly described in two words. To the boy we say, "do"; to the girl, "Don't."

    CHARLOTTE PERKINS GILMAN, *Women and Economics*, 1898

My own experience proves to me that it is a grave mistake to send boys and girls to separate institutions of learning, especially at the most impressible age. The stimulus of sex promotes alike a healthy condition of the intellectual and the moral faculties and gives to both a development they never can acquire alone.

ELIZABETH CADY STANTON, *Eighty Years and More*, 1898

Knowledge and experience have to be gathered by wide and prolonged study; they do not come by an infinite repetition of the same private experiments.

CHARLOTTE PERKINS GILMAN, *The Home*, 1903

There is one "primary explanation" for the fact that women are underpaid, over-worked, and victims of unsanitary conditions. They are, for the most part, untrained workers, and because of this and of certain custom-imposed limitations regarding what is called "women's work," there is a great over-supply of labor in the occupations which are open to them.

The History of Trade Unionism Among Women in Boston, n. d., material suggests 1906

... almost from the cradle an artificial distinction between the sexes is created and fostered: self-reliance and self-control encouraged in the boy, and discountenanced in the girl. How often has a boy been told by his ignorant nurse, his ignorant governess, or his equally ignorant mother: "Don't cry— that is like a girl;" thus sowing the first seed for that contempt for women that some unfortunate men grow up with.

LADY GROVE, *The Human Woman*, 1908

The intelligence, emotions, and desires of the human infant at birth differ not at all perceptibly, as its sex may be male or female; and such psychic differences as appear to exist in later childhood are undoubtedly very largely the result of artificial training, forcing on the appearance of psychic sexual divergencies long before they would tend spontaneously to appear ... as when an infant female is forcibly prevented from climbing or shouting, and the infant male from amusing himself with needle and thread or dolls.

OLIVE SCHREINER, *Woman and Labour*, 1911

Of the diversity of human gifts we had, no doubt, our full share. But the talents which we were not permitted to exercise were folded and laid away in a napkin, to moulder useless and unknown, even to ourselves. For we were not the equals of our brothers. If there is any value in education, it must obtain for women as well as for men.

> JULIA WARD HOWE, "Speech on Equal Rights," *Julia Ward Howe and the Woman Suffrage Movement*, ed. Florence Howe Hall, 1913

To women, driven by need to earn their living in unaccustomed ways, men have all too often opened no front gate through which they could make an honest daylight entrance into a trade, but have left only side-alleys and back-doors through which the guiltless intruders could slip in.

> ALICE HENRY, *The Trade Union Woman*, 1917

Much of the unreal and amateurish quality of women's education is due to the fact that too often it hangs suspended in mid air, as it were, and has no vital connection with their lives.

> ALICE BEAL PARSONS, *Woman's Dilemma*, 1926

... the repression of natural impulse inculcated upon women by their upbringing ... will probably not disappear entirely until the prevailing ideal in bringing up girls shall be to help them to become fully human beings, rather than to make them marriageable; for humanity and market-value have really little in common.

> SUZANNE LA FOLLETTE, *Concerning Women*, 1926

Many societies have educated their male children on the simple device of teaching them not to be women ...

> MARGARET MEAD, *Male and Female*, 1949

Even more than to the boy is the "all-round" ideal held up to girls, and it is not always possible to integrate the roles of good date, good daughter, good sorority sister, good student, good friend, and good citizen. The superior achievements of college men over college women bear witness to the crippling division of energies among women.

> HELEN MAYER HACKER, "Women as a Minority Group," *Social Forces*, 30, October 1951

One might ask: if an education geared to the growth of the human mind weakens femininity, will an education geared to femininity weaken the growth of the mind? What is femininity, if it can be destroyed by an education which makes the mind grow, or induced by not letting the mind grow?

> BETTY FRIEDAN, *The Feminine Mystique*, 1963

In light of the social expectations about women, it is not surprising that women end up where society expects them to; the surprise is that little girls don't get the message that they are supposed to be stupid until they get into high school.

NAOMI WEISSTEIN, "Woman as Nigger," *Psychology Today*, October 1969

Basically, her [the ambitious girl's] problem stems from the inescapable truth that people expect little girls to grow up wanting to be a *mommy*.

LETTY COTTIN POGREBIN, *How to Make It in a Man's World*, 1970.

Like the Indian tribes which exclude women from sacred "secrets," our own culture has kept women from understanding sophisticated machinery and the tricks of a trade businessmen like to call "unpatentable knowhow."

CAROLINE BIRD, *Born Female*, rev. ed., 1971

Sometime in high school a girl learns, often poignantly, that class honors are fine, but attracting boys is what counts with her peers. The message comes over from other girls even more loudly and clearly than it does from boys. Many girls read it and cash in their aspirations.

Ibid.

[Education in sexually segregated schools] does not handicap the men who dominate the profession and can relate among themselves to their project, but it severely isolates the "exceptional" woman, putting intolerable pressures on her to confrom to masculine requirements in her production and to feminine standards in her manners.

JULIET MITCHELL, *Woman's Estate*, 1971

Most women are not short of education—they have got more than enough for anything they are likely to have the opportunity to do with it. In the home, and in their educational acquisitions, women are *redundant*.

Ibid.

The only road to glory this culture offers women is one that cannot last, one that must perish long before they do. The culture discourages women from achieving the kind of glory that does last, the glory that results from using one's mind. The little boy is asked what he's *going to become* when he grows up; the little girl is told she *is*—pretty.

UNA STANNARD, "The Mask of Beauty," *Woman in Sexist Society*, ed. Vivian Gornick and Barbara K. Moran, 1971

There is a sort of attitude that still makes my blood boil. Because you are born a girl you have to be indoctrinated into accepting that you are not worth the time and expense of being trained. If they do train you, they think you are only going to get married and take the edge off any profits they might make from paying out. No thought is given to how this squanders all sorts of abilities that could be useful to society, or the way it stops women leading more satisfying lives on a personal level. It is an attitude which goes right back through school. Girls do cookery, and so all girls have to go to cookery classes. When I asked to do metalwork and woodwork, I was told only boys do those lessons.

MAY HOBBS, *Born to Struggle*, 1973

Boys learn that girls are not where the action is. They learn to cooperate and compete with boys. Sports, cars, masturbation, and secret clubs are the primary outlets for the release of male emotions and affections. This prepares them for the aggressive masculine society and constructs the foundation of positive, exclusive male bonding. . . . Girls learn quickly that boys are where the action is.

ELLEN MINTZ, "The Prejudice of Parents," *Who Discriminates Against Women?*, ed. Florence Denmark, 1974

. . . in cultures where learning is valued for itself, men are apt to be the guardians of culture and the preservers of grammar; in cultures where book larnin' is the schoolmarm's domain, this job will be relegated to the women.

ROBIN LAKOFF, *Language and Woman's Place*, 1975

The Dependent

. . . do you candidly think these wives do not wish to control the wages they earn . . . ? Do you suppose that any woman is such a pattern of devotion and submission that she willingly stitches all day . . . that she may enjoy the unspeakable privilege . . . of paying for her husband's tobacco and rum? Think you the wife of the confirmed, beastly drunkard would consent to share with him her home and bed, if law and public sentiment would release her from such gross companionship? . . . Think you that the woman who has worked hard all her days in helping her husband to accumulate a large property, consents to the law that places this wholly at his disposal?

ELIZABETH CADY STANTON, "Address to the Legislature of the State of New York," 1854, *History of Woman Suffrage*, I, 1881

I do wish that more women would become owners of the soil . . .
> AMELIA BLOOMER, letter, 1855, in D. C. Bloomer, *Life and Writings of Amelia Bloomer*, 1895

. . . woman's poverty does not add to man's wealth, and if, in the plenitude of his power, he should secure to her the exercise of all her God-given rights, her wealth could not bring poverty to him. There is a kind of nervous unrest always manifested by those in power, whenever new claims are started by those out of their own immediate class. The philosophy of this is very plain. They imagine that if the rights of this new class be granted, they must, of necessity, sacrifice something of what they already possess. They can not divest themselves of the idea that rights are very much like lands, stocks, bonds, and mortgages, and that if every new claimant be satisfied, the supply of human rights must in time run low.
> ELIZABETH CADY STANTON, "Address to the Legislature of the State of New York," 1860, *History of Woman Suffrage*, I, 1881

There is not the woman born who desires to eat the bread of dependence, no matter whether it be from the hand of father, husband, or brother; for any one who does so eat her bread places herself in the power of the person from whom she takes it.
> SUSAN B. ANTHONY, American Equal Rights Association Convention, 1869, *History of Woman Suffrage*, II, 1882

Most women in lunatic asylums are there from domestic trouble, from overwork, from inability to earn a living, or from the terrible fear that they may not be able to do so in the future.
> VIRGINIA PENNY, *Think and Act*, 1869

Wherever, on the face of the globe or on the page of history, you show me a disfranchised class, I will show you a degraded class of labor.
> SUSAN B. ANTHONY, "Woman Wants Bread, Not the Ballot," campaign speech, 1870–1880, in Ida Husted Harper, *Life and Work of Susan B. Anthony*, vol. II, 1898

Woman has not only failed to assert her own right to consideration, her right to be herself, she has given herself away, and given herself away for nothing.
> TERESA BILLINGTON-GREIG, *The Militant Suffrage Movement*, 1911

This desire to keep women in economic subjection to themselves—to have women, as it were, at their mercy—is at the root of men's opposition to the industrial and professional employment of women.

CHRISTABEL PANKHURST, *Plain Facts About a Great Evil*, 1913

Probably no man who has not experienced it can conceive the ravages of financial dependence on character, the having nothing in the world he could call his own, except as a gift from someone else, even though he may have worked continually. The home is supposed to be particularly the woman's, and she spends her life caring for it, but she cannot even buy its furnishings, unless her husband chooses to give her the necessary money.

ALICE BEAL PARSONS, *Woman's Dilemma*, 1926

The news of my legacy reached me one night about the same time that the act was passed that gave votes to women.... Of the two—the vote and the money—the money, I own, seemed infinitely the more important.

VIRGINIA WOOLF, *A Room of One's Own*, 1929

It [capitalism] makes marriage precarious and old age perilous. And every inequality which hampers the poor man's son hampers his daughter even more decisively.

MARY AGNES HAMILTON, "Changes in Social Life," *Our Freedom and Its Results*, ed. Ray Strachey, 1936

Women were the first group in history to be enfranchised before gaining their economic independence. It seems scarcely necessary to argue the point that a group of persons who have not attained economic independence cannot reach a position of untrammeled influence. He who steals my purse may steal trash, but he who holds the purse strings controls my life.

HARRIOT STANTON BLATCH AND ALMA LUTZ, *Challenging Years*, 1940

There is a persistent myth that a wife has control over her husband's money because she gets to spend it. Actually, she does not have much more financial autonomy than the employee of a corporation who is delegated to buy office furniture or supplies.

ELLEN WILLIS, " 'Consumerism' and Women," *Voices from Women's Liberation*, ed. Leslie B. Tanner, 1970

I think one of the problems is that all too many men in personnel view every woman who comes before them as an image of their wife and therefore they look at that person and say, "What would I like my wife to be doing?" And if this woman is applying for something they would not like their wife to be doing, they automatically decide that she shouldn't be doing it either.

> AILEEN HERNANDEZ, "Current Report on Equal Employment Opportunities," keynote address (unpublished) to Equal Employment Opportunities in the '70's Meeting, University of California, 1972

The truth is that [Aid to Families with Dependent Children] is like a super-sexist marriage. You trade in *a* man for *the* man. But you can't divorce him if he treats you bad. He can divorce you, of course, cut you off anytime he wants. But in that case, *he* keeps the kids, not you.

> JOHNNIE TILLMON, "Welfare Is a Women's Issue," *Ms.*, Spring 1972

. . . women, black and brown as well as white, suffer from a dimension of economic prejudice that minority men do not; one that prolongs the problem by the very effective device of denying that any problem exists. We are perceived as *already powerful*—at least in relation to men of our own group, and often to society at large.

> GLORIA STEINEM, "If We're So Smart, Why Aren't We Rich?" *Ms.*, I, June 1973

When a woman is financially dependent on a man, even if it is only for one evening, she puts herself, to some extent, in his power.

> ANDRA MEDEA AND KATHLEEN THOMPSON, *Against Rape*, 1974

The woman who has been given sexual freedom without real financial and social independence will find herself still bartering.

> Ibid.

The Wage Earner

Woman has relied heretofore too entirely for her support on the *needle*—that one-eyed demon of destruction that slays its thousands annually; that evil genius of our sex, which, in spite of all our devotion, will never make us healthy, wealthy, or wise.

> ELIZABETH CADY STANTON, letter to Woman's Rights Convention, 1851, *History of Woman Suffrage*, I, 1881

Do you not see, gentlemen, that so long as society says a woman is incompetent to be a lawyer, minister, or doctor, but has ample ability to be a teacher, that every man of you who chooses this profession tacitly acknowledges that he has no more brains than a woman?

> SUSAN B. ANTHONY, New York Convention of Teachers, 1853, *History of Woman Suffrage*, I, 1881

All women need employment, active, useful employment; and if they do not have it, they sink down into a state of listlessness and insipidity and become enfeebled in health and prematurely old simply because denied this great want of their nature. Nothing has tended more to the physical and moral degradation of the race than the erroneous and silly idea that woman is too weak, too delicate a creature to have imposed upon her the more active duties of life . . .

> AMELIA BLOOMER, in *Western Home Visitor*, circa 1854, in D. C. Bloomer, *Life and Writings of Amelia Bloomer*, 1895

The flour-merchant, the house-builder, and the postman charge us no less on account of our sex; but when we endeavor to earn money to pay all these, then, indeed we find the difference.

> LUCY STONE, Women's Rights Convention, 1855, *History of Woman Suffrage*, I, 1881

. . . a want of respect for labor, and a want of respect for woman, lies at the bottom of all our difficulties, low wages included.

> CAROLINE WELLS DALL, lectures 1856–1862, *The College, The Market, and the Court*, 1914

I used to work in the field and bind grain, keeping up with the cradler; but men doing no more, got twice as much pay. . . . We do as much, we eat as much, we want as much.

> SOJOURNER TRUTH, American Equal Rights Association Convention, 1867, *History of Woman Suffrage*, II, 1882

So far from there being no demand for women as physicians, I believe that there is at this moment a large amount of work actually awaiting them; that a large amount of suffering exists among women which never comes under the notice of medical men at all, and which will remain unmitigated till women are ready in sufficient numbers to attend medically to those of their own sex who need them, and this in all parts of the world.

> SOPHIA JEX-BLAKE, "Medicine as a Profession for Women," *Woman's Work and Woman's Culture*, ed. Josephine E. Butler, 1869

101

Men, in most branches of labor are paid such prices that when their health fails, they have something left of their wages, to keep them from starvation. Women receive barely enough to keep them alive while at work.

VIRGINIA PENNY, *Think and Act,* 1869

We have often felt disposed to give men credit for employing women in preference to persons of their own sex, but often the preference is given because they can be had for less wages.

Ibid.

The reason women do not have strikes in the United States, like men, and demand higher wages, is, that many are ignorant; many cannot afford the time and money; some are so despairing they think it useless; some have a false pride about the matter; they think it would look unwomanly; but the principal reason is, they have no one to lead them, on whom they can rely.

Ibid.

You remember the old adage, "Beggars must not be choosers"; they must take what they can get or nothing! That is exactly the position of women in the world of work today; they can not choose.

SUSAN B. ANTHONY, "Woman Wants Bread, Not the Ballot!" campaign speech, 1870–1880, in Ida Husted Harper, *Life and Work of Susan B. Anthony,* vol. II, 1898

. . . there are hundreds of women suffering, not for the ballot but for bread. I have never wanted the ballot. I believe it belongs to the men who have it; but I come to ask you in the name of humanity if there can be any society organized that will repress the unscrupulous employers and let the public know they are oppressing the poor girls. Men are strong; they can get together and ask what they want; they can organize in large bodies, but the working women are the most oppressed race in the United States.

MISS LEONARD, president of the Parasol Makers, American Woman Suffrage Association Convention, 1873, *History of Woman Suffrage,* II, 1882

His [the Rev. Morgan Dix's] declaration that women should not enter professions "already overstocked" makes one think of the remark of a certain physician in England, when the question was mooted whether women should enter the medical profession: "Do these women know that there is not work enough for us men doctors now?"—as if the world must of course belong to men, and that only after they had filled all desirable positions might women expect to be allowed to take some humble places, and perhaps pick up a few of the crumbs which fell from their well-spread table.

      LILLIE DEVEREUX BLAKE, *Women's Place Today*, 1883

It has always been thought perfectly womanly to be a scrub-woman in the Legislature and to take care of the spittoons; that is entirely within the charmed circle of woman's sphere; but for women to occupy any of those official seats would be degrading.

      SUSAN B. ANTHONY, National American Woman Suffrage Association Convention, 1895, *History of Woman Suffrage*, IV, 1902

It is not being a doctor that makes a woman unwomanly, but the treatment which the first women medical students and physicians received was such as to make even men unmanly.

      CHARLOTTE PERKINS GILMAN, *Women and Economics*, 1898

What reason is there to doubt that women would have made rapid strides in every skilled pursuit had they been under the same law as men? The usual answer to this question involves what might be called the invalid theory of woman's emancipation. This theory demands that, on account of their innate weakness, we should regard some trades as women's, others as men's; but in the division the advocates of invalidism pass over to women scrubbing, charring, night sick-nursing, which do indeed demand exceptional strength.

      HARRIOT STANTON BLATCH, "Factory Legislation," *Women in Industrial Life*, ed. Countess of Aberdeen, 1900

The working women have much more need of the ballot than we of the so-called leisure class. We suffer from the insult of its refusal; . . . The working women have not only these insults and privations but they have also the knowledge that they are being destroyed, literally destroyed, body and soul, by conditions which they cannot touch by law . . .

      GERTRUDE BARNUM, "Women as Wage Earners," National American Woman Suffrage Association Convention, 1906, *History of Woman Suffrage*, V, 1922

The girls of the family give in their wages more regularly than the boys, and receive back a smaller portion for their own use.

      KATHARINE ANTHONY, *Mothers Who Must Earn*, 1914

. . . they are not allowed to use long-handled mops. The reason usually given is that it is not possible to clean so thoroughly with mops. However, it was observed in a certain hospital where most of the floors are done by women on

their knees, that a few rooms, including the floor of the antiseptic operating room, were considered sufficiently clean after a porter had gone over them carefully with a long-handled mop.
Ibid.

The scrubbing is done in the most primitive fashion, and as long as the women's labor is as cheap as it is, there is little incentive for employers to adopt improved methods of work. There is also a general belief that women do this sort of work more thoroughly than men,—a fact which has served to prolong their tenure.
Ibid.

Too often we hear these women spoken of as if some perversity of instinct drove them to neglect their homes and go to work at the expense of their homes and children. It is for the sake of their children that they work, as mothers have done from time immemorial. The last penny of their earnings is absorbed by their homes.
Ibid.

These same men who tell us we are angels send vice-commissioners to investigate why girls go wrong. I should think a glance at the pay-roll would give them the answer.
Rose Schneiderman, "The Industrial Woman's Need of the Vote," National American Woman Suffrage Association Convention, 1914, *History of Woman Suffrage*, V, 1922

The young woman who has entered medicine, or law, or dentistry, who paints pictures or writes books, is on very much the same economic basis as the young working-girl. She, too, is accepted as part of the already established order of things, and the present generation has grown up in happy ignorance of the difficulties experienced by the pioneers in all these professions in establishing their right to independent careers. The professional woman who has married finds herself so far on a less secure foundation.
Alice Henry, *The Trade Union Woman*, 1917

As long as there was no recognized way of admitting the home woman to even a tiny corner of the labor field, as long as entry was restricted solely to the wage-earning woman, there seemed no chance of women being ever in anything but a hopeless minority in either local or international union, and that minority, too, composed so largely of young and inexperienced girls. Is it

any wonder, then, that the interests of the working-girls have suffered, and that, as a ready consequence, workingmen's interests have suffered, too.
Ibid.

Work is human. It is not feminine, though women began it. It is not masculine, though men have taken it. But because men have kept women out of it for so long, it has shared in the disadvantages of excessive masculinity.
CHARLOTTE PERKINS GILMAN, *His Religion and Hers*, 1923

The results of these investigations, published in the Bulletin No. 30 of the Women's Bureau, show that the woman in industry is not merely working for pin-money, as thoughtless people assume, but that she is more often not only supporting herself on her inadequate wage, but contributing materially to the support of dependents.
SUZANNE LA FOLLETTE, *Concerning Women*, 1926

[Paraphrasing Ethel Snowden]... woman's invasion of the gainful occupations appears to be found unwomanly in proportion to the importance of the position to which she aspires.
Ibid.

... under a monopolistic economic system the opportunity to earn a living by one's labour comes to be regarded as a privilege instead of a natural right. Women are simply held to be less entitled to this privilege than men.
Ibid.

Possibly one of the greatest deprivations women suffer in their present anomalous situation is that of being shut out from the sociability of the work room. Something very precious grows up among any group of people working together.
ALICE BEAL PARSONS, *Woman's Dilemma*, 1926

The joy and exhilaration of this first plunge is responsible for women's having accepted somewhat uncritically the sort of jobs that were first open to them. To earn from fifteen to one hundred dollars a week all their own represented such an immeasurable advance over their previous financial dependence on husbands and fathers, so transported them into a new world, that women of great ability gratefully accepted positions under men so much their inferiors in intelligence and often in training as well, that they would never have dreamed of marrying them, or even of numbering them among their friends.
Ibid.

You men must know that you cannot get very far or make any real progress, if you have women workers who compete with you, unorganized and working for less wages.

> ELIZABETH GRADY, Building Service Employees International Union Convention, 1935, *Service Employee*, 37, October 1977

It is still commonly assumed that a woman has "nobody to keep but herself." Seldom is that actually the case. More normally . . . the woman's earnings go straight into the family box, whereas the man makes pocket money a first charge on his.

> MARY AGNES HAMILTON, "Changes in Social Life," *Our Freedom and Its Results*, ed. Ray Strachey, 1936

Women have come into all their new spheres of work at the bottom, often bringing abilities much too good for the tasks they have been set to do, and because they have been thankful to get the work at all they have been amenable, if not content, in regard to payment.

> RAY STRACHEY, "Changes in Employment," *Our Freedom and Its Results*, ed. Ray Strachey, 1936

Among the millions who are working for pay there are very few indeed—whether married or not—who wholly escape from material domestic preoccupations: few who can lay the blame of domestic discomfort upon anyone but themselves; few who can expect to be fully "looked after."

The effect of this situation is a double handicap to women workers, on the one hand laying upon them the burden of two simultaneous jobs and on the other predisposing their employers to regard them as casual workers, whose real duty lies elsewhere.

> Ibid.

Working-class women, whether they work at home or outside it, are, of course, the vast majority of their sex. At no time have they been "sheltered." [They] have always, like their men-folk, worked because they had to. . . .

> MARY AGNES HAMILTON, *Women at Work*, 1941

[Women] do not expect to succeed; they do not expect to be decently paid; they take it for granted that they are beasts of burden. Resistance, struggle, initiative, are hard for them, just because the conventional picture does not allow them any of these attributes, and because they are so often condemned to solitude in their effort and in their toil.

> Ibid.

... the status and pay of women in the professions are important to all women who work. ... Here the standard is set. The rule is laid down here: the hard rule of lower pay and fewer chances for the woman, because she is a woman.
    Ibid.

No paradox is, in fact, more characteristic of the Capitalism [sic] system under which we live than the practice of paying workers more in proportion as work grows more interesting and more responsible, and less in proportion as it is disagreeable and dull. From this women suffer acutely.
    Ibid.

The low wages of women at work are not only a burden upon women; they are a drag upon men.
    Ibid.

That time-worn myth, that all single women are supported by their fathers and all married women are supported by their husbands, still prevails. ... Women only work, it is contended, to earn spare cash for cosmetics, movies, cigarettes, and clothes. Even in peace time, this is an out-dated view.
    SUSAN B. ANTHONY II, *Out of the Kitchen—Into the War*, 1943

The key to woman's status at any time, whether in war or peace, is not how many women there are in the factories, at the benches and typists' chairs, but how many there are in policy-making positions in Government and in professional jobs outside.
    Ibid.

... men lose out when women get low wages, for the reason that low wages for women undercut the standards for men too.
    Ibid.

When some new and unprecedented field requiring motor efficiency comes into being, as with the invention of the typewriter and the automobile, there is a certain trial period in which medical and mechanical authorities—all male—discuss whether women are strong enough to handle the new instruments. ... [But when] men woke up to the fact that the typewriter ... was actually extremely tedious to operate, ... they forthwith handed it over to the world of women whom they have never ceased to congratulate for their dexterity and precision in regard to it.
    RUTH HERSCHBERGER, *Adam's Rib*, 1948

It is nonsense to debar women from activities where their physical strength is only slightly inferior to men's when some simple gadget would make them as efficient as men. It is particularly nonsensical when it is accompanied by elaborate social rationalizations about a task's being unwomanly, or—in the opposite case—unmanly.

MARGARET MEAD, *Male and Female,* 1949

So brother and sister, boy and girl, educated together, learn what each wishes from what each can give to the other. The girl learns to discipline and mute an ambition that her society continually stimulates, as all girls working in white-collar jobs are said to have "careers," and careers are glamorous, while most men with similar skills merely have jobs. And we have the situation that looks so strange on the surface, that as more and more women work, women seem on the whole less interested in the battle that permits them to succeed professionally.

Ibid.

. . . exploitation of women workers by paying them substandard wages tends to depress all wage rates, for men as well as women.

ESTHER PETERSON, "Working Women," *The Woman in America,* ed. Robert Jay Lifton, 1965.

Though as often quoted to show progress, one third of all women work, they work in the worst sense of the word; that is, they have merely added a new exploiter to the old one. For they are concentrated in the service occupations, at the bottom rung of the employment ladder . . .

SHULAMITH FIRESTONE, "The Women's Rights Movement in the U.S.: A New View," *Notes from the First Year,* June 1968

Women and blacks have provided a reserve army of unemployed workers, benefiting capitalists and the stable male white working class alike. Yet the system imposes untold suffering on the victims, blacks and women, through low wages and chronic unemployment.

MARLENE DIXON, "Why Women's Liberation?" *Ramparts,* December 1969

Capitol Hill offices swarm with intelligent, Washington-wise, college-trained—and attractive—young women who do most of the work that makes a congressman look good, but often get sub-standard pay for it and have little hope of advancing to a top staff job.

SHIRLEY CHISHOLM, *Unbought and Unbossed,* 1970

There is a big difference between knowing how to type and *really* typing. And for a woman in a man's world, the longest, most arduous journey is from the cold steel typing table to the warm walnut desk of a lady executive. If you become too ensconced at the first, you may never get the chance to feel comfortable and cozy behind the second.

> LETTY COTTIN POGREBIN, *How to Make It in a Man's World*, 1970

[Even gifted] women will face discrimination in admission where they will encounter both official and unofficial quotas; they will face discrimination when they apply for scholarships and financial assistance. When they graduate, their own university will discriminate against them in helping them find jobs. They will be discriminated against in hiring for the faculty. If hired at all, they will be promoted far more slowly than their male counterparts, and they will most likely receive far less money than their colleagues of the other sex.

> DR. BERNICE SANDLER, to Rep. Edith Green's Special Subcommittee on Education, 1970, *Discrimination Against Women*, U.S. Government Printing Office, 1971

Black women have been doubly oppressed. . . . White women have their problems. They're interviewed for secretarial instead of the executive thing. But we're interviewed for mopping floors.

> MARGARET WRIGHT, in "L.A.'s Women Liberationists," *Los Angeles Times, West* magazine, June 7, 1970

. . . we have come to depend on a work force of married women who do not think of themselves as workers and are not treated seriously on the job. Only when we look back into history do we see how they have been pulled into wage work and pushed back home at the convenience of the changing economy.

> CAROLINE BIRD, *Born Female*, rev. ed. 1971

In academic life as elsewhere, rules against nepotism limit professional women and sometimes deprive them of the opportunity to work at all. Men and women meet at work and marry. . . . But as they rise to positions of power the situation becomes uncomfortable, even if it does not violate specific rules, and it is always the wife who withdraws.

> Ibid.

Hypocritical insistence that opportunity is really equal is the cruelest form of discrimination. It implies that the loser in any contest has lost through his own inabilities. And while women and blacks realize that the cards are stacked against them, they are compelled by the prevailing rhetoric to act as if they had actually lost out in fair competition.

Ibid.

Economically, the most elementary demand is not the right to work or receive equal pay for work—the two traditional demands—but *the right to equal work itself*.

JULIET MITCHELL, *Woman's Estate*, 1971

Given the extraordinary status, wealth, power and prestige that physicians have, it is evident that women as workers and patients occupy the wide base of a pyramid with white male doctors at the narrow top, controlling everything and everyone below them for their own interests.

BOSTON WOMEN'S HEALTH BOOK COLLECTIVE, *Our Bodies, Ourselves*, 2d ed., 1976

For us, the superwoman who knits marriage, career, and motherhood into a satisfying life without dropping a stitch is as oppressive a role model as the airbrushed Bunny in the Playboy centerfold . . .

SYLVIA RABINER, "How the Superwoman Puts Women Down," *Village Voice*, May 24, 1976

Tokenism is painful, and either resolution of the problems of integrity and compromise—joining the boys or becoming a token feminist—immerses the woman in the absurdity.

MARILYN FRYE, "Who Wants a Piece of the Pie?" *Quest*, III, Winter 1976–1977

When it comes to women's employment . . . we hear a lot about the first jockey or the first television anchorwoman, the first coal miner or Episcopal priest. What we don't hear is that these exceptions mean almost nothing to the lives of most women because they are still confined to female job ghettos. And so we get a false sense of progress from hearing only about the few exceptions allowed to enter almost totally male worlds.

GLORIA STEINEM, "Pink-Collar Workers," *Progressive*, May 1977

The Consumer

Thus we have painfully and laboriously evolved and carefully maintain among us an enormous class of non-productive consumers,—a class which is half the world, and mother of the other half.
    CHARLOTTE PERKINS GILMAN, *Women and Economics*, 1898

I suddenly realized the significance of the boast that women wield seventy-five per cent of the purchasing power in America. I suddenly saw American women as *victims* of that ghastly gift, that power at the point of purchase.
    BETTY FRIEDAN, *The Feminine Mystique*, 1963

[Motivational researchers] are guilty of persuading housewives to stay at home, mesmerized in front of a television set, their nonsexual human needs unnamed, unsatisfied, drained by the sexual sell into the buying of things.
    Ibid.

Like a primitive culture which sacrificed little girls to its tribal gods, we sacrifice our girls to the feminine mystique, grooming them ever more efficiently through the sexual sell to become consumers of the things to whose profitable sale our nation is dedicated.
    Ibid.

Women in particular *are* good consumers; this follows naturally from their responsibility for matters in the home. Also, the inferior status of women, their general lack of a strong sense of worth and identity, make them more exploitable than men and hence better consumers.
    MARGARET BENSTON, "The Political Economy of Women's Liberation," *Monthly Review*, September 1969

There is nothing like boredom to make one want to buy things, as anyone with an hour to spare in the centre of town must know, and nothing like being at home all day for making one notice that the curtains look drab and the carpet is fraying. The woman who is out at work not only has preoccupations which prevent her from fussing about appearances, except perhaps her own, but she actually has no use for many of the consumer goods that our industries dream up.
    EVA FIGES, *Patriarchal Attitudes*, 1970

To convince a man to buy, an ad must appeal to his desire for autonomy and freedom from conventional restrictions; to convince a woman, an ad must appeal to her need to please the male oppressor.

ELLEN WILLIS, " 'Consumerism' and Women," *Voices from Women's Liberation*, ed. Leslie B. Tanner, 1970

The cad! The traitor! Pretending to believe that fairy tale about her birth from Zeus' head! "Always for the male," indeed! Yet even in this vital moment she acknowledges that she'd *never marry* one.

This is probably the first recorded instance of man's use of the brainwashed enemy to brainwash her fellows. Television-commercial writers and women's magazines have made an art of it.

ELIZABETH GOULD DAVIS, commenting on Athena's casting the deciding vote in favor of acquitting Orestes of the murder of his mother, *The First Sex*, 1971

Because she is the emblem of spending ability and the chief spender, she is also the most effective seller of this world's goods. . . . The gynolatry of our civilization is written large upon its face, upon . . . cinema screens, television, newspapers, . . . all consecrated to the reigning deity, the female fetish. Her dominion must not be thought to entail the rule of women, for she is not a woman.

GERMAINE GREER, *The Female Eunuch*, 1971

Great parts of our economy are directly dependent upon women having a weak self-concept. A multi-billion dollar fashion-cosmetic industry testifies to the validity of this approach. A woman who does not know who she is can be sold anything.

GABRIELLE BURTON, *I'm Running Away from Home, But I'm Not Allowed to Cross the Street*, 1972

The success of the feminine-hygiene spray provides a fascinating paradox in that its manufacturers have taken advantage of the sexual revolution to sell something that conveys an implicit message that sex—in the natural state, at least—is dirty and smelly.

NORA EPHRON, *Crazy Salad*, 1975

Reforms directed at the private sphere can only be tokenism. Women will naturally be pressed into becoming the self-help ecologists in band-aid remedies that increase the dissipation of their energies in trivia. . . . The ecological factor will be built into consumer products in some trivial way and then sold with much advertising to women as a luxury item tacked onto present consumer products to placate the conscience.

ROSEMARY RADFORD RUETHER, *New Woman New Earth,* 1975

7   A Man's World

Language

Last evening we spoke of the propriety of women being called by the names which are used to designate their sex, and not by those assigned to males. You differed with me on the ground that custom had established the rule that a woman must take the whole of her husband's name, particularly when public mention is made of her. . . . I have very serious objections, dear Rebecca, to being called Henry. There is a great deal in a name. . . . Why are slaves nameless unless they take that of their master? Simply because they have no independent existence. . . . Even so with women. The custom of calling women Mrs. John This and Mrs. Tom That . . . is founded on the principle that white men are lords of all. I cannot acknowledge this principle as just; therefore, I cannot bear the name of another.

ELIZABETH CADY STANTON, letter to Rebecca Eyster, 1847, *Elizabeth Cady Stanton: As Revealed in Her Letters Diary and Reminiscences*, II, ed. Theodore Stanton and Harriot Stanton Blatch, 1922

But, it is urged, the use of the masculine pronouns he, his, and him, in all the constitutions and laws, is proof that only men were meant to be included in their provisions. If you insist on this version of the letter of the law, we shall insist that you be consistent, and accept the other horn of the dilemma, which would compel you to exempt women from taxation for the support of the government and from penalties for the violation of laws.

SUSAN B. ANTHONY, "Address to the Citizens of New York State," 1873, *History of Woman Suffrage*, II, 1882

Then, too, have not men, poor fellows, had to do all the talking since the world began? Have we not heretofore been the silent sex? Even to-day a thousand men speak from pulpit and platform where one woman uplifts her voice.

> LILLIE DEVEREUX BLAKE, "The Rights of Men," National Woman Suffrage Association Convention, 1887, *History of Woman Suffrage*, IV, 1902

Ever since the world began all women of note have been known by their own Christian names. Adam named his wife Eve and we have no account of her ever being called Mrs. Adam.

> AMELIA BLOOMER, undated article from *Western Woman's Journal*, in D. C. Bloomer, *Life and Writings of Amelia Bloomer*, 1895

A house does not need a wife any more than it does a husband. Are we never to have a man-wife?

> CHARLOTTE PERKINS GILMAN, *The Home*, 1903

The ground of the modern woman's protest has been precisely the fact that "he" meant in man's mind what the plain word said, and not what he assured her that it meant.

> ELIZABETH ROBBINS, *Ancilla's Share*, 1924

If there is no word for shrew, or slut in male form, is it because there were no bad-tempered, no slovenly men? Or is it because only the male tongue might safely point out defects? If a female did so, was the scold's bridle and the ducking stool the proper repartee?

> Ibid.

. . . most people, no doubt, when they espouse human rights, make their own mental reservations about the proper application of the word "human". . .

> SUZANNE LA FOLLETTE, *Concerning Women*, 1926

For hundreds of years the use of the word "man" has troubled critical scholars, careful translators, and lawyers. Difficulties occur whenever . . . the context gives no intimation whether "man" means just a human being irrespective of sex or means a masculine being and none other.

> MARY RITTER BEARD, *Woman as Force in History*, 1946

A good portion of our language is designed to degrade women to the level where it is permissible to have sexual feelings for them.

> SHULAMITH FIRESTONE, *The Dialectic of Sex*, 1970

Don't let the "man's world" label scare you either. We have to call it by its rightful name because there are mostly men in it.
>   LETTY COTTIN POGREBIN, *How to Make It in a Man's World*, 1970

... matriarchal people "pleasure" the woman, while patriarchal people "ride" her.
>   ELIZABETH GOULD DAVIS, *The First Sex*, 1971

The word *harlot* did not become exclusively feminine until the seventeenth century. There is no male analogue for it in the era of the double standard.
>   GERMAINE GREER, *The Female Eunuch*, 1971

The first symptom of oppression is the repression of words; the state of suffering is so total and so assumed that it is not known to be there.
>   JULIET MITCHELL, *Woman's Estate*, 1971

Words like "old maid" and "spinster," as opposed to "bachelor" and "playboy," illustrate how we view women who do not choose to marry or who miss out on the chance if they want it.
>   CHARLOTTE HOLT CLINEBELL, *Meet Me in the Middle*, 1973

... women have had the power of *naming* stolen from us. We have not been free to use our own power to name ourselves, the world, or God.
>   MARY DALY, *Beyond God the Father*, 1973

When ... I have spoken of "the sisterhood of man" the result has been a sense of contradiction and a jarring of images.
>   Ibid.

If a woman is swept off a ship into the water, the cry is "Man overboard!" If she is killed by a hit-and-run driver, the charge is "manslaughter." If she is injured on the job, the coverage is "workmen's compensation." But if she arrives at a threshold marked "Men Only," she knows the admonition is not intended to bar animals or plants or inanimate objects. It is meant for her.
>   ALMA GRAHAM, "How to Make Trouble: The Making of a Nonsexist Dictionary," *Ms.*, December 1973

For at least some speakers, the more demeaning the job, the more the person holding it (if female, of course) is likely to be described as a *lady*. Thus, *cleaning lady* is at least as common as *cleaning woman, saleslady* as *saleswoman*. But one says, normally, *woman doctor*.

ROBIN LAKOFF, *Language and Woman's Place*, 1975

... if we were to have a married woman president, we would not have any name for her husband parallel to *First Lady*, and why do you suppose that is?

Ibid.

... it is one thing to be an *old master*, like Hans Holbein, and another to be an *old mistress* . . .

Ibid.

Unfortunately, [modern feminists] ... did not anticipate that "liberation" would be caricatured as "lib," "libbie," and "libbest" and contribute to the women's movement, like women, not being taken seriously.

JO FREEMAN, *The Politics of Women's Liberation*, 1975

... a phrase like "feminist bias" makes no sense at all, since evenhanded treatment—commonly known as equality under the law—is what feminism is all about. To be biased in favor of feminism is to be unfair in one's advocacy of fairness; to say something has a feminist bias is like saying it's inequitably egalitarian.

KAREN DURBIN, "The Intelligent Woman's Guide to Sex," *Mademoiselle*, February 1977

It seems the original meaning of *virtue*, male strength, expanded to include both courage and moral worth, but was cleverly narrowed to chastity when applied to women. When a woman had the strength and courage of a man, she was called a virago—which became a bad word in Rome. Today a virago is a "violent, loud-voiced, ill-tempered, scolding woman: a shrew." So much for women of masculine strength or spirit. I don't recall any word for a woman of feminine strength and spirit.

KATHRYN LINDSKOOG, "Roots," *The Christian Century*, XCIV, March 16, 1977

To be named and defined by someone else is to accept an imposed identity—to agree that the way others see us is the way we really are. Naming conventions, like the rest of language, have been shaped to meet the interests of society, and in patriarchal societies the shapers have been men.
 CASEY MILLER AND KATE SWIFT, *Words and Women*, 1977

Those who have grown up with a language that tells them they are at the same time men and not men are faced with ambivalence—not about their sex, but about their status as human beings. For the question "Who is man?" it seems, is a political one, and the very ambiguity of the word is what makes it a useful tool for those who have a stake in maintaining the status quo.
 Ibid.

History/Literature

Alluded to, rather as an incident than a principal in the chronicles of nations, her influence, which cannot be denied, has been turned into a reproach; her genius, which could not be concealed, has been treated as a phenomenon, when not considered a monstrosity!
 LADY SYDNEY MORGAN, *Woman and Her Master*, 1840

. . . while woman is permitted to cultivate the arts which merely please, and which frequently corrupt, she is denounced as a thing unsexed . . . if she directs her thoughts to pursuits which aspire to serve, and which never fail to elevate.
 Ibid.

Will you tell us, that women have no Newtons, Shakespeares, and Byrons? Greater natural powers than even those possessed may have been destroyed in woman for want of proper culture, a just appreciation, reward for merit as an incentive to exertion, and freedom of action . . . ; and yet, amid all blighting, crushing circumstances—confined within the narrowest possible limits, trampled upon by prejudice and injustice, from her education and position forced to occupy herself almost exclusively with the most trivial affairs—in spite of all these difficulties, her intellect is as good as his.
 ERNESTINE L. ROSE, Second National Convention, Friends of Woman Suffrage, 1851, *History of Woman Suffrage*, I, 1881

. . . I seldom have one hour undisturbed in which to sit down and write. Men who can, when they wish to write a document, shut themselves up for days with their thoughts and their books, know little of what difficulties a woman must surmount to get off a tolerable production.

> ELIZABETH CADY STANTON, letter to Susan B. Anthony, 1853, *Elizabeth Cady Stanton: As Revealed in Her Letters Diary and Reminiscences*, II, ed. Theodore Stanton and Harriot Stanton Blatch, 1922

The philosopher, the poet, and the saint, all combine to make the name of woman synonymous with either fool or devil. Every passion of the human soul, which in manhood becomes so grand and glorious in its results, is fatal to womankind. Ambition makes a Lady Macbeth; love, an Ophelia; none but those brainless things, without will or passion, are ever permitted to come to a good end. What measure of content could you draw from the literature of the past?

> ELIZABETH CADY STANTON, letter to Gerrit Smith, 1855, *History of Woman Suffrage*, I, 1881

If men start with the idea that woman is an inferior being, incapable of wide interests, and created for their pleasure alone; if they enact laws and establish customs to sustain these views; if, for the most part, they shut her into hareems, consider her so dangerous that she may not walk the streets without a veil,—they will write history in accordance with such views, and, whatever may be the facts, they will be interpreted to suit them.

> CAROLINE WELLS DALL, Lectures 1856–1862, *The College, The Market, and the Court*, 1914

. . . not only do . . . women suffer . . . ever-recurring indignities in daily life, but the literature of the world proclaims their inferiority and divinely decreed subjection in all history, sacred and profane, in science, philosophy, poetry, and song.

> E. C. STANTON, S. B. ANTHONY, and M. J. GAGE, eds., *History of Woman Suffrage*, II, 1882

Which recalls a saying that was once held to be quite indisputable, that a woman's name should never appear in the newspapers but twice, once when she was married and once when she died. How pleasant it has been for men to monopolize all the attention of the public in the past! No wonder they do not like the idea of sharing their honors—of, possibly, being outrivalled.

> LILLIE DEVEREUX BLAKE, *Women's Place Today*, 1883

119

You may look among the honored names of the nation and you may search in vain for a woman's. Dorothea Dix, and Clara Barton, and Mother Bickerdyke are unrecorded, and after that cruel struggle was over the loyal women of the North received precisely the same portion that was meted out to unpardoned rebels—disfranchisement.

Ibid.

Man's trials, his fears, his losses, all fell on woman with double force; yet history is silent concerning the part woman performed in the frontier life of the early settlers. Men make no mention of her heroism and divine patience; they take no thought of the mental or physical agonies women endure in the perils of maternity, ofttimes without nurse or physician in the supreme hour of their need, going, as every mother does, to the very gates of death in giving life to an immortal being!

ELIZABETH CADY STANTON, *Eighty Years and More*, 1898

All history is a record of man's domination and woman's suffering.

"STELLA," anonymous author of "The Tyranny of Man," *The Burden of Women*, ed. Frank Mond, 1908

. . . lack of recognition of woman's influence in history was not so much the result of intention as of the masculine point of view which has dominated civilization. The impression conveyed by our text books . . . is that this world has been made by men and for men and the ideals they are putting forth are colored by masculine thought.

PAULINE STEINEM, National American Woman Suffrage Convention, 1909, *History of Woman Suffrage*, V, 1922

Men's favourite method of arguing against women is to deny their statements of fact.

CHRISTABEL PANKHURST, *Plain Facts About a Great Evil*, 1913

Dominant early thinkers, being men, and having in their minds as premises the common errors as to the nature and power of women, naturally incorporated these errors in their systems of philosophy. What the women thought, is not recorded, any more than the lion has erected a statue to the victor in the hunt.

CHARLOTTE PERKINS GILMAN, *His Religion and Hers*, 1923

While feminists have, in a large measure, stayed their hand, anybody who has anything abusive to say of women, whether ancient or modern, can command a vast public in the popular press and a ready agreement from the average publisher.
> DORA RUSSELL, *Hypatia*, 1925

... the east wind of indifference which has chilled the fire of many a masculine artist who found himself part of an age indifferent to his order of talent, has always blown its coldest upon the woman who essayed creative work.
> SUZANNE LA FOLLETTE, *Concerning Women*, 1926

The world's literature, from the Sanscrit proverbs to the comic magazine of the twentieth century, is full of disparaging references to the character of women; to their frailty, their cunning, their deceitfulness, their irresponsibility, their treachery—qualities, all of them, which in a fair view they seem bound to have extemporized as their only defence in a social order which was proof against more honourable weapons.
> Ibid.

Man has always liked to have some woman, especially one about eight feet high and of earnest aspect, to represent his ideas or inventions. At the same time, of course, he anxiously thwarted her attempts to utilize the inventions or pursue the theories he held. Thus, he wanted women to be illiterate, but to represent the Spirit of Education; he denied them property rights and painted them as the Spirit of Plenty; he refused them custody of their own children and sculptured them as the Spirit of Motherhood.
> MIRIAM BEARD, "Woman Springs from Allegory to Life," *New York Times Sunday Magazine*, March 20, 1927

When ... one reads of a witch being ducked, of a woman possessed by devils, of a wise woman selling herbs, or even of a very remarkable man who had a mother, then I think we are on the track of a lost novelist, a suppressed poet, of some mute and inglorious Jane Austen, some Emily Brontë who dashed her brains out on the moor or mopped and mowed about the highways crazed with the torture that her gift had put her to. Indeed, I would venture to guess that Anon, who wrote so many poems without signing them, was often a woman.
> VIRGINIA WOOLF, *A Room of One's Own*, 1929

Speaking crudely, football and sport are "important"; the worship of fashion, the buying of clothes "trivial." And these values are inevitably transferred from life to fiction. This is an important book, the critic assumes, because it

121

deals with war. This is an insignificant book because it deals with the feelings of women in a drawing-room.
Ibid.

Intellectual freedom depends upon material things. Poetry depends upon intellectual freedom. And women have always been poor, not for two hundred years merely, but from the beginning of time. Women have had less intellectual freedom than the sons of Athenian slaves. Women, then, have not had a dog's chance of writing poetry.
Ibid.

If the historians of the twenty-fifth century, let us say, should have access to no other fragment of our time in the field of science than the introduction or advertisement of the *Biographical Dictionary of American Men of Science*, they would naturally come to the conclusion that women of this century could not enter laboratories, were not interested in science, and had no deeds, large or small, to their credit, in that realm.
MARY RITTER BEARD, *On Understanding Women*, 1931

To appreciate what it signifies to have no history, let us try to imagine what it would be like to know nothing even of men's past!
MARY RITTER BEARD, *A Changing Political Economy as It Affects Women*, 1934

Children's books, mythology, stories, tales, all reflect the myths born of the pride and desires of men; thus it is that through the eyes of men the little girl discovers the world and reads therein her destiny.
SIMONE DE BEAUVOIR, *The Second Sex*, 1952

In a not-so-subtle way both men and women are told that only men make history and women are not important enough to study.
JO FREEMAN, Rep. Edith Green's Special Subcommittee on Education, 1970, *Discrimination Against Women*, U.S. Government Printing Office, 1971

Perhaps patriarchy's greatest psychological weapon is simply its universality and longevity.
KATE MILLETT, *Sexual Politics*, 1971

... when [historians]... are bound by the necessity for accuracy or logic to include a woman's *name* in the unfolding of a national event, her name is invariably coupled with a belittling adjective designed not only to put down the

122

woman herself but to assure their feminine readers that such women are undesirable and "unfeminine." Thus all outstanding women become in the history books "viragos" (Boadicea), "hussies" (Matilda of Flanders), "hysterics"
(Joan of Arc), "monstrosities" (Tomyris), or merely myths (Martia and Pope
Joan).

> ELIZABETH GOULD DAVIS, *The First Sex*, 1972

These pressures toward censorship, self-censorship; towards accepting, abiding by dominant attitudes, thus falsifying one's own reality, range, vision,
truth, are extreme for women writers (indeed have much to do with the fear,
the sense of powerlessness that pervades some of our books). Not to be able to
come to one's own truth, or not to use it in one's writing, robs one of drive, of
conviction; limits potential stature; results in loss to literature and the compre-
hensions we seek in it.

> TILLIE OLSON, "Women Who Are Writers in Our Century: One Out of
> Twelve," *College English*, October 1972

The habits of a lifetime when everything else had to come before writing are
not easily broken, even when circumstances now often make it possible for
the writing to be first; habits of years: response to others, distractibility, responsibility for daily matters, stay with you, mark you, become you. The cost
of "discontinuity" (that pattern still urged on women by a society that prefers
that *they* adjust, not itself) is such a weight of things unsaid, an accumulation
of material so great, that everything starts up something else in me; what
should take weeks, takes months to write; what should take months, takes
years.

> Ibid.

Women, as all oppressed people, live in a culture of silence . . .

> ROSEMARY RADFORD RUETHER, *Liberation Theology*, 1972

The press treated women's liberation much as society treats women—as en-
tertainment not to be taken seriously.

> JO FREEMAN, *The Politics of Women's Liberation*, 1975

Maintaining history as the exclusive province of the elite not only denies most
women a sense of their past but inevitably diminishes the significance they attach to their own lives.

> SHERNA GLUCK, Introduction, *From Parlor to Prison*, 1976

... the individual artist ethic has been very destructive to women, because when men are alone, they aren't really alone—they are alone in their studios supported by systems. But women are *really* alone, without any system, and that is not just alone—that is isolated and powerless.

> JUDY CHICAGO, in Susan Rennie and Arlene Raven, "The Dinner Party Project: An Interview with Judy Chicago," *Chrysalis*, 4, 1977

Religion

Well do they [ministers of religion] know, that if the daughters of the present and mothers of the future generation, were to drink of the living waters of knowledge, their reign would be ended.... Their own sex, old and young, they see with indifference swim by their nets; but closely and warily are their meshes laid, to entangle the female of every age.

> FRANCES WRIGHT, *Course of Popular Lectures*, 1829

Priestess, prophetess, the oracle of the tripod, the sibyl of the cave, the veiled idol of the temple, the shrouded teacher of the academy, the martyr or missionary of a spiritual truth, the armed champion of a political cause, she has been covertly used for every purpose by which man, when he has failed to reason his species into truth, has endeavoured to fanaticise it into good; whenever mind has triumphed by indirect means over the inertia of masses.

> LADY SYDNEY MORGAN, *Woman and Her Master*, 1840

Women no soul! Then, of course, we are not accountable beings: and if not accountable to our Maker, then surely not to man.

> AMELIA BLOOMER, response to the Tennessee legislature's conclusion that women had no souls, *The Lily*, 1850, in D. C. Bloomer, *Life and Writings of Amelia Bloomer*, 1895

He [man] has brought the Bible to prove that he is her lord and master, and taught her that resistance to his authority is to resist God's will. I deny that the Bible teaches any such doctrine. God made them different in sex, but equal in intellect, and gave them equal dominion.

> AMELIA BLOOMER, response to Mr. T. S. Arthur's "Ruling a Wife," in D. C. Bloomer, *Life and Writings of Amelia Bloomer*, 1895

Man was not pronounced good until woman was created, and God said, Let us make man in our image after our own likeness, and let THEM *have dominion.*

> MARY MOTT, letter to Westchester Convention, 1852, *History of Woman Suffrage*, I, 1881

They [women] have accepted the opinions of men for the commands of their Creator.

> E. C. STANTON, S. B. ANTHONY, M. J. GAGE, eds., *History of Woman Suffrage*, I, 1881

That woman has not thrown off the yoke of religious despotism can be readily appreciated when we recognize the fact that man, from time immemorial, has played upon her religious faith to exalt his own attributes and degrade hers; that through this teaching her abiding belief in his superior capacity to interpret scriptural truths for her has been the means of sacrificing her power of mind, her tender affections, her delicate sensibilities, on the altar of his base selfishness throughout the ages. Orthodoxy recognizes no "inspiration" for woman to-day. She is not "called" save to serve man.

> PHOEBE COUZINS, National Woman Suffrage Association Convention, 1882, *History of Woman Suffrage*, III, 1887

Women are robbed of the right of conscience. Their silence and subjection in the church have been the curse not only of womanhood but of manhood. No other human being should decide for us in questions pertaining to our own moral and spiritual welfare.

> ANNA HOWARD SHAW, sermon, National American Woman Suffrage Association Convention, 1894, *History of Woman Suffrage*, IV, 1902

With the corruption of human nature and the decline of mental power which followed the supremacy of the animal instincts, the earlier abstract idea of God was gradually lost sight of, and man himself in the form of a potentate or ruler, together with the various emblems of virility, came to be worshipped as the Creator.

> ELIZA BURT GAMBLE, *The God-Idea of the Ancients*, 1897

The clerical portion of the [Anti-Slavery] convention [1840] was most violent in its opposition. The clergymen seemed to have God and his angels especially in their care and keeping, and were in agony lest the women should do or say something to shock the heavenly hosts. Their all-sustaining conceit gave them abundant assurance that their movements must necessarily be all-pleasing to the celestials whose ears were open to the proceedings of the World's Convention.

ELIZABETH CADY STANTON, *Eighty Years and More*, 1898

When women understand that governments and religions are human inventions; that Bibles, prayerbooks, catechisms, and encyclical letters are all emanations from the brain of man, they will no longer be oppressed by the injunctions that come to them with the divine authority of "Thus saith the Lord."

Ibid.

... we have an interest in tracing the lessons taught to women in the churches to their true origin and a right to demand from our theologians the same full and free discussion in the church that we have had in the State, as the time has fully come for women to be heard in the ecclesiastical councils of the nation.

ELIZABETH CADY STANTON, letter to the National American Woman Suffrage Association Convention, 1901, *History of Woman Suffrage*, V, 1922

The central falsehood from which ... different forms of slavery spring is the doctrine of original sin and woman as a medium for the machinations of Satan, its author. The greatest block today in the way of woman's emancipation is the church, the canon law, the Bible and the priesthood.

Ibid.

Religion was for man to preach—and women to practise.

CHARLOTTE PERKINS GILMAN, *The Home*, 1903

... the preachers and poets had a habit of talking so exclusively about "the God of our fathers" that there was danger of forgetting that our mothers had any God!

ANNA HOWARD SHAW, National American Woman Suffrage Association Convention, 1904, *History of Woman Suffrage*, V, 1922

Every nation has kept woman in ignorance, and has used its religion as a means of securing her subjection. Is it any wonder then that the world has always been a scene of bloodshed and cruelty?

"STELLA," anonymous author of "The Tyranny of Man," *The Burden of Women*, ed. Frank Mond, 1908

The superior being is the one that has the greater strength of will; and we find that a mysterious supernatural power was needed to overcome the will of Eve, while the man surrendered all his principles at her request.
>   Ibid.

No one suffered more than Paul himself from the absence of female guidance and assistance; for he confesses that he had little ability as an orator, and that he had often to suffer great discomfort, so that it is very evident that he was badly fitted to wander about alone . . .
>   Ibid.

. . . as man accords to woman moral superiority it is his pre-eminent duty to encourage her to speak and teach in religious assemblies.
>   National American Woman Suffrage Association, Resolution of the Convention of 1908, *History of Woman Suffrage*, V, 1922

Puritanism, with its perversion of the significance and functions of the human body, especially in regard to woman, has condemned her to celibacy, or to the indiscriminate breeding of a diseased race, or to prostitution.
>   EMMA GOLDMAN, "The Hypocrisy of Puritanism," *Anarchism and Other Essays*, 1911

Religion, especially the Christian religion, has condemned woman to the life of an inferior, a slave. It has thwarted her nature and fettered her soul, yet the Christian religion has no greater supporter, none more devout, than woman.
>   EMMA GOLDMAN, "Woman Suffrage," *Anarchism and Other Essays*, 1911

In the moral code developed by the Church, women have been so degraded that they have been habituated to look upon themselves through the eyes of men.
>   MARGARET SANGER, *The Pivot of Civilization*, 1922

Had the religions of the world developed through her mind, they would have shown one deep essential difference, the difference between birth and death. The man was interested in one end of life, she in the other. He was moved to faith, fear, and hope for the future; she to love and labor in the present.
>   CHARLOTTE PERKINS GILMAN, *His Religion and Hers*, 1923

A rather conspicuous point to be noted in all these joy-promising futures [heavens] is their naïve masculinity. Never a feminine paradise among them. Happy Hunting-Grounds—no happy Nursing Grounds.
  Ibid.

One religion after another has accepted and perpetuated man's original mistake in making a private servant of the mother of the race.
  Ibid.

The origin of the stupid ideal of womanhood against which men as well as women to-day are still fighting was the asceticism of the Christian religion; and, unless St. Paul was a woman in disguise, I fail to see how woman is to be blamed for a conception of her place and duty from which she has suffered more than anybody else.
  DORA RUSSELL, *Hypatia*, 1925

Religion has persisted in regarding the female body as unclean when engaged in its most important functions, and purifying it afterwards by special prayers to the Deity. We find this savagery current in Judaism as in Christianity, together with an exhortation to be fruitful and multiply, and therefore to pass through shame and uncleanness as often as we can.
  Ibid.

There is nothing more innately human than the tendency to transmute what has become customary into what has been divinely ordained . . .
  SUZANNE LA FOLLETTE, *Concerning Women*, 1926

Religion sanctions woman's self-love; it gives her the guide, father, lover, divine guardian she longs for nostalgically; it feeds her daydreams; it fills her empty hours. But, above all, it confirms the social order, it justifies her resignation, by giving her the hope of a better future in a sexless heaven.
  SIMONE DE BEAUVOIR, *The Second Sex*, 1952

When man substituted God for the Great Goddess he at the same time substituted authoritarian for humanistic values.
  ELIZABETH GOULD DAVIS, *The First Sex*, 1971

It has been the custom of Christian historians for eighteen centuries to bewail the freedom of Roman women and to hold them responsible for the decline of the Roman Empire. But the facts do not bear out this accusation. Rome did not fall until *after* it had adopted Christianity, a fact which suggests . . . that

128

Christianity itself caused the decline and fall of the empire and the Dark Ages that followed . . .
Ibid.

. . . would-be pacifiers of women seem to be fond of quoting the Pauline text which proclaims that "in Christ there is neither male nor female." This invites the response that *even if* this were true, the fact is that everywhere else there certainly is.
Mary Daly, *Beyond God the Father*, 1973

. . . in patriarchy, with the aid of religion, women have been the primordial scapegoats.
Ibid.

It might be interesting to speculate upon the probable length of a "depatriarchalized Bible." Perhaps there would be enough salvageable material to comprise an interesting pamphlet.
Ibid.

The witch was a triple threat to the Church: She was a woman, and not ashamed of it. She appeared to be part of an organized underground of peasant women. And she was a healer whose practice was based in empirical study. In the face of the repressive fatalism of Christianity, she held out the hope of change in this world.
Barbara Ehrenreich and Deirdre English, *Witches, Midwives and Nurses*, 1973

Even in our own overrational age, the medium of the all-male priesthood continues to convey the ancient message that women and mystery are a dangerous combination.
Emily Hewitt and Suzanne Hiatt, *Women Priests: Yes or No?*, 1973

. . . Christian women do no favor for Christian men when they try to "protect" men's position in the church by limiting that of women.
Ibid.

The fiction of fatherhood is a giant religion called christianity.
Jill Johnston, *Lesbian Nation*, 1973

Men are of this world, but women are of the Spirit. The net effect of this piety . . . has been that women have been effectively removed from public influence in the Church.

> CONSTANCE F. PARVEY, "The Theology and Leadership of Women in the New Testament," *Religion and Sexism*, ed. R. R. Ruether, 1974

. . . *sexist* conceptualizations, images, and attitudes concerning God, spawned in a patriarchal society, tend to breed *more* sexist ideas and attitudes, and together these function to legitimate and perpetuate sexist institutions and behavior. Briefly, if God is male, then the male is God.

> MARY DALY, new introduction, *The Church and the Second Sex*, 1975

The Professions

The science of Obstetrics is a branch of the profession which should be monopolized by women. The fact that it is now almost wholly in the hands of the male practitioner, is an outrage on common decency that nothing but the tyrant *custom* can excuse.

> ELIZABETH CADY STANTON, letter to Woman's Convention, 1851, *History of Woman Suffrage*, I, 1881

Those who are most anxious to see women waiting upon male patients as nurses, consider it an outrage upon propriety that they should attend their own sex as physicians.

> EMILY DAVIES, LL.D., "Medicine as a Profession for Women," Annual Meeting of the National Association for the Promotion of Social Science, 1862, *Thoughts on Some Questions Relating to Women, 1860–1908*, 1910

One general fact that stands out is the large number of women more or less injured after confinement who seem to consider it is a woman's lot in life always to suffer from various aches and pains and never to expect really good health. While on the whole the treatment of women at the women's special hospitals or hospital departments is excellent again on the whole, the general practitioners' treatment of gynaecological conditions is very often worse than useless.

> MAUDE E. KERSLAKE, "On Some Special Points of Interest in Our 'Difficult Cases,'" in Marie Carmichael Stopes, "*The First Five Thousand*," 1925

Doctors are always enemies of women. They are an ultra-conservative group resisting any kind of social change. They consistently adopt an infuriating and patronizing attitude toward women. This is especially true of most obstetricians who elect to play the role of father and god to their patients, forcing women into the role of helpless, stupid, ridiculous little girls.

VICKI POLLARD, "Producing Society's Babies," *Women: A Journal of Liberation*, Fall 1969

Psychology has nothing to say about what women are really like, what they need and what they want, for the simple reason that psychology does not know. Yet psychologists will hold forth endlessly on the true nature of woman, with dismaying enthusiasm and disquieting certitude.

NAOMI WEISSTEIN, "Woman as Nigger," *Psychology Today*, October 1969

When one imagines the orthodox disciple of Freud in his bedchamber, refusing to acknowledge the function, teleological or otherwise, of his wife's clitoris, one can understand the nervous preoccupation with frigidity. But Freudian feminine psychology, with its emphasis on female passivity in general and exclusively vaginal excitation in particular, must have caused more frigidity than it ever cured.

EVA FIGES, *Patriarchal Attitudes*, 1970

Education, social work, sociology, anthropology, all the related behavioral sciences, remained for years pseudo-sciences, overburdened with a double function: the indoctrination of women . . .

SHULAMITH FIRESTONE, *The Dialectic of Sex*, 1970

As far as the woman is concerned, psychiatry is an extraordinary confidence trick: the unsuspecting creature seeks aid because she feels unhappy, anxious and confused, and psychology persuades her to seek the cause in *herself*. The person is easier to change than the status quo which represents a higher value in the psychologists' optimistic philosophy.

GERMAINE GREER, *The Female Eunuch*, 1971

The essential factor in the liberation of the married woman is understanding of her condition. . . . She must know her enemies, the doctors, psychiatrists, social workers, marriage counselors, priests, health visitors, and popular moralists.

Ibid.

. . . all clinicians are involved in the *institution* of private practice—an institution which, like a mental asylum, is structurally modeled upon that of marriage and the family.

PHYLLIS CHESLER, *Women and Madness*, 1972

Publicly, [psychologists] . . . have behaved like any other group [about feminism]: they have engaged in nervous laughter, purposeful misunderstanding, hairsplitting, malicious cruelty, misguided sympathy, boredom, hostility, condescension, and commercial and academic capitalism.
    Ibid.

The medical profession helped to create the popular notion of women as sickly in the first place; now it seems to have turned around and blamed the victim. Women patients are seen as silly, self-indulgent, and superstitious. . . . How many times do we go to a doctor feeling sick and leave, after a diagnosis of "psychosomatic," feeling *crazy?*
    BARBARA EHRENREICH AND DEIRDRE ENGLISH, *Complaints and Disorders*, 1973

. . . you are limited irrevocably in what you can get from the [health care] system because you are a woman. The value placed on your health, the respect given your complaints or requests, the general way in which treatment is prescribed and administered are not the same as for male patients. . . . Women's complaints are even labeled "neurotic" and dismissed.
    BOSTON WOMEN'S HEALTH BOOK COLLECTIVE, *Our Bodies, Ourselves*, 2d ed., 1976

. . . many male doctors, like many other men, have created myths about the female character and personality which blind them to us as a group and as individuals. What is frightening is how much power male doctors hold over many aspects of our lives, and how their *official* ideas about women affect the medical care we get and thus our very survival.
    Ibid.

The loneliness, the sense of abandonment, of being imprisoned, powerless, and depersonalized is the chief collective memory of women who have given birth in American hospitals.
    ADRIENNE RICH, *Of Woman Born*, 1976

Like premenstrual syndrome, menopausal syndrome does not generate a sense of drama—at least not for the physician . . .
    PAULA WEIDEGER, *Menstruation and Menopause*, 1976

In his capacity as physician/shaman, the gynecologist has taken control of both the medical and spiritual guidance of the lives of many women. In his role as witch doctor, the gynecologist uses his medical-school training but

combines it, in a peculiar admixture, with a watered-down version of psychoanalytic theory.
>Ibid.

Dress/Fashion

Taught from infancy that beauty is woman's sceptre, the mind shapes itself to the body, and roaming round its gilt cage, only seeks to adorn its prison.
>MARY WOLLSTONECRAFT, A *Vindication of the Rights of Woman*, 1792

... one of the chief obstacles in the way of woman's elevation to the same platform of human rights, and moral dignity, and intellectual improvement, with her brother, on which God placed her ... is her love of dress.
>SARAH GRIMKÉ, Letter XI, 1837, *Letters on the Equality of the Sexes*, 1838

... why keep up these distinctions in dress? Surely, whatever dress is convenient for one sex must be for the other also. Whatever is necessary for the perfect and full development of man's physical being, must be equally so for woman.
>ELIZABETH CADY STANTON, letter to Gerrit Smith, 1855, *History of Woman Suffrage*, I, 1881

The second fashion was made by God himself, and it would be supposed that if He intended the sexes to be distinguished by their garments explicit directions would have been given as to the style of each.
>AMELIA BLOOMER, review of sermon by the Rev. Dr. Talmage, undated, in D. C. Bloomer, *Life and Writings of Amelia Bloomer*, 1895

Common sense teaches us that the dress which is the most convenient, and best adapted to our needs, is the proper dress for both men and women to wear.
>Ibid.

The most casual observer could see how many pleasures young girls were continually sacrificing to their dress: In walking, running, rowing, skating, dancing, going up and down stairs, climbing trees and fences, the airy fabrics and flowing skirts were a continual impediment and vexation. We can not estimate how large a share of the ill-health and temper among women is the result of the crippling, cribbing influence of her costume.
>ELIZABETH CADY STANTON, "Reminiscences," 1848–1861, *History of Woman Suffrage*, I, 1881

133

... girls have to study under all sorts of disadvantages that boys do not have to contend with. Hang a hoop-skirt on a boy's hips; lace him up in a corset; hang pounds of clothing and trailing skirts upon him; puff him out with humps and bunches behind; pinch his waist into a compass that will allow his lungs only half their breathing capacity; load his head down with superfluous hair ... and stick it full of hair pins; and then set him to translating Greek and competing for prizes in a first-class university. What sort of a chance would he stand in running that race or any other!!

> FRANCES ELLEN BURR, report on National Woman Suffrage Association Meeting, 1874, *History of Woman Suffrage*, II, 1882

... instead of being a useful servant wisely fulfilling the purposes of its existence, our dress has become a terrible tyrant, subjecting the human body to its inconvenient, unsightly, and even tormenting control, and bringing into subjection, also, the noble faculties of the mind.

> MERCY B. JACKSON, M.D., Lecture III, *Dress-Reform*, ed. Abba Goold Woolson, 1874

Our only hope for the redemption of woman from the thralldom of dress lies in the belief that her hitherto limited sphere of activities has been so insufficient for her intellectual occupations that she has been forced to expend her thoughts in decorating her person, instead of in enlarging her mind.

> Ibid.

If it be true that the New Testament and the Parisian fashion-book do necessarily go hand in hand, we might well hesitate before sending more missionaries abroad to the happy heathen, endeavoring to save their souls while making sure of ruining their bodies.

> ABBA GOOLD WOOLSON, Lecture V, *Dress-Reform*, ed. Abba Goold Woolson, 1874

For [women] ... nothing could be right which was not fashionable; and nothing could be fashionable which had not come from Paris. They were strengthened in their hostility [to the Bloomer costume] by that half of humanity whose favor they chiefly sought, and who, as they had never experienced the miseries of the old attire, could never appreciate the comforts of the new.

> Ibid.

It is rather amusing to note the custom of the newspaper reporters to give a detailed description of the dress of each one of the speakers, usually to the exclusion of the subject-matter of her speech.

> SUSAN B. ANTHONY AND IDA HUSTED HARPER, eds., referring to reports on the National Woman Suffrage Association Convention, 1885, *History of Woman Suffrage*, IV, 1902

. . . great are the penalties of those who dare resist the behests of the tyrant Custom.

> ELIZABETH CADY STANTON, *Eighty Years and More*, 1898

There is a very real point, however, in the circumstance that as long as men do not find women attractive unless they are "feminine," unless they possess attributes of "self attention" which are at present considered feminine, the woman who wishes to have a mate as well as a career will have to devote much of her attention to herself—her hair, her skin, her emotions, and so will be handicapped by a double strain.

> ALICE BEAL PARSONS, *Woman's Dilemma*, 1926

Each change woman has ventured has been denounced as treason to her sex. It is only about twenty years ago that the first rash, unwomanly creatures began to put off corsets. To hear the comment their doing so aroused one would have supposed that the corset was a sexual organ with which a woman was born, and that in laying it off she was deliberately unsexing herself.

> Ibid.

By permitting man's legs to remain visible, and incidentally free, and by insisting that woman's shall be concealed, and so restricted, civilization has not only created a marked difference of appearance, but it has seriously impaired woman's health. For a woman confined by skirts loses her agility and speed, necessarily forfeiting to a greater or less extent, determined by the character of the skirt, the free play of her muscles. Her heart and lungs are thereby prevented from developing as fully as man's.

> Ibid.

Even so, the care of the face is typical of traditional women's work, in that it is never done.

> MARY AGNES HAMILTON, "Changes in Social Life," *Our Freedom and Its Results*, ed. Ray Strachey, 1936

You may at times have the sensation you are being written down to. This is because your Beauty Quotient is supposed to be twice your Intelligence Quotient. It is a little hard for some girls to take at first, but it's no worse than smoking opium. The first time or two you get really sick at your stomach, but later the vomiting wears off and the dreams, They Say, are out of this world.
ELIZABETH HAWES, *Anything But Love*, 1948

The function of ornamental attire is very complex; with certain primitives it has a religious significance; but more often its purpose is to accomplish the metamorphosis of woman into idol.
SIMONE DE BEAUVOIR, *The Second Sex*, 1952

The significance of woman's attire is evident: it is decoration, and to be decorated means to be offered.
Ibid.

The purchase of a wedding gown is the creation of a memory and the wedding itself an elevation into the ecstasy and acceptability of wifehood. They sell and sell and sell, and the mothers and daughters buy eagerly, focused as they are on proving how much they are worth on the marriage market.
CELESTINE WARE, *Woman Power: The Movement for Women's Liberation*, 1970

The point at which I started countering strange men who approached me for dates with "yes, for a price" was, in a sense, a natural outgrowth of the grooming in make-up, poise, clothing and conversation that was an integral part of my upbringing. This was the first time that all that training was able to serve a useful purpose for me, rather than just getting me into hot water and hang-ups.
CATHY NOSSA, "Prostitution: Who's Hustling Whom?" *Women: A Journal of Liberation*, III, circa 1972

A woman who is constantly worrying about how her behavior and clothing might appear to a censorious world is a hobbled woman: she might as well stay at home.
EMILY HAHN, *Once Upon a Pedestal*, 1974

When we become teenagers our developing bodies are usually a mystery to us. We discover there is only one norm for beauty—a commercial norm, a Hollywood norm. TV sells us products as we agonize over breasts, hair, legs and skin that will never—ever—measure up. We lose respect for our uniqueness, our own smells and shapes and ways of doing things. We look to others to reassure us that we are, despite all this, okay. We learn to judge ourselves in relation to others and images from the media. The constant comparing leads to a competitiveness that separates us from each other.

BOSTON WOMEN'S HEALTH BOOK COLLECTIVE, *Our Bodies, Ourselves,* 2d ed., 1976

PART II

The Feminist As Rebel and Visionary

We proclaimed a peaceful revolution . . .
PAULINA WRIGHT DAVIS, Twentieth
Anniversary Woman's Rights Convention,
1870, *History of Woman Suffrage*, II, 1882

8 Leaders

Leadership

Those who are bold enough to advance before the age they live in, and to throw off, by the force of their own minds, the prejudices which the maturing reason of the world will in time disavow, must learn to brave censure. We ought not to be too anxious respecting the opinion of others.
MARY WOLLSTONECRAFT, *A Vindication of the Rights of Woman*, 1792

Happy, most happy shall it be for human kind, when all independent individuals, male or female, citizens or foreigners, shall feel the debt of kindness they owe to their fellow beings, and fearlessly step forth to reveal unbought truths and hazard unpopular opinions.
FRANCES WRIGHT, *Course of Popular Lectures*, 1829

I was born and lived almost forty years in South Bristol, Ontario County—one of the most secluded spots in Western New York; but from the earliest dawn of reason, I pined for that freedom of thought and action that was then denied to all womankind. I revolted in spirit against the customs of society and the laws of the State that crushed my aspirations and debarred me from the pursuit of almost every object worthy of an intelligent, rational mind. But not until that meeting at Seneca Falls in 1848, of the pioneers in the cause, gave this feeling of unrest form and voice, did I take action.
EMILY COLLINS, "Reminiscences," circa 1848, *History of Woman Suffrage*, I, 1881

We are said to be a "few disaffected, embittered women, met for the purpose of giving vent to petty personal spleen and domestic discontent." I repel the charge; and I call upon every woman here to repel the charge. If we have personal wrongs, here is not the place for redress. If we have private griefs . . . we do not come here to recount them. The grave will lay its cold honors over the hearts of all here present, before the good we ask for our kind will be realized to the world.

> ELIZABETH OAKES SMITH, Woman's Rights Convention, 1852, *History of Woman Suffrage*, I, 1881

The woman who first departs from the routine in which society allows her to move must suffer. Let us bravely bear ridicule and persecution for the sake of the good that will result, and when the world sees that we can accomplish what we undertake, it will acknowledge our right.

> LUCY STONE, Woman's Rights Convention, 1852, *History of Woman Suffrage*, I, 1881

We hear a great deal about the heroism of the battle-field . . . . Compare it with the heroism of the woman who stands up for the right, and it sinks into utter insignificance. To stand before the cannon's mouth . . . encouraged by . . . [the] leader, stimulated by the sound of the trumpet, and sustained by the still emptier sound of glory, requires no great heroism; . . . but to face the fire of an unjust and prejudiced public opinion . . . to brave not only the enemy abroad but often . . . your own friends at home, requires a heroism that the world has never yet recognized, that the battle-field can not supply, but which woman possesses.

> ERNESTINE L. ROSE, Woman's Rights Convention, 1856, *History of Woman Suffrage*, I, 1881

We shall never get what we ask for until the majority of women are openly with us; and they will never claim their civil rights until they know their social wrongs.

> ELIZABETH CADY STANTON, letter to Lucy Stone, Woman's Rights Convention, 1856, *History of Woman Suffrage*, I, 1881

Cautious, careful people, always casting about to preserve their reputation and social standing, never can bring about a reform. Those who are really in earnest must be willing to be anything or nothing in the world's estimation, and publicly and privately, in season and out, avow their sympathy with despised and persecuted ideas and their advocates, and bear the consequences.

> SUSAN B. ANTHONY, 1860, in Ida Husted Harper, *Life and Work of Susan B. Anthony*, vol. I, 1898

... Lucretia Mott made a few closing remarks, showing that all great achievements in the progress of the race must be slow, and were ever wrought out by the few, in isolation and ridicule—but, said she, let us remember in our trials and discouragements, that if our lives are true, we walk with angels...

E. C. STANTON, S. B. ANTHONY, M. J. GAGE, eds., on Woman's Rights Convention, 1866, *History of Woman Suffrage*, II, 1882

A few of us must suffer sharply for the sake of that great future which God shows us to be possible, when goodness shall join hands with power. But we do not like our pain. We would gladly be sheltered, and comforted, and cheered, and we warn you, by what passes in our own hearts, that women will never express a "general" desire for suffrage until men have ceased to ridicule and despise them for it...

CAROLINE WELLS DALL, letter to *The Nation*, 1866, *History of Woman Suffrage*, II, 1882

Remember, the gay and fashionable throng who whisper in the ears of statesmen, judges, lawyers, merchants, *"We have all the rights we want,"* are but the mummies of civilization, to be brought back to life only by earthquakes and revolutions. Would you know what is in the soul of woman, ask not the wives and daughters of merchant princes; but the creators of wealth—those who earn their bread by honest toil—those who, by a turn in the wheel of fortune, stand face to face with the stern realities of life.

ELIZABETH CADY STANTON, "Address to New York Constitutional Convention," 1867, *History of Woman Suffrage*, II, 1882

... examine ancient and modern history ... and you will find there never has been a time when all men of any country—white or black—have ever asked for a reform. Reforms have to be claimed and obtained by the few, who are in advance, for the benefit of the many who lag behind. And when once obtained and almost forced upon them, the mass of the people accept and enjoy their benefits as a matter of course.

ERNESTINE L. ROSE, letter to Woman Suffrage Convention, 1869, *History of Woman Suffrage*, II, 1882

Though still in the minority, there is hope; for with a radical truth one shall chase a thousand, and two put ten thousand to flight.

PAULINA WRIGHT DAVIS, letter to Elizabeth Cady Stanton, 1869, *History of Woman Suffrage*, II, 1882

I wish it were felt that women who are labouring especially for women are not one-sided or selfish. We are human first; women secondarily. We care for the evils affecting women most of all because they react upon the whole of society, and abstract from the common good.

JOSEPHINE E. BUTLER, ed., Introduction, *Woman's Work and Woman's Culture*, 1869

The promised land of justice and equality is not to be reached by a short cut. I fear we have a large part of the forty years of struggle and zigzagging before us yet. I am pretty sure our Moses has not appeared. I think he will be a woman.

GRACE GREENWOOD, *New York Times*, circa 1873, *History of Woman Suffrage*, II, 1882

There is something very significant to the student of progress, in the history of the forerunners of revolutions. Their eager confidence in their own immediate success, their pathetic bewilderment at the mystery of their apparent failures, are rich with suggestion to any one who means work for an unpopular cause. No reform marches evenly to its consummation.

ELIZABETH STUART PHELPS, letter to Lucy Stone, 1873, *History of Woman Suffrage*, II, 1882

Our cause is half won when we find that people are willing to hear it . . .

LUCY STONE, American Woman Suffrage Association Convention, 1873, *History of Woman Suffrage*, II, 1882

Fortunately for all reforms, the leaders, not seeing the obstacles which block the way, start with the hope of a speedy success. Our demands at the first seemed so rational that I thought the mere statement of woman's wrongs would bring immediate redress. I thought an appeal to the reason and conscience of men against the unjust and unequal laws for women that disgraced our statute books, must settle the question. But I soon found, while no attempt was made to answer our arguments, that an opposition, bitter, malignant, and persevering, rooted in custom and privilege, grew stronger with every new demand made, with every new privilege granted.

ELIZABETH CADY STANTON, letter to Lucretia Mott, 1876, *History of Woman Suffrage*, III, 1887

The leaders in this movement have been women of superior mental and physical organization, of good social standing and education, remarkable alike for their domestic virtues, knowledge of public affairs, and rare executive ability; good speakers and writers, inspiring and conducting the genuine reforms of the day; everywhere exerting themselves to promote the best interests of society; yet they have been uniformly ridiculed, misrepresented, and denounced in public and private by all classes of society.

> E. C. STANTON, S. B. ANTHONY, M. J. GAGE, eds., *History of Woman Suffrage, I,* 1881

The people who demand authority for every thought and action, who look to others for wisdom and protection, are those who perpetuate tyranny. The thinkers and actors who find their authority within, are those who inaugurate freedom.

> Ibid.

The ignorance and indifference of the majority of women, as to their status as citizens of a republic, is not remarkable, for history shows that the masses of all oppressed classes, in the most degraded conditions, have been stolid and apathetic until partial success had crowned the faith and enthusiasm of the few.

> Ibid.

No man or woman has ever sought to lead his fellows to a higher and better mode of life without learning the power of the world's ingratitude; and though at times popularity may follow in the wake of a reformer, yet the reformer knows popularity is not love.

> ANNA HOWARD SHAW, sermon, International Council of Women, 1888, *History of Woman Suffrage, IV,* 1902

The greatest test of the reformer's courage comes when, with a warm, earnest longing for humanity, she breaks for it the bread of truth and the world turns from this life-giving power and asks instead of bread a stone.

> Ibid.

The moment we begin to fear the opinions of others and hesitate to tell the truth that is in us, and from motives of policy are silent when we should speak, the divine floods of light and life flow no longer into our souls. Every truth we see is ours to give the world, not to keep for ourselves alone, for in so doing we cheat humanity out of their rights and check our own development.

> ELIZABETH CADY STANTON, National American Woman Suffrage Association Convention, 1890, *History of Woman Suffrage, IV,* 1902

Reformers who are always compromising, have not yet grasped the idea that truth is the only safe ground to stand upon. The object of an individual life is not to carry one fragmentary measure in human progress, but to utter the highest truth clearly seen in all directions, and thus to round out and perfect a well-balanced character.

ELIZABETH CADY STANTON, ed., *The Woman's Bible*, 1895

It is so much easier to speak when brickbats are flying.

SUSAN B. ANTHONY, National American Woman Suffrage Association Convention, 1897, *History of Woman Suffrage*, IV, 1902

That only a few, under any circumstances, protest against the injustice of long-established laws and customs, does not disprove the fact of the oppressions, while the satisfaction of the many, if real, only proves their apathy and deeper degradation.

ELIZABETH CADY STANTON, *Eighty Years and More*, 1898

. . . if we who do see the absurdities of the old superstitions never unveil them to others, how is the world to make any progress in the theologies? I am in the sunset of life, and I feel it to be my special mission to tell people what they are not prepared to hear, instead of echoing worn-out opinions.

Ibid.

The seers and leaders of all times have been dreamers. Every step of progress the world has made is the crystallization of a dream into reality. To look forward to a time when men shall be just, when "fair play and a square deal for all" will include women, when our republic shall in truth become what its dreamers have hoped it would be, a government "of the people, by the people and for the people,"—this *is* a dream but it is a dream which we are helping to make real, and the result will come not alone because a vision has been revealed but by following it steadfastly to its fruition.

ANNA HOWARD SHAW, National American Woman Suffrage Association Convention, 1905, *History of Woman Suffrage*, V, 1922

Of all the people who block the progress of woman suffrage the worst are the women of wealth and leisure who never knew a day's work and never felt a day's want, but who selfishly stand in the way of those women who know what it means to earn the bread they eat by the sternest toil and who, with a voice in the Government, could better themselves in every way.

HARRIOT STANTON BLATCH, convention of Self-Supporting Women's Suffrage League, 1908, *History of Woman Suffrage*, V, 1922

For her . . . who sees beyond the present, though in a future which she knows she will never enter, an enlarged and strengthened womanhood . . . it is not so hard to renounce and labour with unshaken purpose: but for those who have not that view, and struggle on, animated at most by a vague consciousness that somewhere ahead lies a large end, towards which their efforts tend; . . . who carve away all their lives to produce a corbel of some reform in sexual relations, in the end to find it break under the chisel; who out of many failures attain, perhaps, to no success, or but to one . . . ; for such as these, it is perhaps not so easy to labour without growing weary.

OLIVE SCHREINER, *Woman and Labour*, 1911

It is the swimmer who first leaps into the frozen stream who is cut sharpest by the ice; those who follow him find it broken, and the last find it gone. It is the man or woman who first treads down the path which the bulk of humanity will ultimately follow, who must find themselves at last in solitudes where the silence is deadly.

Ibid.

I had set out in the militant struggle sure of the great work we should do for the ultimate emancipation of women, but doubtful to the last degree of any early acknowledgment or success. I looked forward to a pilgrimage of protest in which we should prepare the way for the women who came after us and should see but little of the harvest ourselves. I felt that our work would not be understood or valued until, like other rebel pioneers, we had been dead a few hundred years. The parliamentary vote would, of course, be granted much earlier because of our efforts, but it would appear to the world to be granted in spite of us rather than by means of us. We must be prepared to be execrated, misrepresented, condemned, to the end.

TERESA BILLINGTON-GREIG, *The Militant Suffrage Movement*, 1911

Let us go out and make them [men and women] want things; let us show them the reasonableness and the justice of the things they already want but of which they have not dared to speak; and let us go seeking for the right outlet along the many ways that are blind now both to us and to them. We may never reach the big movement for which we seek, but we shall be going towards it; we shall not be buying one liberty at the price of others; we shall not be losing hold of ourselves under the sway of dangerous emotion; we shall not be playing political tricks.

Ibid.

It is always found by those who take part in political warfare that the roughest and least civilised members of society are invariably opposed to the pioneer and the reformer and usually support the Government in power, to whatever party it may belong, just as they try to "back the winner" in a race.

E. SYLVIA PANKHURST, *The Suffragette*, 1911

The change in the position of women which this country has witnessed, appears to those who take note of it little less than miraculous. This change has been brought about in great part by women themselves ... who have valorously striven to win for themselves and their fellows the outlook of a larger liberty, and the inspiration of a loftier interpretation of womanly duty.

JULIA WARD HOWE, "The Change in the Position of Women," *Julia Ward Howe and the Woman Suffrage Movement*, ed. Florence Howe Hall, 1913

[Emmeline Pankhurst] voiced in a language new to the timid and the ladylike, all the revolt that was gnawing at the hearts of women. To many women it must have seemed that their deepest unuttered thoughts and the unuttered thoughts of generations of women had found expression, and anyone who has had this experience knows what intense devotion is felt towards the person who has the courage and the genius to utter the words.

H. M. SWANWICK, *The Future of the Women's Movement*, 1913

Any movement with fear lurking in the background, fear of the press, of public opinion, of our neighbors, or of the enemy, can not have that spirit which fearlessness of opposition brings. It is not for rights women should ask, all rights are here—rather is it for you to inculcate into her the desire to get these rights.

MARGARET SANGER, "The New Feminists," *The Woman Rebel*, I, March 1914

... I returned to America, determined, since the exclusively masculine point of view had dominated too long, that the other half of the truth should be made known.

MARGARET SANGER, *The Pivot of Civilization*, 1922

To tell these women that they are as good as their men, to tell them to free themselves from their oppression and to take charge of their own destinies, to tell them they are being weak and parasitic, existing in a degraded state, is to make them feel inexplicably slapped in the face ...

DANA DENSMORE, "The Slave's Stake in the Home," *No More Fun and Games*, 2, February 1969

... those of us who have enough to eat have the option and the responsibility to discover new ways of doing things. We can't wait until every one is fed to start talking about equality for women or any other group.

> CHARLOTTE HOLT CLINEBELL, *Meet Me in the Middle*, 1973

Movement History

We have all been thrown down so low that nobody thought we'd ever get up again; but we have been long enough trodden now; we will come up again ...

> SOJOURNER TRUTH, Woman's Rights Convention, 1853, *History of Woman Suffrage*, I, 1881

Dear Mrs. Stanton: Well, I have been and gone and done it! positively voted the Republican ticket—straight—this a.m. at seven o'clock, and *swore my vote in, at that* ...

> SUSAN B. ANTHONY, letter, 1872, *History of Woman Suffrage*, II, 1882

Let it be remembered by our daughters in future generations that Lucretia Mott, in the eighty-fourth year of her age, asked permission, as the representative woman of this great movement for the enfranchisement of her sex, to present at the centennial celebration of our national liberties, Woman's Declaration of Rights, and was refused.

> ELIZABETH CADY STANTON, letter to Lucretia Mott, 1876, History of Woman Suffrage, III, 1887

[The women's leaders'] work was not for themselves alone, nor for the present generation, but for all women of all time. The hopes of posterity were in their hands and they determined to place on record for the daughters of 1976, the fact that their mothers of 1876 had asserted their equality of rights, and impeached the government of that day for its injustice toward woman. Thus, in taking a grander step toward freedom than ever before, they would leave one bright remembrance for the women of the next centennial.

> E. C. STANTON, S. B. ANTHONY, M. J. GAGE, eds., recounting the silent presentation of the Declaration of Rights for Women at the official July 4, 1876, centennial celebration in Philadelphia, *History of Woman Suffrage*, III, 1887.

... we have aroused public thought to the many disabilities of our sex, and our countrywomen to higher self-respect and worthier ambition, and in this struggle for justice we have deepened and broadened our own lives and extended the horizon of our vision . . . we have learned to place a just estimate on popular opinion, and to feel a just confidence in ourselves.

> ELIZABETH CADY STANTON, address, 1878, *History of Woman Suffrage*, III, 1887

Those who have not been through the conflict will never realize how dark the prospect was in starting. Denied education, and a place in the world of work, denied the rights of property, whether of her own earnings, or her inheritance, with the press and the pulpit, custom, and public opinion sustaining the law, was there ever a struggle entered upon, which at its beginning seemed more hopeless than this for woman?

> E. C. STANTON, S. B. ANTHONY, M. J. GAGE, eds., *History of Woman Suffrage*, I, 1881

. . . her work for woman . . . has kept her young and fresh and happy all these years.

> SUSAN B. ANTHONY, writing of Elizabeth Cady Stanton, 1881, in Ida Husted Harper, *Life and Work of Susan B. Anthony*, vol II, 1898

The humiliation of our children has been the bitterest drop in the cup of reformers.

> ELIZABETH CADY STANTON, "Lucretia Mott," *History of Woman Suffrage*, I, 1881

. . . the advocates of suffrage who labored there in that first woman's suffrage campaign . . . have forgotten, in part, the bitterness of disappointment and defeat; we think no more of the long and wearisome journeys under the hot sun of southern Kansas; the anxiety and uncertainty; the nervous tremor when night has overtaken us wandering on the prairie, not knowing what terrible pitfalls might lie before; the mobs which sometimes made the little log schoolhouse shake with their missiles; the taunts and jeers of the opposition; all this is passed, but the great principle of human rights which we advocated remains, commending itself more and more to the favor of all good men . . .

> OLYMPIA BROWN, letter to Susan B. Anthony, 1882, *History of Woman Suffrage*, II, 1882

We . . . feel a peculiar tenderness for the young women on whose shoulders we are about to leave our burdens. Although we have opened a pathway to the promised land and cleared up much of the underbrush of false sentiment, logic and rhetoric intertwisted with law and custom, which blocked all avenues in starting, yet there are still many obstacles to be encountered before the rough journey is ended. The younger women are starting with great advantages over us. They have the results of our experience; they have superior opportunities for education; they will find a more enlightened public sentiment for discussion; they will have more courage to take the rights which belong to them. Hence we may look to them for speedy conquests. When we think of the vantage-ground woman holds today, in spite of all the artificial obstacles placed in her way, we are filled with wonder as to what the future mothers of the race will be when free to have complete development.

Thus far women have been the mere echoes of men. Our laws and constitutions, our creeds and codes, and the customs of social life are all of masculine origin. The true woman is as yet a dream of the future.

> ELIZABETH CADY STANTON, International Council of Women, 1888, *History of Woman Suffrage*, IV, 1902

... to be a woman of the Negro race in America ... is to have a heritage ... unique in the ages. In the first place, the race is young and full of the elasticity and hopefulness of youth. All its achievements are before it. It does not look on the masterly triumphs of nineteenth century civilization with that *blasé* world-weary look which characterizes the old washed out and worn out races which have already ... seen their best days.

> [ANNA JULIA COOPER] A Black Woman of the South, *A Voice from the South*, 1892

It seems remarkable to those standing, as I do, one of a generation almost ended, that so many of these young people know nothing of the past; they are apt to think they have sprung up like somebody's gourd, and that nothing ever was done until they came. So I am always gratified to hear these reminiscences, that they may know how others have sown what they are reaping today.

> SUSAN B. ANTHONY, National American Woman Suffrage Association Convention, 1893, *History of Woman Suffrage*, IV, 1902

There never yet was a young woman who did not feel that if she had had the management of the work from the beginning the cause would have carried long ago. I felt just so when I was young.

> SUSAN B. ANTHONY, National American Woman Suffrage Association Convention, 1895, *History of Woman Suffrage*, IV, 1902

Every energy of her [Susan B. Anthony's] soul is centered upon the needs of this world. To her, work is worship. She has not stood aside, shivering in the cold shadows of uncertainty, but has moved on with the whirling world, has done the good given her to do, and thus, in the darkest hours, has been sustained by an unfaltering faith in the final perfection of all things.

ELIZABETH CADY STANTON, *Eighty Years and More*, 1898

If I had had the slightest premonition of all that was to follow that convention [Seneca Falls, 1848] I fear I should not have had the courage to risk it . . .

Ibid.

When [Susan B. Anthony] rose to call the meeting to order she was deluged with many beautiful floral tributes and drolly peering over the heap of flowers she said: "Well, this is rather different from the receptions I used to get fifty years ago. They threw things at me then—but they were not roses . . ."

IDA HUSTED HARPER, describing Anthony's reception at 1905 convention of National American Woman Suffrage Association, *History of Woman Suffrage*, V, 1922.

"There have been others also just as true and devoted to the cause . . . but with such women consecrating their lives"—here she paused for an instant and seemed to be gazing into the future, then dropping her arms to her sides she finished her sentence—"failure is impossible!" These were the last words Miss Anthony ever spoke in public and from that moment they became the watchword of those who accepted as their trust the work she laid down.

IDA HUSTED HARPER, recounting Susan B. Anthony's birthday party in 1906, immediately following the National American Woman Suffrage Association Convention, *Life and Work of Susan B. Anthony*, vol. III, 1908

To speak of the [woman's] movement as a transitory wave already on the decline seems due to an extraordinary inability to grasp the goal towards which the human race is inevitably creeping.

LADY GROVE, *The Human Woman*, 1908

It is a commonplace that many people who rise to the heights in adversity and live lives of simple usefulness and dignity under ordinary conditions cannot stand the strain of success. It is the same with movements.

TERESA BILLINGTON-GREIG, *The Militant Suffrage Movement*, 1911

. . . the movement became conventionalised and narrowed and hypocritical. We were accepted for what we were not, and immediately began to live up— or down—to the standard expected of us. There came to be one speech for the council chamber and another for the platform; the propaganda of the society suffered a sudden loss of breadth; the industrial evils which had formed the basis of much of our appeal were gradually pushed aside for the consideration

of technical, legal, and political grievances; the advocacy of reformed sex-relations was reduced to the vaguest generalities, and even these were discouraged; the working-class women were dropped without hesitation and the propaganda of the organisation confined to the middle and upper classes; the "advanced" women, an eminently undesirable class in a socially superior society, were even more speedily driven out or silenced.
Ibid.

Those women who claim equal rights and are eager to accept the full burdens which sex equality must bring are the promise of the whole movement. But they are submitting to a policy of avoidance of fundamentals, a policy of suppression, which must be an ill-preparation for the future. I do not speak lightly in this matter. I have had the evasion and hypocrisy forced upon myself. I have quibbled with questioners. I have spoken on the edge of self-committal and held myself back. I have found myself under the influence of the audience I addressed whittling down what I should have said into what I knew was as much as I dared to say. Such evasion has become a habitual use in the movement. The forces that would make for the best kind of legislation, which would prepare the future elector to destroy and to construct with knowledge and insights, are dammed up at their source; they are sacrificed for a mere temporary advantage.
Ibid.

So far as I have been able to study history, I have never found that there was a strong, virtuous nation in which the women of that nation were not something more than mere appendages to men in domestic life. They were also strong for public duty, unwavering in principle, and courageous (in crises of danger) for the national defence.
JOSEPHINE E. BUTLER, *Personal Reminiscences of a Great Crusade*, 1911

It is this . . . consciousness on the part of the women taking their share in the Woman's Movement . . . that their efforts are not . . . of immediate advantage to themselves, but that they . . . lead to loss and renunciation, which gives to this movement its very peculiar tone; setting it apart from the large mass of economic movements, placing it rather in a line with those vast religious developments which at the interval of ages have swept across humanity, irresistibly modifying and reorganising it.
OLIVE SCHREINER, *Woman and Labour*, 1911

Our woman's movement resembles strongly . . . the gigantic religious and intellectual movement which for centuries convulsed the life of Europe; and had, as its ultimate outcome, the final emancipation of the human intellect

153

and the freedom of the human spirit. Looked back upon from the vantage-point of the present, this past presents the appearance of one vast, steady, persistent movement proceeding always in one ultimate direction, as though guided by some controlling human intellect.
Ibid.

That the Woman's Movement of our day has not taken its origin from any mere process of theoretic argument; that it breaks out . . . in forms divergent and at times superficially almost irreconcilable; that the majority of those taking part in it are driven into action as the result of the immediate pressure of the conditions of life, and are not always able logically to state the nature of all causes which propel them, or to paint clearly all results of their action; so far from removing it from the category of the vast reorganising movements of humanity, places it in a line with them, showing how vital, spontaneous, and wholly organic and unartificial is its nature.
Ibid.

[The militant suffrage movement's] greatest achievement . . . is that it woke people up and opened their purses, in a way totally unprecedented. It made those who had never cared realise that some women cared intensely, and made them ask why. It made those who had been working for long years realise that there were many yet untried methods, and that some of them were good. Above all, it made many women feel that, if they desired the enfranchisement of women, and if they did not like the methods of the W.S.P.U. [Women's Social and Political Union], the only respectable thing to do was to work as hard, and give as much for what they thought right, as these other women did.
H. M. SWANWICK, *The Future of the Women's Movement*, 1913

Looking back now, we can see that whatever thinkers and statesmen fifty years ago may have argued for as best meeting the immediate needs of the hour, the organized suffrage movement in all the most advanced countries should long ago have broadened their platform, and explicitly set before their own members and the public as their objective not merely "the vote," but "the political, legal and social equality of women."
ALICE HENRY, *The Trade Union Woman*, 1917

This was the most unequal contest that ever was waged, for one side had to fight without weapons. It was held against women that they were not educated, but the doors of all institutions of learning were closed against them; that they were not taxpayers, although money-earning occupations were barred to them and if married they were not allowed to own property. They were kept in subjection by authority of the Scriptures and were not permitted to expound them from a woman's point of view, and they were prevented from pleading their cause on the public platform. When they had largely overcome these handicaps they found themselves facing a political fight without political power.

IDA HUSTED HARPER, Introduction, *History of Woman Suffrage*, V, 1922

It is doubtful if any man, even among suffrage men, ever realized what the suffrage struggle came to mean to women before the end was allowed in America. How much of time and patience, how much work, energy and aspiration, how much faith, how much hope, how much despair went into it. It leaves its mark on one, such a struggle.

CARRIE CHAPMAN CATT AND NETTIE ROGERS SHULER, *Woman Suffrage and Politics*, 1923

It is a strange thing, and to some people an unaccountable one, that of those women who played a prominent part in winning the Vote not one of them sits in Parliament, and most of them are out of the political world altogether. Why is this? I think on a final analysis it will be found that most of them gave all they had to give in winning the Vote. The others, who kept themselves free from the political turmoil, were more ready to enter into the new realm of politics. Both Suffragist and Suffragette leaders had spent their vital force working for Women's independence, but once that freedom was theirs it was necessary for them to withdraw to recuperate and revitalize themselves for the next piece of work in hand.

ANNIE KENNEY, *Memories of a Militant*, 1924

The unswerving zeal of the hundreds of thousands of women who laboured in their solitary fields alone and unsupported was one of the hidden causes of the success of the Movement. All women owe a debt of gratitude to those women who worked in silence, suffered in silence, unknown to any save the odd speakers who visited their tiny hamlets or villages. . . . They were met with ridicule and scorn, and yet they continued their work as though the whole village had erected a tablet in their honour.

Ibid.

Movements are built up by silent followers, and few realize the sacrifices they make, the secret suffering they endure, in their effort to be true to a great principle which has stirred their hearts. For the first few years the Militant Movement was more like a religious revival than a political movement. It stirred the emotions, it aroused passions, it awakened the human chord which responds to the battle-call of Freedom. It was a genuine reform for emancipation, led by earnest, unselfish, self-sacrificing women. A cause that works for emancipation must always draw to itself those who feel the need of freedom, and those who consciously feel their position rouse in others the same desire for liberty. The call was universal. All women were appealed to. Class barriers were broken down; political distinctions swept away; religious differences forgotten. All women were as one.

     Ibid.

... the very same ladies who stated with so much emphasis that women were totally unfit to take part in political life were always ready to take part in it themselves; they wrote and spoke on political platforms, canvassed electors, published election literature, and even started classes intended to train young women in the art of speaking, so that they should be able to proclaim on public platforms that "women's place is home."

     MILLICENT GARRETT FAWCETT, *What I Remember,* 1925

It is because of [a] ... myopic view of the nature of freedom that all revolutions have accomplished nothing more than a shifting of power from one class to another.... If the woman's movement should resolve itself into a similar scramble, it would be unfortunate but not surprising, for women may hardly be expected to rise at once above the retaliatory spirit which is one of the common curses of humanity.

     SUZANNE LA FOLLETTE, *Concerning Women,* 1926

It is a misfortune of the woman's movement that it has succeeded in securing political rights for women at the very period when political rights are worth less than they have been at any time since the eighteenth century.... No system of government can hope long to survive the cynical disregard of both law and principle which government in America regularly exhibits. Under these circumstances, no legal guarantee of rights is worth the paper it is written on, and the women who rely upon such guarantees to protect them against prejudice and discrimination are leaning on a broken reed.

     Ibid.

Instead of being "conscious" of status, in reality, however, neither the pioneers nor the succeeding generations of feminists who derived their inspiration from 1848 were sufficiently conscious of status to take account of the economic forces which condition it. In other words, the founders of the latest historical woman movement—of the democratic movement—saw only men in their crystal-gazing and overlooked the natural resources of the nation. That is, in their quest for privilege, they failed to reckon with probabilities, such as, for example that the ruthless exploitation of American natural resources and the concentration of wealth in the hands of a few privileged persons would be the true arbiters of their destiny.

MARY RITTER BEARD, *A Changing Political Economy as It Affects Women,*
1934

Here in the United States the drive to defeat women is no longer a menace; it is a condition in fact. . . . These flaws [reasons for women's defeat] have been the cleavage in the women's organizations, their acute inaction as a whole, their indifference to the needs of the great body of wage-earning women, a dearth of inspiring and inspired leaders, too great a variety of self-interests . . .

GENEVIEVE PARKHURST, "Is Feminism Dead?" *Harper's Magazine,* 170,
May, 1935

. . . these gallant fighters of the past must . . . admit that in the old days almost the hardest aspect of their fight was the intrinsic absurdity of the position they were then attacking. They had constantly to concentrate on passionately proclaiming the obvious. Women were human beings.

MARY AGNES HAMILTON, "Changes in Social Life," *Our Freedom and Its Results,* ed. Ray Strachey, 1936

That the acceptance of women as people should, as it does, constitute a revolution, is certainly the most amazing paradox of our day, and it is well that we should look at it, before its features blur and become incredible. Successful revolutions have a trick of blurring their own outlines; in proportion as they are successful, their early stages vanish in the mists of the past. With revolutions in opinion, accomplished as they are by slow stages and largely underground, this is specially the case. People forget that they ever held opinions once universal, when those opinions are universal no longer.

Ibid.

It [suffrage] was the great barrier which had got to be surmounted. Until it was surmounted, women spoke as though, from its summit, they would survey the kingdoms of heaven and earth and enter into possession of a goodly heritage. They have found that on the other side of that barrier dwell the dragons, and that freedom means, in the main, freedom to participate in the fight with them [men], on common terms.

Ibid.

Not all women were suffragists, but the majority were affected by the propaganda and became more independent, more able to stand up for themselves, more self-respecting and respected.

> ALISON NEILANS, "Changes in Sex Morality," *Our Freedom and Its Results,* ed. Ray Strachey, 1936

... the struggle for the right to become politicians in itself made women into politicians.

> ELEANOR F. RATHBONE, M.P., "Changes in Public Life," *Our Freedom and Its Results,* ed. Ray Strachey, 1936

After suffrage was won, many women who had been engrossed in the suffrage campaign turned their attention to improving women's working conditions. ... They failed to see that in working for protective legislation for adult women and not also for men, they were shutting the door tight against the economic independence of women.

> HARRIOT STANTON BLATCH AND ALMA LUTZ, *Challenging Years,* 1940

It was one of the major hardships of the suffrage fight that it compelled women to think and act in sex terms. That phase is over, and well over. It is good that the young ones breathe naturally in an air in which women and men are working comrades.

> MARY AGNES HAMILTON, *Women at Work,* 1941

True reform [after 1920] experienced a general lassitude of morale. The excitement of the last-ditch fight being over, the great masses of women who had united in the common struggle for an immediate goal, split off into segments. One cause of their disintegration was that these women who had come from all walks of life were still not sufficiently fused by a common theory, a common class or a long-run objective. Yes, they could cooperate on an immediate political battle; but no, they were not ready to cooperate to push forth the basic economic demands of a full-fledged woman movement.

> SUSAN B. ANTHONY II, *Out of the Kitchen—Into the War,* 1943

Reactionaries insist that suffrage and the entry of women into industry have actually achieved nothing, that modern women are miserably unhappy, frustrated and hysterical, and go insane at a faster rate than ever before. ... The solution, if we are to believe them, seems to be to hurry back to what's left of the home, which is something like going all out for the horse as a means of modern transportation.

> JOYCE [COWLEY] MAUPIN, "Pioneers of Women's Liberation," *The International Socialist Review*, 1955, in *Voices of the New Feminism*, ed. Mary Lou Thompson, 1970

Few people today are aware that the early feminism was a true grass-roots movement: They haven't heard of the torturous journeys made by feminist pioneers into backwoods and frontiers, or door to door in the towns to speak about the issues or to collect signatures for petitions that were laughed right out of the Assemblies.

> SHULAMITH FIRESTONE, *The Dialectic of Sex*, 1970

. . . the United States cannot afford to repeat the costly errors of the nineteenth century in the shrunken world of twentieth century crises. One of these errors was the failure to grant universal suffrage at the end of the Civil War, a failure the political consequences of which are still being suffered today.

> PAULI MURRAY, to Rep. Edith Green's Special Subcommittee on Education, 1970, *Discrimination Against Women*, U.S. Government Printing Office, 1971

. . . none were quite so surprised as the suffragists when women proceeded to take their newfound political equality in stride rather than use it to revolutionize their lives.

> JO FREEMAN, *The Politics of Women's Liberation*, 1975

The average life of most movement activists is about two years, after which they retire in exhaustion to be replaced by new converts who try to make up in enthusiasm what they lack in experience.

> Ibid.

. . . the evolution of the totally free woman in our society will be possible only when we repossess the true dignity of our history and re-integrate it into our lives. Only then will we be able to move beyond this particular struggle, instead of being condemned to repeat it with each succeeding generation. The knowledge that my grandmother's contemporaries were not just good wives, mothers, housekeepers, and cooks but rather a generation of potentially revolutionary freedom fighters gives a new dimension to their lives and a new strength to mine.

> MIDGE MACKENZIE, *Shoulder to Shoulder*, 1975

The Militants

If particular care and attention is not paid to the ladies, we are determined to [foment] a rebellion, and will not hold ourselves bound by any laws in which we have no voice or representation.

> ABIGAIL ADAMS, to John Adams, 1776, *Familiar Letters of John Adams and His Wife, Abigail Adams During the Revolution,* ed. Charles Francis Adams, 1876

Women's crusades against saloons, brothels and gambling-dens, emptying kegs and bottles into the streets, breaking doors and windows and burning houses, all go to prove that disfranchisement, the denial of lawful means to gain desired ends, may drive even women to violations of law and order.

> SUSAN B. ANTHONY, "Woman Wants Bread, Not the Ballot," campaign speech, 1870–1880, in Ida Husted Harper, *Life and Work of Susan B. Anthony,* vol. II, 1898

. . . I will never pay a dollar of your unjust penalty. . . . And I shall earnestly and persistently continue to urge all women to the practical recognition of the old Revolutionary maxim, "Resistance to tyranny is obedience to God."

> SUSAN B. ANTHONY, addressing Judge Hunt at her trial for voting, 1873, in Ida Husted Harper, *Life and Work of Susan B. Anthony,* vol. I, 1898

If all the heroic deeds of women recorded in history and our daily journals, and the active virtues so forcibly illustrated in domestic life, have not yet convinced our opponents that women are possessed of superior fighting qualities, the sex may feel called upon in the near future to give some further illustrations of their prowess. Of one thing they may be assured, that the next generation will not argue the question of woman's rights with the infinite patience we have had for half a century, and to so little purpose.

> ELIZABETH CADY STANTON, letter to National Woman Suffrage Association Convention, 1887, *History of Woman Suffrage,* IV, 1902

. . . like every other step in progress, it [the woman question] will eventually be settled by violence. The wild enthusiasm of women can be used for evil as well as good.

> ELIZABETH CADY STANTON, to Senate Committee on Woman Suffrage, 1888, *History of Woman Suffrage,* IV, 1902

What . . . shall we do to hasten the work? I answer, the pioneers have brought you through the wilderness in sight of the promised land; now, with active, aggressive warfare, take possession. Instead of rehearsing the old arguments which have done duty fifty years, make a brave attack on every obstacle which stands in your way . . .

> ELIZABETH CADY STANTON, letter to National American Woman Suffrage Association Convention, 1898, *History of Woman Suffrage*, IV, 1902

They [the women] were awake at last. They were prepared to do something that women had never done before—fight for themselves. Women had always fought for men, and for their children. Now they were ready to fight for their own human rights.

> EMMELINE PANKHURST, after march on House of Commons, 1906, *My Own Story*, 1914

At the door the Governor spoke to me, and asked me if I had any complaints to make. "Not of you," I replied, "nor of any of the wardresses. Only of this prison, and all of men's prisons. We shall raze them to the ground."

> EMMELINE PANKHURST, upon release from Holloway Gaol after serving her first sentence, *My Own Story*, 1914

How can modern educated women agitate? The thing is unthinkable. But oppose them with a touch of uncivilised barbarity; to even a small extent make martyrs of them;—and the thing is made easy for them at once.

> CONSTANCE LYTTON, letter, 1909, *Letters of Constance Lytton*, ed. Betty Balfour, 1925

. . . we are like an army . . . we are deputed to fight for a cause, and for other people, and in any struggle or any fight weapons must be used. The weapons for which we ask are simple,—a fair hearing; but that is refused us. . . . Then we must have other weapons. What do other people choose when they are driven to the last extremity? What do men choose? They have recourse to violence.

> CONSTANCE LYTTON, speech, 1910, *Letters of Constance Lytton*, ed. Betty Balfour, 1925

To the mob mind woman, being woman, is ever required to seek even her soul's salvation decorously, and it was a thing of shame that she should cast off her immemorial chains of correct behaviour for any right on the face of the earth or any star out of the heavens.

> TERESA BILLINGTON-GREIG, *The Militant Suffrage Movement*, 1911

... only a minority of rebels are capable of distinguishing between their desire for retaliation and their desire for reform.
> Ibid.

We were accepted into respectable circles not as rebels but as innocent victims, and as innocent victims we were led to pose. If we had frankly and strongly stated that we had set out to make the Government imprison us, that we had deliberately chosen just those lines of protest and disorder that would irritate those in authority into foolish retaliation, if we had told the truth, the very proper persons who became our champions would have spent many weary months and years in condemning us before they had finally realised the value and intention of our efforts.
> Ibid.

Revolution should never be ashamed of itself.
> Ibid.

If militancy is impolitic,—harmful to our Cause,—one would see on looking back, that at any rate our militant union would be smaller, poorer, less powerful than the non-militant organisations;—that politicians would enquire anxiously whether the non-militant societies were satisfied with their promises, and ignore the attitude of the militants. You know there are no such proofs,—only proofs to the contrary.
> CONSTANCE LYTTON, letter, circa 1911, *Letters of Constance Lytton*, ed. Betty Balfour, 1925

Votes for Women in those days was regarded by the majority of sober, level-headed men as a ladies' fad which would never come to anything and the idea that it could ever be a question upon which governments would stand or fall, or be associated with persecution, rioting and imprisonment had been alike unthinkable to them.
> E. SYLVIA PANKHURST, *The Suffragette*, 1911

Suffering born for a cause begets sympathy with that cause and coercion arouses sympathy with the coerced.
> Ibid.

... we have made more progress with less hurt to ourselves by breaking glass than ever we made when we allowed them to break our bodies.
> EMMELINE PANKHURST, Women's Social and Political Union, 1912, *My Own Story*, 1914

. . . every bit of work that is done to get the vote ought to be done in such a way as to make the use of the vote run smoothly, when at last it is attained. Militant methods, whether of martyrdom or war, are useless for that.

H. M. SWANWICK, *The Future of the Women's Movement*, 1913

Our highest regard is given to those who made the history of the past glorious and became law-breakers for the freedom of the people. That the women who are rebels and law-breakers to-day are carrying on the same fight and suffering for the same human liberty is not recognized.

TERESA BILLINGTON-GREIG, *The Woman Rebel*, I, May 1914

We never went to prison in order to be martyrs. We went there in order that we might obtain the rights of citizenship. We were willing to break laws that we might force men to give us the right to make laws. That is the way men have earned their citizenship.

EMMELINE PANKHURST, *My Own Story*, 1914

. . . every advance of men's political freedom has been marked with violence and the destruction of property. Usually the advance has been marked by war, which is called glorious. Sometimes it has been marked by riotings, which are deemed less glorious but are at least effective.

Ibid.

There is something that governments care far more for than human life, and that is the security of property, and so it is through property that we shall strike the enemy. From henceforward the women who agree with me will say, "We disregard your laws, gentlemen, we set the liberty and the dignity and the welfare of women above all such considerations, and we shall continue this war, as we have done in the past; and what sacrifice of property, or what injury to property accrues will not be our fault."

Ibid.

Why is it that men's blood shedding militancy is applauded and women's symbolic militancy punished with a prison cell and the forcible feeding horror? It means simply this, that men's double standard of sex morals, whereby the victims of their lust are counted as outcasts, while the men themselves escape all social censure, really applies to morals in all departments of life. Men make the moral code and they expect women to accept it. They have decided that it is entirely right and proper for men to fight for their liberties and their rights, but that it is not right and proper for women to fight for theirs.

Ibid.

I break the law from no selfish motive. I have no personal end to serve, neither have any of the other women who have gone through this court during the past few weeks. . . . They seriously believe that the welfare of humanity demands this sacrifice; they believe that the horrible evils which are ravaging our civilisation will never be removed until women get the vote.
        Ibid.

. . . if it is justifiable to fight for common ordinary equal justice, then women have ample justification, nay, have greater justification, for revolution and rebellion, than ever men have had in the whole history of the human race.
        Ibid.

Only one class has the right to condemn the use of violence by women, the Society of Friends, who have always condemned it equally in men and women. The Quakers have never canted about brute force being noble and patriotic when used by men and abominable when used by women, but have said flatly that it was uncivilized, unchristian and degrading in any case.
        MARY WINSOR, "The Militant Suffrage Movement," *The Annals of the American Academy of Political and Social Science*, LVI, November 1914

The heavy dignity of the Senate forbade their meddling much in this controversy. . . . Also they were more interested in the sporting prospect of our going into the world war. There was no appeal to blood-lust in the women's fight. There were no shining rods of steel. There was no martial music. We were not pledging precious lives and vast billions in our crusade for liberty. The beginning of our fight did indeed seem tiny and frail by the side of the big game of war . . .
        DORIS STEVENS, *Jailed for Freedom*, 1920

The Administration [Woodrow Wilson's] pinned its faith on jail—that institution of convenience to the oppressor when he is strong in power and his weapons are effective. When the oppressor miscalculates the strength of the oppressed, jail loses its convenience.
        Ibid.

We were what are known as fanatics, people who really want to see a thing carried through—perhaps too quickly.
        ANNIE KENNEY, *Memories of a Militant*, 1924

"No matter what your fight," I said, "don't be ladylike! God Almighty made women and the Rockefeller gang of thieves made the ladies."

> MOTHER [MARY HARRIS] JONES, to group of suffragists, *Autobiography of Mother Jones,* 1925

... indeed the upholders of law and order have always common sense on their side, but fanatics continue their stormy way to create another order.

> E. SYLVIA PANKHURST, *The Suffrage Movement,* 1931

Susan B. Anthony, Carrie Nation, and Sojourner Truth were not evolutionaries. They were revolutionaries ...

> SHIRLEY CHISHOLM, "Women Must Rebel," *Voices of the New Feminism,* ed. Mary Lou Thompson, 1970

All of them [Murray's students] ... are asking themselves the question whether our legal system is flexible enough to accommodate necessary social change. What I have to say ... is influenced by my own desperate need to answer this question in the affirmative coupled with the apprehension that in the area of women's rights as in other areas of human rights, our lawmakers will respond only when there is violence and disruption of nationwide proportions.

> PAULI MURRAY, to Rep. Edith Green's Special Subcommittee on Education, 1970, *Discrimination Against Women,* U.S. Government Printing Office, 1971

If anyone should ask a Negro woman what is her greatest achievement, her honest answer would be: "I survived!"

> Ibid.

The time for a woman to start fighting is before she gives it all up—fighting for the right to herself, her pride, her body, her time.

> ANDRA MEDEA AND KATHLEEN THOMPSON, *Against Rape,* 1974

There's a strange fear that if women ever learn to fight, every man would be in imminent danger, which may say something about the guilt of the ruling class.

> Ibid.

You don't get rid of oppression just by merely recognizing it.

> NANCY MYRON, "Class Beginnings," *Class and Feminism,* ed. Charlotte Bunch and Nancy Myron, 1974

165

Equal Rights

Yes . . . our souls are by nature *equal* to yours; the same breath of God animates, enlivens and invigorates us; and that we are not fallen lower than yourselves, let those witness who have greatly towered above the various discouragements by which they have been so heavily oppressed . . .

    JUDITH SARGENT MURRAY, "On the Equality of the Sexes," *The Massachusetts Magazine,* March 1790

I may excite laughter by dropping a hint which I mean to pursue some future time, for I really think that women ought to have representatives, instead of being arbitrarily governed without having any direct share allowed them in the deliberations of government.

    MARY WOLLSTONECRAFT, *A Vindication of the Rights of Woman,* 1792

. . . woman's rights are not the gifts of man—no! nor the *gifts* of God. His gifts to her may be recalled at his good pleasure—but her *rights* are an integral part of her moral being; they cannot be withdrawn; they must live with her forever.

    ANGELINA GRIMKÉ, Letter XI, *Letters to Catherine E. Beecher,* 1837

I recognize no rights but *human* rights—I know nothing of men's rights and women's rights; for in Christ Jesus, there is neither male nor female.

    Ibid., Letter XII

The question is often asked, "What does woman want, more than she enjoys? What is she seeking to obtain? Of what rights is she deprived? What privileges are withheld from her?" I answer, she asks nothing as favor, but as right; she wants to be acknowledged a moral, responsible being.

    LUCRETIA MOTT, discourse, circa 1849, *History of Woman Suffrage,* I, 1881

The tyrant sex, if such we choose to term it, holds such natural and necessary relations to the victims of injustice, that neither rebellion nor revolution, neither defiance nor resistance, nor any mode of assault or defence incident to party antagonism, is either possible, expedient, or proper. Our claim must rest on its justice, and conquer by its power of truth.

    PAULINA WRIGHT DAVIS, Address, *Proceedings of the Woman's Rights Convention, Held at Worcester, October 23 & 24, 1850,* 1851

Humanity recognizes no sex; virtue recognizes no sex; mind recognizes no sex; life and death, pleasure and pain, happiness and misery, recognize no sex. Like man, woman comes involuntarily into existence; like him, she possesses physical and mental and moral powers . . . like him she has to pay the penalty for disobeying nature's laws, and far greater penalties has she to suffer from ignorance . . . like him she enjoys or suffers with her country. Yet she is not recognized as his equal!

> ERNESTINE L. ROSE, Second National Convention, Friends of Woman Suffrage, 1851, *History of Woman Suffrage*, I, 1881

There are certain natural rights as inalienable to civilization as are the rights of air and motion to the savage in the wilderness. The natural rights of the civilized man and woman are government, property, the harmonious development of all their powers, and the gratification of their desires.

> ELIZABETH CADY STANTON, "Address to the New York State Legislature," 1860, *History of Woman Suffrage*, I, 1881

. . . if there is but one woman in this State who feels the injustice of her position, she should not be denied her inalienable rights, because the common household drudge and the silly butterfly of fashion are ignorant of all laws, both human and Divine.

> Ibid.

. . . before our Government can be a true democracy . . . the civil and political rights of every citizen must be practically established.

> SUSAN B. ANTHONY, Women's National Loyal League Meeting, 1863, *History of Woman Suffrage*, II, 1882

. . . woman is full-grown to-day, whether man knows it or not, equal to her rights, and equal to the responsibilities of the hour. I want to be identified with the negro; until he gets his rights, we never shall have ours.

> ANGELINA GRIMKÉ, Women's National Loyal League Meeting, 1863, *History of Woman Suffrage*, II, 1882

We are here to endeavor to help the cause of human rights and human freedom. We ought not to be afraid.

> ERNESTINE L. ROSE, Women's National Loyal League Meeting, 1863, *History of Woman Suffrage*, II, 1882

If the right of one single human being is to be disregarded by us, we fail in our loyalty to the country.

> Lucy Stone, Women's National Loyal League Meeting, 1863, *History of Woman Suffrage*, II, 1882

... we ... conjure you to act not for the passing hour, not with reference to transient benefits, but to do now the one grand deed that shall mark the progress of the century—proclaim EQUAL RIGHTS TO ALL.

> Susan B. Anthony, address to Congress, 1866, *History of Woman Suffrage*, II, 1882

I remember that in one of our earliest Woman's Rights Conventions, in Syracuse, a resolution was offered to the effect that as the assertion that the slave did not want his freedom, and would not take it if offered to him, only proved the depth of his degradation, so the assertion that woman had all the rights she wanted only gave evidence how far the influence of the law and customs, and the perverted application of the Scriptures, had encircled and crushed her.

> Lucretia Mott, American Equal Rights Association Convention, 1867, *History of Woman Suffrage*, II, 1882

"Principles, not policy; justice, not favor; men, their rights and nothing more; women, their rights and nothing less."

> Motto of *The Revolution*, 1868, periodical edited by Elizabeth Cady Stanton, published by Susan B. Anthony

We have declared in favor of a government of the people, for the people, by the people, the whole people. Why not begin the experiment?

> Elizabeth Cady Stanton, to Senate Judiciary Committee, 1872, *History of Woman Suffrage*, II, 1882

It was we, the people, not we, the white male citizens, nor yet we, the male citizens, but we, the whole people, who formed this Union.

> Susan B. Anthony, "Address to the Citizens of New York State," 1873, *History of Woman Suffrage*, II, 1882

Political power would withdraw women from their proper sphere—i.e. the home. This allegation is a very odd one. Men are lawyers, doctors, merchants; every hour of the day is pledged. . . . Yet men vote. If occupation be a fatal disqualification, let us pass a law that only idle people shall have votes.

> Annie Besant, speech, "The Political Status of Women," 1874, in Constance Rover, *Love, Morals and the Feminists*, 1970

The people are beginning to regard the idea of woman's equality with man as not only a political, but a religious truth.

ELIZABETH CADY STANTON, letter to *Golden Age*, 1874, *History of Woman Suffrage*, III, 1887

In the territories of Wyoming and Utah, woman suffrage still continues after five years' experiment, and we have not learned that households have been broken up or that babies have ceased to be rocked.

BELVA A. LOCKWOOD, Annual Report, National Woman Suffrage Association Convention, 1876, *History of Woman Suffrage*, III, 1887

I care nothing for suffrage merely to stand beside men, or rush to the polls, or to take any privilege outside of my home, only . . . for humanity. I never realized the importance of this cause, until we were beaten back on every side in the work of reform.

ELIZABETH L. SAXON, to Senate Judiciary Committee, 1880, *History of Woman Suffrage*, III, 1887

Liberty for one's self is a natural instinct possessed alike by all, but to be willing to accord liberty to another is the result of education, of self-discipline.

SUSAN B. ANTHONY, to House Judiciary Committee, 1884, *History of Woman Suffrage*, IV, 1902

I accept no authority of either Bibles or constitutions which tolerate the slavery of women. My rights were born with me and are the same over the whole globe.

ELIZABETH CADY STANTON, letter to Susan B. Anthony, circa 1884, in Alma Lutz, *Created Equal*, 1940

So long as women have no voice in the Government under which they live they will be an ostracised class, and invidious distinctions will be made against them in the world of work. Thrown on their own resources they have all the hardships that men have to encounter in earning their daily bread, with the added disabilities which grow out of disfranchisement.

ELIZABETH CADY STANTON, "Self-Government," to Senate Committee on Woman Suffrage, 1884, *History of Woman Suffrage*, IV, 1902

Lucy Stone always asked for suffrage because it is right and just that women should have it, and not on the ground of a swiftly-coming millennium which should follow it . . .

JULIA WARD HOWE, National American Woman Suffrage Association Convention, 1894, *History of Woman Suffrage*, IV, 1902

169

[The women of the Middle West] are determined to have the ballot if they have to bear and raise the sons to give it to them. This scheme is in active operation. I myself have raised three—eighteen feet for woman suffrage—and others have done better.

> MARY J. COGGESHALL, "Word from the Middle West," National American Woman Suffrage Association Convention, 1905, *History of Woman Suffrage*, V, 1922

Only one thing can make me see the justness of woman being classed with the idiot, the insane and the criminal and that is, if she is willing, if she is satisfied to be so classed, if she is contented to remain in the circumscribed limits which corrupt customs and perverted application of the Scriptures have marked out for her. It is idiotic not to want one's liberty; it is insane not to value one's inalienable rights and it is criminal to neglect one's God-given responsibilities.

> JUDITH HYAMS DOUGLAS, National American Woman Suffrage Convention, 1908, *History of Woman Suffrage*, V, 1922

We have never tried universal suffrage but if that which we have is a failure the cure for it is not to restrict it but to extend it, because no class of men is able to represent another class and it is much truer that no class nor all classes of men are capable of representing any class or all classes of women.

> ANNA HOWARD SHAW, to Senate Judiciary Committee, 1910, *History of Woman Suffrage*, V, 1922

To deny the franchise because it is capable of leading to mischievous action, would be like standing beside a new-born babe and saying: "It will probably be a sinner, let us hinder it once and for all."

> JULIA WARD HOWE, "Speech at a Suffrage Hearing before the Massachusetts Legislature," n.d., from *Julia Ward Howe and the Woman Suffrage Movement*, ed. Florence Howe Hall, 1913

Let us either stop our pretence before the nations of the earth of being a republic and having "equality before the law" or else let us become the republic that we pretend to be.

> HELEN H. GARDENER, "brief" submitted to House and Senate Judiciary Committees, 1914, *History of Woman Suffrage*, V, 1922

... the woman suffrage movement in the United States was a movement of *the spirit of the Revolution which was striving to hold the nation to the ideals which won independence.*

CARRIE CHAPMAN CATT AND NETTIE ROGERS SHULER, *Woman Suffrage and Politics*, 1923

[To] blot out of every law book in the land, to sweep out of every dusty court-room, to erase from every judge's mind that centuries-old precedent as to women's inferiority and dependence and need for protection; to substitute for it at one blow the simple new precedent of equality, that is a fight worth making if it takes ten years.

CRYSTAL EASTMAN, "Feminists Must Fight," letter to the editor, *The Nation*, 119, November 12, 1924

... it seems ... most emphatically not true that the battle for "equal rights" must be fought within party lines. It can never be won there. It must be fought and it will be fought by a free-handed, nonpartisan minority of ener-getic feminists to whom politics in general, even "reform" politics, will con-tinue to be a matter of indifference so long as women are classed with chil-dren and minors in industrial legislation, so long as even in our most advanced States a woman can be penalized by the loss of her job when she marries.

Ibid.

The ultimate emancipation of woman, then, will depend not upon the aboli-tion of the restrictions which have subjected her to man—that is but a step, though a necessary one—but upon *the abolition of all those restrictions of natural human rights that subject the mass of humanity to a privileged class.*

SUZANNE LA FOLLETTE, *Concerning Women*, 1926

For the feminist the goal is an equal moral standard; that law, custom and public opinion should accord to women as a natural and inalienable right the same liberty of action and the same standard of responsibility, neither more nor less, that are accorded to men.

ALISON NEILANS, "Changes in Sex Morality," *Our Freedom and Its Results*, ed. Ray Strachey, 1936

The "war-horses" of the fight for the suffrage sometimes complain, indeed, that the young take the vote, and so on, for granted. So they should. Its denial was an outrage. Its possession is elementary justice and common sense. The younger women have a hard enough task before them. They have got to win the next stage—real equality of opportunity and freedom of choice.

MARY AGNES HAMILTON, *Women at Work*, 1941

The argument that this amendment will not solve the problem of sex discrimination is not relevant. If the argument were used against a civil rights bill—as it has been used in the past—the prejudice that lies behind it would be embarrassing. Of course laws will not eliminate prejudice from the hearts of human beings. But that is no reason to allow prejudice to continue to be enshrined in our laws—to perpetuate injustice through inaction.

SHIRLEY CHISHOLM, House floor debate on the Equal Rights Amendment, August 1970, *Congressional Record*, vol. 116, part 21

It has been said that if this amendment is passed it will create profound social changes. May I say to you, it is high time some profound social changes were made in our society.

EDITH GREEN, House floor debate on the Equal Rights Amendment, August 1970, *Congressional Record*, vol. 116, part 21

... women don't have hang-ups, they have political problems.

LOWER EAST SIDE WOMEN'S LIBERATION COLLECTIVE, "Love Is Just a Four-Letter Word," from *Hip Culture, Six Essays on Its Revolutionary Potential*, in *The American Sisterhood*, ed. Wendy Martin, 1972

... women's liberation is not a debatable issue ...

JILL JOHNSTON, *Lesbian Nation*, 1973

I think that whereas women felt it definitely unfair that they couldn't vote, I think women now conceive of the inequality as something a great deal more serious than a personal affront. They realize that it has a lot to do with the kind of world we have and the mess we're in, and that the only valid hope for the future lies in *true* equality.

LAURA ELLSWORTH SEILER, interview with Sherna Gluck, *From Parlor to Prison*, 1976

It's time to listen to that different drummer: equality—equality in all employment. And it's time to get away from the circular reasoning of the unmerit system where women are denied admission to merit system examinations because we lack the required experience, and we lack the required experience because of sex discrimination. We need the ERA.

ELINOR BROKAW GRANT, speech (unpublished) at Women's Day, California Men's Colony, San Luis Obispo, 1977

... standing alone we learned our power; we repudiated man's counsels forevermore; and solemnly vowed that there should never be another season of silence until woman had the same rights everywhere on this green earth, as man.

E. C. STANTON, S. B. ANTHONY, M. J. GAGE, eds., *History of Woman Suffrage*, II, 1882

9   Talking Back

... one reason why men have superior judgment, and more fortitude than women, is undoubtedly this, that they give a freer scope to the grand passions, and by more frequently going astray enlarge their minds.

MARY WOLLSTONECRAFT, *A Vindication of the Rights of Woman*, 1792

Men are strange machines; and their whole system of morality is in general held together by one grand principle, which loses its force the moment they allow themselves to break with impunity over the bounds which secured their self-respect. A man ceases to love humanity, and then individuals, as he advances in the chase after wealth; as one clashes with his interest, the other with his pleasures: to business, as it is termed, every thing must give way; nay, is sacrificed; and all the endearing charities of citizen, husband, father, brother, become empty names.

MARY WOLLSTONECRAFT, *Letters Written During a Short Residence in Sweden, Norway, and Denmark*, 1796

If God has assigned a sphere to man and one to woman, we claim the right to judge ourselves of His design in reference to *us*, and we accord to man the same privilege. We think a man has quite enough in this life to find out his own individual calling, without being taxed to decide where every woman belongs; and the fact that so many men fail in the business they undertake, calls loudly for their concentrating more thought on their own faculties, capabilities, and sphere of action. We have all seen a man making a jackass of himself in the pulpit, at the bar, or in our legislative halls, when he might have shone as a general in our Mexican war, captain of a canal boat, or as a tailor on his bench. Now, is it to be wondered at that woman has some doubts about the present position assigned her being the true one, when her everyday experience shows her that man makes such fatal mistakes in regard to himself.

> ELIZABETH CADY STANTON, reply to "newspaper objections" to women's rights conventions in Seneca Falls and Rochester, *National Reformer*, 1848, *History of Woman Suffrage*, I, 1881

Thousands of girls are born with mechanical fingers. Thousands of girls have a muscular development that could do the work of the world as well as men; and there are thousands of men born to effeminacy and weakness.

> FRANCES D. GAGE, American Equal Rights Association Convention, 1867, *History of Woman Suffrage*, II, 1882

The editors of the New York press have made known their dissatisfaction that no gentlemen were to be admitted into this charmed circle [the Sorosis club]. ... For the comfort of these ostracised ones, we would suggest a hope for the future. After these ladies become familiar with parliamentary tactics, and the grave questions that are to come before them for consideration, it is proposed to admit gentlemen to the galleries, that they may enjoy the same privileges vouchsafed to the fair sex in the past, to look down upon the feast, to listen to the speeches, and to hear "the pale, thoughtful brow," "the silken moustache," "the flowing locks," "the manly gait and form" toasted in prose and verse.

> ELIZABETH CADY STANTON, ed., periodical *The Revolution*, 1868, *History of Woman Suffrage*, III, 1887

I believe that by nature men are no more unjust than women. If from the beginning women had maintained the right to rule not only themselves but men also, the latter today doubtless would be occupying the subordinate places with inferior pay in the world of work; women would be holding the higher positions with the big salaries; widowers would be doomed to a "life interest of one-third of the family estate"; husbands would "owe service" to their wives, so that every one of you men would be begging your good wives, "Please be so kind as to 'give me' ten cents for a cigar."

> SUSAN B. ANTHONY, "Woman Wants Bread, Not the Ballot," campaign speech, 1870–1880, in Ida Husted Harper, *Life and Work of Susan B. Anthony*, vol. II, 1898

Nature has not rendered it impossible for [men] ... to assume those splendors of the toilet which they are so fond of in us. Once they made themselves magnificent with scarlet velvets slashed with gold, with embroidered ruffs,

174

flashing knee-buckles, and long, powdered hair. Why does not a full-dress occasion demand this of them to-day, as rigorously as it does the trains, the laces, the coiffures of our sex? ... And if some people must agonize as lay-figures for the sake of others' eyes, let the suffering be equally divided. We will bear our half, let the men bear theirs!

> ABBA GOOLD WOOLSON, Lecture V, *Dress-Reform*, ed. Abba Goold Woolson, 1874

Single-handed they saw they were helpless against this incoming tide of feminine persuasiveness, and so it seems they called a meeting of faint-hearted men, and bound themselves together by a constitution and by-laws to protect the franchise from the encroachment of women.

> ELIZABETH CADY STANTON, speaking of English men's club formed to oppose woman suffrage, circa 1875, *History of Woman Suffrage*, III, 1887

At other polls I saw colored men, once slaves, electioneering and voting against the rights of women. When remonstrated with, one said: "We want the women at home cooking our dinners." A shrewd colored woman asked whether they had provided any dinner to cook, and added that most of the colored women there had to earn their dinners as well as cook it.

> LUCY STONE, letter to *Woman's Journal* describing franchise election in Colorado, 1877, *History of Woman Suffrage*, III, 1887

[A certain minister's arguments] remind one of the story of Baron Munchausen's horn, into which a certain coach-driver blew all manner of wicked tunes. The weather being very cold, these tunes remained frozen in the horn. When hung by the fire, the horn began to thaw out, and these wicked tunes came pealing forth to the great amazement of the by-standers. The reverend gentleman seems to think women are full of frozen wickedness, which if they enter public life will be thawed out to the utter demolition of their "dignity and delicacy" and the disgust of society. He deems it "too hazardous" to allow women to vote. "Bad women would vote." Well, what of it? Have they not equal right with bad men, to self-governnent?

> MATILDA JOSLYN GAGE, ed., periodical *National Citizen*, 1878, *History of Woman Suffrage*, III, 1887

... we would warn the young women of the coming generation against man's advice as to their best interests, their highest development. We would point for them the moral of our experiences: that woman must lead the way to her own enfranchisement, and work out her own salvation with a hopeful courage and determination that knows no fear or trembling. She must not put

175

her trust in man in this transition period, since, while regarded as his subject, his inferior, his slave, their interests must be antagonistic.

> E. C. STANTON, S. B. ANTHONY, M. J. GAGE, eds., *History of Woman Suffrage*, II, 1882

"Adam was first formed, then Eve." What does that prove? Either nothing, or that man is inferior to the fishes.

> LILLIE DEVEREUX BLAKE, *Women's Place Today*, 1883

Surely it is time that some one on this platform should say something for this half of humanity, which we really must confess after all is an important half. Ought we not admit that men have wrongs to complain of? Are they not constantly declaring themselves our slaves?

> LILLIE DEVEREUX BLAKE, "The Rights of Men," National Woman Suffrage Association Convention, 1887, *History of Woman Suffrage*, IV, 1902

The subjugation of woman doubtless arose fron an honest desire of man to protect her. His mistake lay in assuming that his mind and will could do private and public duty for both. Woman's mistake lay in assuming that she might with safety permit man's mind and will to discharge the duties nature meant to be fulfilled by her own.

> ELLEN BATTELLE DIETRICK, "Best Methods of Interesting Women in Suffrage," National American Woman Suffrage Association Convention, 1893, *History of Woman Suffrage*, IV, 1902

The political superiors of women have again been demonstrating their superior calmness and freedom from excitability. This time it is two Congressmen who have been throwing inkstands and spongecups at each others' heads.

> ALICE STONE BLACKWELL, ed., *The Woman's Column*, May 2, 1896

Women will never win so long as they consent to barter their services for vague promises of what will be done for them in the future, or to subordinate woman suffrage to the interests of any party.

> LAURA CLAY, National American Woman Suffrage Association Convention, 1897, *History of Woman Suffrage*, IV, 1902

The beautiful coloring of male birds and fishes, and the various appendages acquired by males throughout the various orders below man, and which, so far as they themselves are concerned, serve no other useful purpose than to aid them in securing the favors of the females, have by the latter been turned to account in the processes of reproduction. The female made the male beautiful that she might endure his caresses.

ELIZA BURT GAMBLE, *The God-Idea of the Ancients*, 1897

"Don't you think that the best thing a woman can do is to perform well her part in the role of wife and mother? My wife has presented me with eight beautiful children: is not this a better life-work than that of exercising the right of suffrage?"

... "I have met few men, in my life, worth repeating eight times."

ELIZABETH CADY STANTON, in encounter with a man from Nebraska, *Eighty Years and More*, 1898

True, those gentlemen were all quite willing that women should join their societies and churches to do the drudgery; to work up the enthusiasm in fairs and revivals, conventions and flag presentations; to pay a dollar apiece into their treasury for the honor of being members of their various organizations; to beg money for the Church; to circulate petitions from door to door; to visit saloons; to pray with or defy rumsellers; to teach school at half price, and sit round the outskirts of a hall, in teachers' State conventions, like so many wallflowers; but they would not allow them to sit on the platform, address the assembly, or vote for men and measures.

Ibid.

If we must keep on continually building monuments to great men, they should be handsome blocks of comfortable homes for the poor.... Surely sanitary homes and schoolhouses for the living would be more appropriate monuments to wise statesmen that the purest Parian shafts among the sepulchers of the dead.

Ibid.

American men have had a hard struggle for their own liberty, and some of them are afraid there will not be liberty enough to go around.

JOSEPHINE K. HENRY, National American Woman Suffrage Association Convention, 1899, *History of Woman Suffrage*, IV, 1902

My grandmother taught me to spin ... but the men have relieved womankind from that task and as they have taken so many industrial burdens off of our hands it is our duty to relieve them of some of their burdens of State.

REV. ANTOINETTE BROWN BLACKWELL, "Suffrage and Education," National American Woman Suffrage Association Convention, 1905, *History of Woman Suffrage*, V, 1922

... my reason for believing in the necessity of a vote, from the very fact that men's and women's interests are identical is not based on a belief in men's injustice, brutality, or selfishness at all, but merely in their inadequacy and incompetence.

LADY GROVE, *The Human Woman*, 1908

Why is it that, whenever it is a question of men entering public life, the ideals held out are those of self-sacrifice, attention to duty, disinterested concern for the welfare of others, and a wise discretion in weighing the comparative merits of different measures? When it is a question of women taking an interest in the same things, we hear from opponents of nothing but the demoralising influence of the "hustings," ... of the sordid atmosphere of political life, of its meanness, its pettiness, the unworthiness of the motives that govern public men, and the generally degrading effect that "politics" have on those participating in them.

Ibid.

Men are not able to govern themselves; and it is only when women are consulted and honoured that civilization can exist.

"STELLA," anonymous author of "The Tyranny of Man," *The Burden of Women*, ed. Frank Mond, 1908

Perchance the poor quality of the material whence woman comes is responsible for her inferiority.

EMMA GOLDMAN, on the myth that woman was made out of Adam's rib, "Marriage and Love," *Anarchism and Other Essays*, 1911

It is not the woman, who, on hands and knees, at tenpence a day, scrubs the floors of the public buildings, or private dwellings, that fills [the lofty theorist] with anguish for womanhood: that somewhat quadrupedal posture is for him truly feminine, and does not interfere with his ideal of the mother and child-bearer.... It is not the labour, or the amount of labour, so much as the amount of reward that interferes with his ideal of the eternal womanly ...

OLIVE SCHREINER, *Woman and Labour*, 1911

We are having to hammer out for ourselves the right principles of government. We can take them ready-made from no man.

H. M. SWANWICK, *The Future of the Women's Movement*, 1913

Men are very human. God made them to match the women.

ABIGAIL SCOTT DUNIWAY, *Pathbreaking*, 1914

I can assure the American women that our long alliance with the great parties, our devotion to party programmes, our faithful work at elections, never advanced the suffrage cause one step. The men accepted the services of the women, but they never offered any kind of payment.
    EMMELINE PANKHURST, *My Own Story*, 1914

These young and aspiring statesmen have to attract attention in some fashion, and the espousal of advanced causes, such as labour or women's suffrage, seems an easy way to accomplish that end.
    Ibid. [speaking of Sir Edward Grey, who first appeared to support woman suffrage and later became a "bitter foe"]

It was rapidly becoming clear to my mind that men regarded women as a servant class in the community, and that women were going to remain in the servant class until they lifted themselves out of it. I asked myself many times in those days what was to be done. I had joined the Labour Party, thinking that through its councils something vital might come, some such demand for the women's enfranchisement that the politicians could not possibly ignore. Nothing came.
    Ibid.

... when the anti-suffrage members of the Government criticise militancy in women ... it is very like beasts of prey reproaching the gentler animals who turn in desperate resistance when at the point of death.
    Ibid.

One of the compliments or insults that has been hurled during the sex-war is that the feminine mind is pervaded by the physical harmony of the feminine body. One may perhaps retort that the dualism of mind and matter is a very masculine philosophy; and one which, moreover, men have translated into their everyday lives by the sharp division they like to make between fighters and thinkers, games-playing idiots and thin intellectuals.
    DORA RUSSELL, *Hypatia*, 1925

... among the Hebrews the subordination of woman gave rise to the notion that she was fashioned out of man's rib. ... Since the Divine Artist had had good practice in creating Adam, it might logically have been expected that His second sex would turn out even better than His first; we must therefore lay His failure to the somewhat sketchy nature of the materials He chose to work with.
    SUZANNE LA FOLLETTE, *Concerning Women*, 1926

Few men can function alone. They have been brought up, poor dears, not to do little, personal things for themselves. In daily processes, they've been taught that the greater their helplessness, the more their masculinity. Women have been their teachers. They enjoy the sense of man's dependence.

> FLORENCE GUY SEABURY, in *Laughing Their Way*, ed. Martha Bruère and Mary R. Beard, 1934

Woman's success in lifting men out of their way of life nearly resembling that of the beasts—who merely hunted and fished for food, who found shelter where they could in jungles, in trees, and caves—was a civilizing triumph. It involved infinite experimentation with natural resources, infinite patience, especial responsibility for offspring, peculiar taste, a sense of esthetics, extraordinary manual skill, and the highest quality of creative intelligence.

> MARY RITTER BEARD, *Woman as Force in History*, 1946

. . . men who are physically and mentally strong are but rarely anti-feminists.

> HANNAH MITCHELL, *The Hard Way Up*, 1946, published 1968

In a canvass made during a recent election, a group of husbands were asked if they ever discussed politics with their wives; most of them said no. Their wives were asked the same question, if they ever discussed politics with their husbands, and answered yes. It was the women who were under the delusion that there had been an exchange of ideas.

> RUTH HERSCHBERGER, *Adam's Rib*, 1948

. . . here was a gentleman [an English judge] who condemned others for theft, for taking what was someone else's property and yet he felt quite entitled to rob his own wife of her individuality. He, I felt, was guilty of sequestering a mind—possibly a soul—but he went unpunished.

> MARY R. RICHARDSON, *Laugh a Defiance*, 1953

If reproduction were the chief and only fact of human life, would all men today suffer from "uterus envy"?

> BETTY FRIEDAN, *The Feminine Mystique*, 1963

The fight against unequal power relationships between men and women necessitates fighting unequal power everyplace: between men and women, . . . between men and men, and women and women, between black and white, and rich and poor.

> TI-GRACE ATKINSON, "Resignation from N.O.W.," October 1968, *Amazon Odyssey*, 1974

180

. . . Revolutions anywhere are always glad to use any help they can get, even from women. But unless women also use the Revolution to further their own interests as well as everyone else's, unless they make it consistently clear that all help given now is expected to be returned, both now and after the Revolution, they will be sold out again and again . . .

> SHULAMITH FIRESTONE, "The Women's Rights Movement in the U.S.: A New View," *Notes from the First Year*, 1968

The worship of muscular male forms is a weakness of men and not of women.

> ELIZABETH GOULD DAVIS, *The First Sex*, 1971

. . . the reason for segregation has got so obvious that we forget the excuses. It's simply that we are (in this case) the oppressed people and around this we organize.

> JULIET MITCHELL, presenting reasons for keeping men out of the Women's Movement, *Woman's Estate*, 1971

Whatever their physical type, educational level, temperament or mentality, all homosexual women are *one* in their rejection of bondage to the male. They refuse to be the second sex.

> CHARLOTTE WOLFF, M.D., *Love Between Women*, 1971

Lesbianism is too near the bone for many women, and too disorientating to the arrogance of most men.

> Ibid.

This crippled emotional condition found in males, which I call "testeria" (> testes, L. for balls) accounts in part for the ability of the male ruling class to efficiently, calmly, and maturely carry out planetary catastrophe. . . .

Testeria is mostly a matter of repression or reserve: the inability to feel. . . . Penisolence is the *active* phase of male emotional disease. . . . It is a pushy and invasive attempt to master one's own distress by mastering other people.

> JULI LOESCH, "Testeria and Penisolence—A Scourge to Humankind," *Aphra*, IV, Winter 1972–1973

Surely the basic family unit was once mother and child, and surely, to primitive people, the ability to give birth must have seemed a far greater miracle than the mere possession of an observable, push-me, pull-me, shrink-and-grow penis, however interesting and even worthwhile this organ may be.

> BARBARA SEAMAN, *Free and Female*, 1972

If there *is* a place for guilt, it is for not recognizing that a male-dominated "liberation" movement cannot essentially change the situation of the more than 50 percent female membership of all down-trodden, poor, and oppressed races and minority groups. Recognizing this, women may well decide that independent "bonding" with each other and cooperation on this basis with male-governed groups is the better choice.

MARY DALY, *Beyond God the Father*, 1973

The liberation of women is for women, not for men. We don't have to have anything to do with the men at all. They've taken excellent care of themselves.

JILL JOHNSTON, *Lesbian Nation*, 1973

... what is done or learned by one class of women, becomes, by virtue of their common womanhood, the property of all women.
ELIZABETH BLACKWELL
and EMILY BLACKWELL, *Medicine as a Profession for Women*, 1860

10   Sisterhood

Love Among Women

Therefore these poor young women, who have, through extreme necessity, been driven to criminal and unlawful pursuits, are not to be despised or sunk beneath our care, but cherished and supported, in order to reclaim their wicked course of life.
MARY ANN RADCLIFFE, *The Female Advocate*, 1799

Art thou afraid to trust the women of this country with discretionary power as to petitioning? Is there not sound principle and common sense enough among them, to regulate the exercise of this right? I believe they will always use it wisely. I am not afraid to trust my sisters—not I.
ANGELINA GRIMKÉ, Letter XI, *Letters to Catherine E. Beecher*, 1837

I believe that, at present, women are the best helpers of one another. Let them think; let them act; till they know what they need. We only ask of men to remove arbitrary barriers.
MARGARET FULLER, *Woman in the Nineteenth Century*, 1845

It is so true that a woman may be in love with a woman, and a man with a man. It is pleasant to be sure of it, because it is undoubtedly the same love that we shall feel when we are angels ...
Ibid.

My whole life is devoted unreservedly to the service of my sex. The study and practice of medicine is in my thought but one means to a great end, for which my very soul yearns with intensest passionate emotion, of which I have dreamed day and night, from my earliest childhood, for which I would offer up my life with triumphant thanksgiving, if martyrdom could secure that glorious end:—the true ennoblement of woman, the full harmonious development of her unknown nature, and the consequent redemption of the whole human race.

> ELIZABETH BLACKWELL, letter to Emily Collins, 1848, *History of Woman Suffrage*, I, 1881

I read, with intense interest, everything that indicated an awakening of public or private thought to the idea that woman did not occupy her rightful position in the organization of society; and, when I read the lectures of Ernestine L. Rose and the writings of Margaret Fuller, and found that other women entertained the same thoughts that had been seething in my own brain, and realized that I stood not alone, how my heart bounded with joy!

> EMILY COLLINS, "Reminiscences," circa 1848, *History of Woman Suffrage*, I, 1881

... I will not be excepted. I stand in the ranks, liable to all the penalties of the calling—exposed to the hot shot of satire and the stinging arrows of ridicule. I will not be received as an exception, where full justice is not done to the class to which I belong.

> GRACE GREENWOOD, letter to *Evening Post*, 1850, *History of Woman Suffrage*, I, 1881

It is cruel selfishness to fold our hands in idle contempt for the needs of others, because the Good Father has cast our lines in pleasant places.

> ELIZABETH OAKES SMITH, *Woman and Her Needs,* 1851

We must be true to each other. We must stand by the woman whose work of hand or brain removes her from the customary sphere.

> LUCY STONE, Woman's Rights Convention, 1852, *History of Woman Suffrage*, I, 1881

We must suffer, to learn to benefit those that have suffered. To endure privations ourselves, is the only sure way, in which to know the wants of others, and how best to meet those wants.

> VIRGINIA PENNY, *Think and Act, 1869*

Women joined in the hue and cry against her [Frances Wright], little thinking that men were building the gallows and making them the executioners. Women have crucified in all ages the redeemers of their own sex, and men mock them with the fact. It is time now that we trample beneath our feet this ignoble public sentiment which men have made for us; and if others are to be crucified before we can be redeemed, let men do the cruel cowardly work; but let us learn to hedge womanhood round with generous, protecting love and care. Then men will learn, as they should, that this system of traducing women is no longer to be used as a means for their subjugation.

> PAULINA WRIGHT DAVIS, Twentieth Anniversary Woman's Rights Convention, 1870, *History of Woman Suffrage*, II, 1882

So entirely one are we [Susan B. Anthony and Elizabeth Cady Stanton] that in all our associations, ever side by side on the same platform, not one feeling of jealousy or envy has ever shadowed our lives. We have indulged freely in criticism of each other when alone, and hotly contended whenever we have differed, but in our friendship of thirty years there has never been a break of one hour.

> ELIZABETH CADY STANTON, "Reminiscences," *History of Woman Suffrage*, I, 1881

Ah, my sisters, because we have dear homes and good husbands, shall we not be able to see those others of our sex who are suffering? Even if we are happy, shall we not have pity on the unhappy ones? A woman need not have endured any wrong herself to feel the wrongs of others.

> LILLIE DEVEREUX BLAKE, *Women's Place Today*, 1883

We have jogged along pretty well for forty years or more. Perhaps mid the wreck of thrones and the undoing of so many friendships, sects, parties, and families, you and I deserve some credit for sticking together through all adverse winds, with so few ripples on the surface. . . . Tell our suffrage daughters to brace up and get ready for a long pull, a strong pull, and a pull all together when I come back.

> ELIZABETH CADY STANTON, letter to Susan B. Anthony, winter of 1887–1888, in Ida Husted Harper, *Life and Work of Susan B. Anthony*, vol. II, 1898

I never expect to know any joy in this world equal to that of going up and down the land, getting good editorials written, engaging halls, and circulating Mrs. Stanton's speeches. If I ever have had any inspiration she has given it to me, for I never could have done my work if I had not had this woman at my right hand.

> SUSAN B. ANTHONY, remarks at her seventieth birthday celebration, 1890, in Ida Husted Harper, *Life and Work of Susan B. Anthony*, vol. II, 1898

Women who have all the rights they want should consider that there are other women who have not all the rights they want . . .

> CARRIE CHAPMAN CATT, conclusion to story about a slave prostitute, "A True Story," *A Woman's Suffrage Leaflet*, 1891

I have never yet met a woman that I was afraid of, or from whom I feared contamination.

> AMELIA BLOOMER, "Woman's Right to the Ballot," undated, in D. C. Bloomer, *Life and Writings of Amelia Bloomer*, 1895

The woman's movement rests not alone on her larger personality, with its tingling sense of revolt against injustice, but on the wide, deep sympathy of women for one another. It is a concerted movement, based on the recognition of a common evil and seeking a common good.

> CHARLOTTE PERKINS GILMAN, *Women and Economics*, 1898

The love of mother and child is beautiful; but there is a higher law than that—the love of one another.

> CHARLOTTE PERKINS GILMAN, *The Home*, 1903

. . . I had seen the misery of the poor, of my sister-women with children crying for bread; the wages of the workmen were often sufficient for four, but eight or ten they could not maintain. Should I set my own safety, my own good name, against the helping of these? Did it matter that my reputation should be ruined, if its ruin helped to bring remedy to this otherwise hopeless wretchedness of thousands?

> ANNIE BESANT, *An Autobiography*, 1908

Corrupt custom has rent the sacred, seamless robe of womanhood and cast out part of the women, abandoning them to degradation. We must learn to recognize the responsibility of pure women for the fallen women, of the woman whose circumstances have enabled her to stand, for the woman whom adverse conditions have borne down . . .

> ANNA GARLIN SPENCER, National American Woman Suffrage Association Convention, 1908, *History of Woman Suffrage*, V, 1922

I sometimes feel as if words could not express the comfort and instruction which have come to me in the later years of my life from two sources. One of these has been the better acquaintance with my own sex; the other, the experience of the power resulting from associated action in behalf of worthy objects. . . . The new domain now made clear to me was that of true womanhood. . . . This discovery was like the addition of a new continent to the map of the world, or of a new testament to the old ordinances.

> JULIA WARD HOWE, "Reminiscences," *Julia Ward Howe and the Woman Suffrage Movement*, ed. Florence Howe Hall, 1913

There is this foundation at least for the frequent statement that women "do not wish to be ruled by women." They do not wish to be ruled by women who have been selected by men, because they know from experience that a man's woman and a woman's woman are not the same.

> H. M. SWANWICK, *The Future of the Women's Movement*, 1913

I . . . tasted the delights of that full, unfettered companionship which is among the greatest immediate rewards of those who work actively in this [the women's militant] cause. No drudgery of preliminary acquaintanceship has to be got through, no misleading inquiries as to kindred temperaments or interests. The sense of unity and mutual confidence is complete and begins from the first unhesitatingly.

> CONSTANCE LYTTON, *Prisons & Prisoners*, 1914

If women, free in mind, can carry the power to care intensely beyond the narrow boundaries of their intimate affections, and make it available for others in widest commonalty spread, they may help, and that potently, to clear our society of its gravest sin. That sin is exploitation—the use of human beings as means and not as ends. It is the other face of possession.

> MARY AGNES HAMILTON, "Changes in Social Life," *Our Freedom and Its Results*, ed. Ray Strachey, 1936

. . . women cannot accept the old division of their own sex into "good" women and "bad" women. There are only women . . .

> ALISON NEILANS, "Changes in Sex Morality," *Our Freedom and Its Results*, ed. Ray Strachey, 1936

Individually, the feminists seem to have had no more nor less reason than all women of their time to envy or hate man. But what they did have was self-respect, courage, strength. Whether they loved or hated man, escaped or suffered humiliation from men in their own lives, they identified with women.

> BETTY FRIEDAN, *The Feminine Mystique*, 1963

187

The charge of homosexuality . . . stands for a fear of something greater, as did the charge of communism against Southern blacks and whites getting together: that they might get together.

>JUDITH BROWN, Part II of "Toward a Female Liberation Movement," by Beverly Jones and Judith Brown, 1968, *Voices from Women's Liberation*, ed. Leslie B. Tanner, 1970

. . . every time we don't struggle we make it harder for a woman who does. But only when we have a movement, only when women can offer each other real support, can we begin to make such demands on each other. To blame women for not struggling is to forget what the risks of struggle are for us all.

>JENNIFER GARDNER, "False Consciousness," *Tooth and Nail*, October 1969

If you love women then you are in revolt against male supremacy.

>RITA MAE BROWN, "The Shape of Things to Come," *Women: A Journal of Liberation*, II, circa 1971

From a psychological point of view, it is only women who can "make up" to each other for their lack of mothering. . . . only women can (if they will) support the entry or re-entry of women into the human race.

>PHYLLIS CHESLER, *Women and Madness*, 1972

. . . when [women] . . . first come into the women's movement, they want to do so much . . . and for the first time in their lives, they do become totally involved and fulfill themselves. Women become happy for the first time in their lives. . . . You feel that you are not only working for yourself, but for every other woman, and it's a total revolution in your life.

>CAROLINE LUND, "Female Liberation and Socialism, An Interview," *Feminism and Socialism*, ed. Linda Jenness, 1972

As one (heterosexual) NOW member put it to us, "I believe deeply that female sexuality is a key issue in the women's movement. Until every woman is able to say, 'Okay, so you think I'm a Lesbian. Fuck you—I will neither confirm nor deny it,' the women's movement will go nowhere. You see, I want liberation, not just equality."

>DEL MARTIN AND PHYLLIS LYON, *Lesbian/Woman*, 1972

The odd thing about these deep and personal connections of women is that they often ignore barriers of age, economics, worldly experience, race, culture—all the barriers that, in male or mixed society, had seemed so difficult to cross.

>GLORIA STEINEM, "Sisterhood," *Ms.*, Spring 1972

188

The concept of a bond among women is key if women are going to work together in a steady and organized fashion to reshape society, but emotional "sisterhood" alone—awareness of common suffering—is not sufficient, based as it is on recognition of a common powerlessness, and may reinforce powerlessness.
> SIDNEY ABBOTT AND BARBARA LOVE, *Sappho Was a Right-On Woman*, 1973

Lesbians understand that sisterhood does not consist only of warm feelings for another who has suffered too; it means working together on specific goals; it means solidarity.
> Ibid.

The "bonding" phenomenon among women, expressed by the word "sisterhood," is ... essential to the battle against false consciousness. Only women hearing each other can create a counterworld to the prevailing sense of reality.
> MARY DALY, *Beyond God the Father*, 1973

A personal solution or exceptional adjustment to a political problem is a collusion with the enemy. The solution is getting it together with women.
> JILL JOHNSTON, *Lesbian Nation*, 1973

"Sister" really means something like: "You who are one with me in our oppression," rather than merely being an expression of pure unity.
> ROBIN LAKOFF, *Language and Woman's Place*, 1975

Women seek a reconstruction of relationships for which we have neither words nor models: a reconstruction which can give each person the fullness of their being.... We seek a new concept of relationships between persons, groups, life systems, a relationship which is not competitive or hierarchical but mutually enhancing.
> ROSEMARY RADFORD RUETHER, *New Woman New Earth*, 1975

The loss of the daugher to the mother, the mother to the daughter, is the essential female tragedy.
> ADRIENNE RICH, *Of Woman Born*, 1976

Women are made taboo to women—not just sexually, but as comrades, cocreators, coinspiritors. In breaking this taboo, we are reuniting with our mothers; in reuniting with our mothers, we are breaking this taboo.
> Ibid.

189

Union and Division

They [women] lose all simplicity, all dignity of mind, in acquiring power, and act as men are observed to act when they have been exalted by the same means.

MARY WOLLSTONECRAFT, A *Vindication of the Rights of Woman*, 1792

... women must leave off ... being influenced by them [men], but retire within themselves, and explore the groundwork of life till they find their peculiar secret. Then, when they come forth again, renovated and baptized, they will know how to turn all dross to gold, and will be rich and free though they live in a hut, tranquil if in a crowd. Then their sweet singing shall not be from passionate impulse, but the lyrical overflow of a divine rapture, and a new music shall be evolved from this many-chorded world.

MARGARET FULLER, *Woman in the Nineteenth Century*, 1845

Oh, if all women could be impressed with the importance of their own action, and with one united voice, speak out in their own behalf, in behalf of humanity, they could create a revolution without armies, without bloodshed, that would do more to ameliorate the condition of mankind ... than all that has been done by reformers in the last century.

FRANCES D. GAGE, Woman's Rights Convention, 1851, *History of Woman Suffrage*, I, 1881

What organization in the world's history has not encumbered the unfettered action of those who created it? Indeed, has not been used as an engine of oppression.

ANGELINA GRIMKÉ, letter to Woman's Rights Convention, 1852, *History of Woman Suffrage*, I, 1881

Woman must be willing to see herself as she is, the slave of fashion, assuming all the Proteus forms she invents, without reference to health or convenience. She must remember how few of us give evidence of sufficient development to warrant our claims ...

SARAH GRIMKÉ, Letter to Woman's Rights Convention, 1852, *History of Woman Suffrage*, I, 1881

You may say that the mass of the women of this State do not make the demand; it comes from a few sour, disappointed old maids and childless women. You are mistaken; the mass speak through us.

> ELIZABETH CADY STANTON, "Address to the Legislature of the State of New York," 1854, *History of Woman Suffrage*, I, 1881

In the United States the government is in the hands of the people, and though we would not, for a moment, encourage the slightest disregard for the laws of the country, yet we would say to the laboring classes, particularly of women, when your wages are such that you cannot, by constant labor, earn the necessaries of life, make a strike—call for higher wages—but to do so, you must be united in effort.

> VIRGINIA PENNY, *Think and Act*, 1869

Women want moral and mental courage. They receive such wages as men offer, without considering whether it is a fair compensation. They feel that to demand higher wages is a barrier they cannot surmount. And perhaps they cannot, in individual cases, as matters now stand; but if they would unite, and work *earnestly, unselfishly,* and *persistently*, they could level the mountains, and fill the valleys, that impede their progress.

> Ibid.

. . . we have felt no temptation to linger over individual differences. These occur in all associations, and may be regarded in this case as an evidence of the growing self-assertion and individualism in woman.

> E. C. STANTON, S. B. ANTHONY, M. J. GAGE, ed., *History of Woman Suffrage*, I, 1881

. . . so long as women are practically arrayed against women, any adjustment of the questions involved in all work is impossible. Hours, wages, all the points at issue that make up the sum of wrong represented by many phases of modern industry, wait for the organization among women themselves; and such organization is impossible till the sense of kinship and mutual obligation has been born.

> HELEN CAMPBELL, *Prisoners of Poverty Abroad*, 1890

When this platform is too narrow for all to stand on, I shall not be on it.

> SUSAN B. ANTHONY, defense of E. C. Stanton, National American Woman Suffrage Association Convention, 1896, in Alma Lutz, *Created Equal*, 1940

If when you go out to organize, you go with a broad spirit, you will create and call out breadth and toleration. You had better organize one woman on a broad platform than 10,000 on a narrow platform of intolerance and bigotry.

Ibid. (This same speech appears in slightly different form in Ida Husted Harper, ed., *Life and Work of Susan B. Anthony*, vol. II, 1898, and in *History of Woman Suffrage*, IV, 1902.)

Every woman can do something for the cause. She who is true to it at her own fireside, who speaks the right word to her guests, to her children and her neighbors' children, does an educational work as valuable as that of the woman who speaks from the platform.

SUSAN B. ANTHONY, National American Woman Suffrage Association Convention, 1899, *History of Woman Suffrage*, IV, 1902

The hardest of the battles have been fought, and while there is still need for both generals and soldiers, the greatest necessity is for the body of women to take possession and hold the ground that has been won.

SUSAN B. ANTHONY, "The Position of Women in the Political Life of the United States," *Women in Politics*, ed. Countess of Aberdeen, 1900

["Our movement"] represents an organic living force with all the strength behind it which vitality and vitality alone can give. We do not seek to drive into society something foreign to its own nature. We claim to be a part of the society in which we live, a living outgrowth of its energy . . .

SUSAN B. ANTHONY, "Political Enfranchisement of Women," *Women in Politics*, ed. Countess of Aberdeen, 1900

Girls, we ought to organize for them that comes after us.

MAGGIE CONDON, organizing Local 183, a union of women working in Chicago packing plants, circa 1902, in Alice Henry, *The Trade Union Woman*, 1917

. . . it cannot be too strongly emphasized that to many women the trade union, with the opportunity that it offers of serving a great cause, and making personal sacrifices for the good of a great class, makes rich with idealism and hope lives that are poor enough in all ways but this.

History of Trade Unionism Among Women in Boston, n.d., material suggests 1906

[A labor] organization means much too for women because it gives them the business experience of which they stand often in such bitter need, and which through the ages they have been denied, and if properly managed, it should awaken a class interest, a desire to improve what is wrong, not only for themselves, but for those who come after them.

Ibid.

The shirt-waist makers' strike was characteristic of all strikes in which women play an active part. It was marked by complete self-surrender to a cause, emotional endurance, fearlessness, and entire willingness to face danger and suffering.

HELEN MAROT, "A Woman's Strike—An Appreciation of the Shirtwaist Makers of New York," *Proceedings of the Academy of Political Science*, I, 1910

I have not a great deal of trust in either men or women in the mass myself, but I have less trust in the leaders of the mass. There is far more danger of corruption and one-sidedness, of narrowness and final shipwreck in absolutely unlimited autocracy than in the stupidest forms of democracy.

TERESA BILLINGTON-GREIG, *The Militant Suffrage Movement*, 1911

I do not believe that the best avenue for the emancipation of women is through emotionalism, personal tyranny, and fanaticism.

Ibid.

. . . I am deeply convinced that our cause will cease to make such rapid progress as heretofore if individual propagandism . . . is altogether abandoned, while we, sitting at home, or largely absorbed in other business, leave the cause mainly to the working of office machinery, and expect its triumph to be achieved by agencies. . . . It is not by official machinery that we shall conquer, though that is necessary *as a scaffolding of operations*, but by self-sacrifice and unwearying missionary zeal, without which no great cause was ever won.

JOSEPHINE E. BUTLER, *Personal Reminiscences of a Great Crusade*, 1911

I have observed that we are sometimes even betrayed into the error . . . of discouraging the initiative of honest and humble persons who have been filled with the desire to do something independently for the cause. Their ardour must have been checked rather than stimulated by being directed to follow in the path of a centralised organisation, the very existence of which tends to make people think their own personal efforts are not required.

Ibid.

It is this abiding consciousness of an end to be attained, reaching beyond her personal life and individual interests, which constitutes the religious element of the Woman's Movement of our day, and binds with the common bond of an impersonal enthusiasm into one solid body the women of whatsoever race, class, and nation who are struggling after the readjustment of woman to life.
    OLIVE SCHREINER, *Woman and Labour*, 1911

Many ... [women], even the older ones, are being made slowly conscious of the subtle and impalpable filaments that secretly bind their experiences and moods into larger relations, and they are filled with a new happiness analogous to that of little children when they are first taught to join hands in ordered play.
    Is such enthusiastic participation in organized effort but one manifestation of that desire for liberty and for a larger participation in life, found in great women's souls all over the world?
    JANE ADDAMS, *The Long Road of Woman's Memory*, 1916

Possibly women's organizations of all types are but providing ever-widening channels through which woman's moral energy may flow, revivifying life by new streams fed in the upper reaches of her undiscovered capacities. In either case, we may predict that to control old impulses so that they may be put to social uses, to serve the present through memories hoarding woman's genuine experiences, may liberate energies hitherto unused and may result in a notable enrichment of the pattern of human culture.
    Ibid.

No committee ever has, or ever will, run a revolution.
    ANNIE KENNEY, *Memories of a Militant*, 1924

It is difficult to argue with those in favour of a cause, easy with those against.
    Ibid.

To be autocratic, self-assertive, dictatorial is necessary on the battlefield, whether the fight be waged in Parliament Square or in Flanders, but once Peace is signed each soldier must be free to act as he thinks best and to judge for himself.
    Ibid.

The Women's Social and Political Union leapt into being like a flame. It released vast stores of unconscious energy, just as the war did. It cohered fiercely, ignoring thinking, feeling, and good order. It was not premeditated nor

194

controllable—*it happened* at the bidding of the unconscious. It swept where it listed, and when its work was done it died down and out . . .
>Dr. MARY GORDON, letter to Betty Balfour, *Letters of Constance Lytton*, ed. Betty Balfour, 1925

[The working mother] cannot now destroy industrialism, which dragged her work and her after it to the mill; but she can claim her right to control it in the name of life and the destiny of her children.
>DORA RUSSELL, *Hypatia*, 1925

I believed, then and always, that the movement required, not more serious militancy by the few, but a stronger appeal to the great masses to join the struggle.
>E. SYLVIA PANKHURST, *The Suffrage Movement*, 1931

Loyalty and comradeship, like the lift given by association to daily action and daily endurance through their connexion with a great idea, are precious gains that Trade Unionism can bring to women. To them, perhaps, they are even more important than to men.
>MARY AGNES HAMILTON, *Women at Work*, 1941

. . . the task of the organiser of women has got to be, in the main, that of organising scattered and often isolated domestic, clerical, commercial and casual workers, since it is among them that the bulk of women workers are found.
>Ibid.

The Trade Union is as important to the woman in the home as to the woman in industry. In its steady struggle for better conditions and for the just price for the job, it is fighting her battle, as well as that of the paid worker. In its struggle for political change that will cause both a fairer distribution of the national product, and a greater product, it is also fighting her battle.
>Ibid.

Dominance and leadership are not the prerogatives of the male sex—not even among mammals. Dominance and aggressiveness shift back and forth according to the species and according to individuals. In some species, one sex is dominant during one season, the other during the next.
>ELISABETH MANN BORGESE, *Ascent of Woman*, 1963

Insofar as evolution proceeds through co-operation, it proceeds through the female.
> Ibid.

Any revolutionary theory or theory of women that doesn't include me is by definition wrong because it must spell my name too . . . I do not accept a revolution that will make me a special class of person and say that eighty-five percent of other women are going to be in a drone class.
> BETTY FRIEDAN, panel discussion, *Proceedings at the Cornell Conference on Women*, ed. Sheila Tobias, Ella Kusnetz, Deborah Spitz, 1969

This standard hierarchical structure entailed that the decisions, thus the views of a few, determined the labors of the majority. This was unfair and thus demoralizing to the bulk of the membership.
> TI-GRACE ATKINSON, discussing the structure of NOW, "Juaniata II: The Equality Issue," February 1970, *Amazon Odyssey*, 1974

Women don't admit to backing off issues because it threatens their personal lives. Instead, it's only because those poor slobs "out there" aren't ready for it.
> TI-GRACE ATKINSON, "University of Rhode Island: Movement Politics and Other Sleights of Hand," March 1970, *Amazon Odyssey*, 1974

Women's Liberation is finally only personal. It is hard to fight an enemy who has outposts in your head.
> SALLY KEMPTON, "Cutting Loose: A Private View of the Women's Uprising," *Esquire*, July 1970

Because we have lived so intimately with our oppressors, in isolation from each other, we have been kept from seeing our personal suffering as a political condition. This creates the illusion that a woman's relationships with her man is a matter of interplay between two unique personalities, and can be worked out individually. In reality, every such relationship is a *class* relationship, and the conflicts between individual men and women are *political* conflicts that can only be solved collectively.
> "Redstockings Manifesto," reprinted in *Notes from the Second Year*, 1970

There is a sense in which diversity within a movement is a decided strength, for there is no one problem and no one solution to the kinds of changes necessary in American society to improve the status of women.
> ALICE S. ROSSI, "Women in the Seventies: Problems and Possibilities," keynote speech, Barnard College Conference on Women, April 1970

... women enjoy each other's company when they are not rivals for the attention of a man. They can work together for a common cause; they like and trust each other.

> MARY LOU THOMPSON, "Forecast for Feminism," *Voices of the New Feminism*, ed. Mary Lou Thompson, 1970

Consciousness raising undoes what the sociologists call "the privatization of women." Since their political status depends on men, their grievances are by definition personal, private, and trivial. . . . Once women express these feelings to each other in a group of women only, it becomes obvious that they are political, the consequences of a power structure, and hence a political system. . . . The remedy lies not in grinning and bearing it, "learning to accept one's role as a woman," as the psychoanalysts put it, but in political action.

> CAROLINE BIRD, *Born Female*, rev. ed., 1971

The sight of women talking together has always made men uneasy; nowadays it means rank subversion.

> GERMAINE GREER, *The Female Eunuch*, 1971

Women, having been trained and socialized to passivity and demureness, are particularly vulnerable to any offer to take a back seat once more. Many groups rotate organizational positions, interviews with the press, radio and television, speaking engagements, etc., so that no one develops a too powerful expertise and no one confirms her own inhibitions. . . . collective work countermands both the hierarchic nature of the oppressive society and the isolation and/or subservience that women are forced into within the home and in their personal relationships.

> JULIET MITCHELL, *Woman's Estate*, 1971

"Consciousness-raising" is speaking the unspoken . . .

> Ibid.

If women don't risk dealing with structures and leadership, we will essentially accept male supremacist rule: without assertive female leadership, men will continue not only to rule in world power terms, but to determine, as they have been doing for the last few years, what is the women's movement, what are the movement structures that get recognition, and who are the women's leaders.

> CHARLOTTE BUNCH, interview, Feminist Radio Network, December 1972, in *Quest*, II, Spring 1976.

Women who are interested in politics join the League of Women Voters; men who are interested in politics run for office.
> CHARLOTTE HOLT CLINEBELL, *Meet Me in the Middle*, 1973

... structurelessness becomes a way of masking power ...
> JO FREEMAN, "The Tyranny of Structurelessness," *Berkeley Journal of Sociology*, XVII, 1973

A laissez-faire group is about as realistic as a laissez-faire society; the idea becomes a smoke screen for the strong or the lucky to establish unquestioned hegemony over others.
> Ibid.

The energy expended in convincing or persuading or working on the man ... is energy best directed toward the building and refining of new interactive structures among the very people, namely women, who form the subject of this new offensive revolution.
> JILL JOHNSTON, *Lesbian Nation*, 1973

The present feminist revolution is a battle not only to wrest control from the men but to confront the women ourselves with the spectacle of our collaboration with the men in maintaining our helpless position. The tool of revolution is consciousness.
> Ibid.

The selfsufficiency of women in the end will have to mean much more than any apparent individual solution to the problem. We remain fugitives.
It is the banding together of fugitives which constitutes the phenomenon of revolutionary opposition.
> Ibid.

Usually either the woman is isolated or the opponent difficult to confront. It is hardly feasible to take concerted group action against a family, a lover, or a boss; it is equally difficult to take on such elusive oppressors as Madison Avenue or pornographic filmsters. Women rarely find themselves naturally grouped, and each woman must to a great extent fight her battles alone. The support of her sisters may not be available until the rap session next Wednesday.
> NANCY MCWILLIAMS, "Contemporary Feminism, Consciousness-Raising, and Changing Views of the Political," *Women in Politics*, ed. Jane S. Jaquette, 1974

The sad fact is that women . . . are organizationally far stronger than they dare realize. . . . We seem to be waiting for God to show us through some dramatic sign how to combine these forces, and they would indeed be formidable forces.

CLARA MARIA HENNING, "Canon Law and the Battle of the Sexes," *Religion and Sexism*, ed. R. R. Ruether, 1974

In making rape a *speakable* crime, not a matter of shame, the women's movement has already fired the first retaliatory shots in a war as ancient as civilization.

SUSAN BROWNMILLER, *Against Our Will*, 1975.

There is a tendency throughout the movement to overindulge in confession, to elevate The Rap to a religious end in itself, to reach a point where self-knowledge dissolves into high-grade narcissism.

NORA EPHRON, *Crazy Salad*, 1975

The rap groups have become mechanisms for social change in and of themselves. They are structures created specifically for the purpose of altering the participants' perceptions and conceptions of themselves and society at large.

JO FREEMAN, *The Politics of Women's Liberation*, 1975

Most women came into the movement via the rap groups; and most go out from there. There is no easy way to move from a rap group to a project; women either stumble onto one or start their own. Most don't do either.

Ibid.

The deliberate withdrawal of women from men has almost always been seen as a potentially dangerous or hostile act, a conspiracy, a subversion, a needless and grotesque thing, while the exclusion of women from men's groups is rationalized by arguments familiar to us all, whether the group is a priesthood, a dining club, a fishing expedition, an academic committee, or a Mafioso rendezvous.

ADRIENNE RICH, *Of Woman Born*, 1976

When women associate with men in serious
matters, as they do now in frivolous, both will
grow stronger and the world's work will be better done.

SUSAN B. ANTHONY, interview with a reporter
for *Cleveland Leader*, 1884, in Ida Husted
Harper, *Life and Work of Susan B. Anthony*,
vol. II, 1898

11   Reformation

Education

Let us then, by being allowed to take the same exercise as boys, not only during infancy, but youth, arrive at perfection of body, that we may know how
far the natural superiority of man extends.

MARY WOLLSTONECRAFT, *A Vindication of the Rights of Woman*, 1792

There is no reason for maintaining any sexual distinctions in the bodily exer-
cises of children; if it is right to give both sexes all the corporal advantages,
which nature has formed them to enjoy, let them both partake of the same
national means of obtaining a flow of health and animal spirits, to enable
them to perform the functions of life. Let girls be no longer confined to sed-
entary employments in a nursery, or at best permitted to take a gentle walk in
a garden, as an apology for more vigorous exertions; whilst their brothers are
allowed the unrestrained enjoyment of their active powers, regardless of soil-
ing their clothes, or the inconveniences of the various seasons.

PRISCILLA WAKEFIELD, *Reflections on the Present Condition of the Female
Sex*, 1798

... though it is by no means requisite that the American women should emu-
late the men in the pursuit of the whale, the felling of the forest, or the shoot-
ing of wild turkeys, they might, with advantage, be taught in early youth to

excel in the race, to hit a mark, to swim, and in short to use every exercise which could impart vigor to their frames and independence to their minds.

FRANCES WRIGHT, *Views of Society and Manners in America*, 1821

I often lament that in the rearing of women so little attention should be commonly paid to the exercise of the bodily organs; to invigorate the body is to invigorate the mind, and Heaven knows that the weaker sex have much cause to be rendered strong in both.

Ibid.

. . . as respects their daughters, they [parents] have nothing to do with the unjustice of laws, nor the absurdities of society. Their duty is plain, evident, decided. In a daughter they have in charge a human being; in a son, the same. Let them train up these *human beings*, under the expanded wings of liberty. Let them seek *for* them and *with* them just knowledge; encouraging, from the cradle upwards, that useful curiosity which will lead them unbidden in the paths of free enquiry; and place them, safe and superior to the storms of life, in the security of well regulated, self-possessed minds, well grounded, well reasoned, conscientious opinions, and self-approved, consistent practice.

FRANCES WRIGHT, *Course of Popular Lectures*, 1829

Rights are not dependent upon equality of mind; nor do we admit inferiority, leaving that question to be settled by future developments, when a fair opportunity shall be given for the equal cultivation of the intellect, and the stronger powers of the mind shall be called into action.

LUCRETIA MOTT, letter to Woman's Suffrage Convention, 1850, *History of Woman Suffrage*, I, 1881

It is the fault of education that she [woman] is now intellectually inferior. Give her the same advantages as men, throw open the door of our colleges and schools of science and bid her enter, teach her that she was created for a higher purpose than to be a parlor ornament or mere plaything for man, show her that you regard her as an equal and that her opinions are entitled to consideration, in short, treat her as an intelligent, accountable being, and when all this has been done, if she prove herself not man's equal in intellect I will yield the point and admit her inferiority.

AMELIA BLOOMER, reply to Mr. T. S. Arthur's "Ruling a Wife," 1851, in D. C. Bloomer, *Life and Writings of Amelia Bloomer*, 1895

Women, like men, must be educated with a view to action, or their studies can not be called education, and no judgment can be formed of the scope of their faculties. The pursuit must be life's business, or it will be mere pastime or irksome task.

> HARRIET MARTINEAU, letter to Paulina Wright Davis, Second National Convention, Friends of Woman Suffrage, 1851, *History of Woman Suffrage*, I, 1881

Begin with the girls of *to-day,* and in twenty years we can revolutionize this nation. The childhood of woman must be free and untrammeled. The girl must be allowed to romp and play . . . ; her clothing must be more like that of the boy . . . that she may be out at all times, and enter freely into all kinds of sports. Teach her to go alone, by night and day, if need be, on the lonely highway, or through the busy streets of the crowded metropolis. The manner in which all courage and self-reliance is educated *out* of the girl, her path portrayed with dangers and difficulties that never exist, is melancholy indeed. Better, far, suffer occasional insults or die outright, than live the life of a *coward,* or never move without a protector. The best protector any woman can have, one that will serve her at all times and in all places, is *courage;* this she must get by her own experience, and experience comes by exposure.

> ELIZABETH CADY STANTON, letter to Woman's Suffrage Convention, 1851, *History of Woman Suffrage*, I, 1881

In . . . education, in industry, let woman's sphere be bounded only by her capacity. We desire there should no walls be thrown about it.

> LUCY STONE, Second National Convention, Friends of Woman Suffrage, 1851, *History of Woman Suffrage*, I, 1881

We should have a literature of our own, a printing-press and a publishing-house, and tract writers and distributors, as well as lectures and conventions; and yet I say this to a race of beggars, for women have no pecuniary resources.

> ELIZABETH OAKES SMITH, Woman's Rights Convention, 1852, *History of Woman Suffrage*, I, 1881

We think it all-important that woman obtain the right of suffrage, but she cannot do this at once. She must gradually prepare the way for such a step by showing that she is worthy of receiving and capable of exercising it. If she do this, prejudices will gradually give way and she will gain her cause.

> AMELIA BLOOMER, article in *The Lily*, 1853, in D. C. Bloomer, *Life and Writings of Amelia Bloomer*, 1895

Let the talents of women be fully developed, and no man will lose any place that he is qualified to fill in consequence, and no woman will obtain that place who has not peculiar fitness.

> Mrs. Elizabeth Jones, Woman's Suffrage Convention, 1860, *History of Woman Suffrage*, I, 1881

There is reason to hope, however, that the prejudices of medical authorities are gradually giving way, and that ere long they will be prepared to aid women in the acquirement of a thorough knowledge of a science which, as mothers and nurses, they are already so frequently called upon to practise.

> Emily Davies, LL.D., "Letters Addressed to a Daily Paper at Newcastle-upon-Tyne, 1860," *Thoughts on Some Questions Relating to Women, 1860–1908*, 1910

What we claim is, that no one knows, as yet, what women are, or what they can do,—least of all, those who have been wedded for years to that low standard of womanly achievement, which classical study tends to sustain. Because we do not know, because experiment is necessary, we claim that all educational institutions should be kept open for her; that she should be encouraged to avail herself of these, according to her own inclination; and that, so far as possible, she should pursue her studies, and test her powers, in company with man.

> Caroline Wells Dall, lectures 1856–1862, *The College, the Market, and the Court*, 1914

Here is the great difficulty in the education of woman, to lead her to a point from which she shall naturally develop self-respect, and learn self-help.

> Ibid.

Those who entertain the fear that an enlarged course of study would, by overworking the female brain, eventually produce wide-spread idiocy, should remember that mental disease is produced by want of occupation as well as by an excess of it.

> Emily Davies, LL.D., "The Influence of University Degrees on the Education of Women," 1863, *Thoughts on Some Questions Relating to Women, 1860–1908*, 1910

Our danger lies, not in the direction of despotism, in the one-man power, in centralization; but in the corruption of the people . . . .

It is in vain to look for a genuine republic in this country until the women are baptized into the idea, until they understand the genius of our institutions . . .

ELIZABETH CADY STANTON, American Equal Rights Association Convention, 1867, *History of Woman Suffrage*, II, 1882

The education which most women need is one which will fit them for business in professions or in industries.

JOSEPHINE E. BUTLER, ed., Introduction, *Woman's Work and Woman's Culture*, 1869

Let a girl be raised with a thorough, practical, but limited knowledge of household duties. It will not then be difficult if she becomes a wife, or takes charge of a house, to improve and extend her knowledge. But let her by all means gain a knowledge of some employment that she can turn to account, if remaining a single lady, or left a penniless widow.

VIRGINIA PENNY, *Think and Act*, 1869

To me the future looks hopeful, when women realize the cause of this tendency to disease, when they ask for knowledge of their own organisms, and inquire the way back to Nature. Let them but understand what they seek to know,—give them a knowledge of their own organisms, of the relation of one part to another, and a knowledge of the functions these organs are called upon to perform,—let them understand also the unvarying physical laws, and the certain retribution that follows their perversion, and thus enlightened, with their naturally quick perceptions, and their skill in adapting means to ends, they will soon render the dress of every woman and child conformable to the requirements of health.

ARVILLA B. HAYNES, M.D., Lecture IV, *Dress-Reform*, ed. Abba Goold Woolson, 1874

Let us insist then on special encouragement for the education of our [Black] women and special care in their training. . . . Teach them that there is a race with special needs which they and only they can help . . .

[ANNA JULIA COOPER] A Black Woman of the South, *A Voice from the South*, 1892

I feel . . . that we shall never become an immense power in the world until we concentrate all our money and editorial forces upon one great national daily newspaper, so we can sauce back our opponents every day in the year . . .

SUSAN B. ANTHONY, National American Woman Suffrage Association Convention, 1893, *History of Woman Suffrage*, IV, 1902

You say "women must be emancipated from their superstitions before enfranchisement will be of any benefit," and I say just the reverse, that women must be enfranchised before they can be emancipated from their superstitions. Women would be no more superstitious today than men, if they had been men's political and business equals and gone outside the four walls of home and the other four of the church into the great world, and come in contact with and discussed men and measures on the plane of this mundane sphere, instead of living in the air with Jesus and the angels.

> SUSAN B. ANTHONY, letter from California to Elizabeth Cady Stanton, 1896, in Ida Husted Harper, *Life and Works of Susan B. Anthony*, vol. II, 1898

Though motherhood is the most important of all the professions,—requiring more knowledge than any other department in human affairs,— yet there is not sufficient attention given to the preparation for this office.

> ELIZABETH CADY STANTON, *Eighty Years and More*, 1898

One of the greatest obstacles . . . can be overcome only by recognizing it as fundamental that if women are to compete with men, they must be given the same training as men. If girls as well as boys are going to enter industrial life they must be trained to enter it self-respectingly.

> *History of Trade Unionism Among Women in Boston*, n.d., material suggests 1906

It matters nothing, and less than nothing, to us as women, whether of those children we bring into the world, our sons should excel in virtue, intelligence, and activity, our daughters, or our daughters our sons; so that, in each child we bring to life, not one potentiality shall be lost, nor squandered on a lesser when it might have been expended on a higher and more beneficent task.

> OLIVE SCHREINER, *Woman and Labour*, 1911

We may make a pretty shrewd guess at the reasons why some scientific men do not wish women to study science, for have not the medical and scientific women already, by their work, exploded many of the old fictions about women, and so put heart and hope into millions of women who felt their powers, but hardly dared believe in them, because of the dead weight of what they were told was science? They have now learned that all that is put forth by a scientific man is not science, and that when sex comes into his calculations it is apt to be a very serious disturbance to clear thought.

> H. M. SWANWICK, *The Future of the Women's Movement*, 1913

.. education is not won for woman, till it brings to her precisely the same blessings that it bears to the feet of man; till it gives her honor, respect, and bread; till position becomes the rightful inheritance of capacity, and social influence follows a knowledge of mathematics and the languages.
CAROLINE WELLS DALL, *The College, The Market, and the Court,* 1914

Just like the new learning of the Renaissance to men's minds in Europe was the opening of high school and university to the feminine mind of to-day.
DORA RUSSELL, *Hypatia,* 1925

There is no reason to expect that women, emerging from tutelage, will be wiser than men. One should expect the contrary. It is necessary to grow accustomed to freedom before one may walk in it sure-footedly.
SUZANNE LA FOLLETTE, *Concerning Women,* 1926

I should prefer in many respects to make the boy's education more like that of an old-fashioned girl! On the girl and woman devolved almost all the home-making arts, the boy having his socks darned for him, his food cooked, his bed made. These are not *sex* requirements: both men and women require stockings, food and beds. The boy would be an immensely better husband and member of the community if he at first hand had some of the education given to most girls in the domestic arts.
MARIE CARMICHAEL STOPES, *Sex and the Young,* 1926

Educated women have shown a tendency to raise questions rather than children.
ELIZABETH HAWES, *Anything But Love,* 1948

Free education threatens the caste boundaries in a society. Students discover that alternatives of action can be contemplated by a simple exercise of the mind. Contemplating alternative modes of behavior may mean choosing a mode that goes against the grain of the caste system. Women are supposed to remain childlike and intuitive. If insights remain haphazard and are a vague feeling-things-out, the caste status feels safe.
RUTH HERSCHBERGER, *Adam's Rib,* 1948

Other factors also must be considered if any predictions are attempted—the availability of education, training and counseling, the willingness of employers to hire and promote on the basis of merit and capacity—but there is no denying that the educated woman will be the pacesetter for the future.

ESTHER PETERSON, "Working Women," *The Woman in America*, ed. Robert Jay Lifton, 1965

If we want more women to enter science, not only as teachers of science but as scientists, some quite basic changes must take place in the ways girls are reared. If girls are to develop the analytic and mathematical abilities science requires, parents and teachers must encourage them in independence and self-reliance instead of pleasing feminine submission; stimulate and reward girls' efforts to satisfy their curiosity about the world as they do those of boys; encourage in girls not unthinking conformity but alert intelligence that asks why and rejects the easy answer.

ALICE S. ROSSI, "Women in Science: Why So Few?" *Science*, 148, May 28, 1965

. . . what women require is *ludic cerebration*, the free play of intuition in our own space, giving rise to thinking that is vigorous, informed, multidimensional, independent, creative, tough. Ludic cerebration is thinking out of experience.

MARY DALY, new introduction, *The Church and the Second Sex*, 1975

Economics

. . . women of rank and fortune . . . should determine to employ women only, wherever they can be employed; they should procure female instructors for their children; they should frequent no shops that are not served by women; they should wear no clothes that are not made by them; they should reward them as liberally as they do the men who have hitherto supplanted them.

PRISCILLA WAKEFIELD, *Reflections on the Present Condition of the Female Sex*, 1798

Farming . . . is commensurate with the powers of the female mind; nor is the practice of inspecting agricultural processes, incompatible with the delicacy of their frames, if their constitution be good.

Ibid.

... I trust the time is coming, when the occupation of an instructer [*sic*] to children will be deemed the most honorable of human employment.

> ANGELINA E. GRIMKÉ, Letter XIII, 1837, *Letters to Catherine E. Beecher,* 1837

It would afford women great pleasure to be able to pay their own expense on pleasure excursions and to the concert-room, instead of being always compelled to allow the gentlemen to foot the bills for them. Women must have equal pay for equal work.

> MRS. COE, Woman's Rights Convention, 1854, *History of Woman Suffrage,* I, 1881

I was disappointed when I came to seek a profession worthy an immortal being—every employment was closed to me, except those of the teacher, the seamstress, and the housekeeper. In education, in marriage, in religion, in everything, disappointment is the lot of woman. It shall be the business of my life to deepen this disappointment in every woman's heart until she bows down to it no longer. I wish that women, instead of being walking show-cases, instead of begging of their fathers and brothers the latest and gayest new bonnet, would ask of them their rights.

> LUCY STONE, Woman's Rights Convention, 1855, *History of Woman Suffrage,* I, 1881

I ask for woman, then, free, untrammelled access to all fields of labor; and I ask it, first, on the ground that she needs to be fed, and that the question which is at this moment before the great body of working women is "death or dishonor:" for lust is a better paymaster than the mill-owner or the tailor, and economy never yet shook hands with crime.

> CAROLINE WELLS DALL, lectures 1856–1862, *The College, The Market, and the Court,* 1914

Let no man taunt woman with inability to labor, till the coal-mines and the metal-works, the rotting cocoons and fuzzing-cards, give up their dead; till he shares with her, equally at least, the perils of manfactures and the press of the market. As partners, they must test and prove their comparative power.

> Ibid.

Woman will always be dependent until she holds a purse of her own. I would therefore have every girl of sixteen begin this day some profitable business. ... Encourage our young girls, therefore, to enter all honest and profitable employment, and you will have struck a blow at vice and licentiousness, stronger and more effectual than any that has yet been dealt.

> ELIZABETH CADY STANTON, periodical *Una*, circa 1860, in Alma Lutz, *Created Equal*, 1940

. . . we wish and confidently expect, to see the day when idleness will be considered not ladylike, but unwomanly, and when those at least who desire to learn and to follow some honourable calling will not be debarred by the false pride of parents or the prejudices of trade.

> EMILY DAVIES, LL.D., 1861, *Thoughts on Some Questions Relating to Women, 1860–1908*, 1910

I recognize for myself no narrow sphere. Where you may work, my brother, I may work.

> LUCY N. COLEMAN, Women's National Loyal League, 1863, *History of Woman Suffrage*, II, 1882

A proper education must prepare woman for labor, skilled or manual; and the experience of a laborer should introduce her to citizenship, for it provides her with rights to protect, privileges to secure, and property to be taxed. If she is a laborer, she must have an interest in the laws which control labor.

> CAROLINE WELLS DALL, Woman's Rights Convention, 1866, *History of Woman Suffrage*, II, 1882

. . . if you enact laws against social evils, whatever those laws are, let them be alike for man and for woman. . . . Do not degrade woman any more than she is already degraded. Perchance she is driven, through your injustice, to that step to maintain her wretched existence, because every office of emolument is barred against her. Let woman have the franchise; let all the avenues of society be thrown open before her, according to her powers and her capacities, and there will be no need to talk about social evils.

> ERNESTINE L. ROSE, American Equal Rights Association Convention, 1867, *History of Woman Suffrage*, II, 1882

The ballot in the hand of woman will bring neither the millennium nor pandemonium the next day; but it will surely right many wrongs. It will open to her the colleges, the professions, the profitable and honorable walks of life, and give her better wages for her work.

> ELIZABETH CADY STANTON, criticism of Horace Greeley's report on the Constitutional Convention, *New York Independent*, 1867, *History of Woman Suffrage*, II, 1882

If women could earn their bread and buy the houses over their heads, in honorable and lucrative avocations; if they stood in the eye of the law men's equals, there would be better work, more hopeful hearts, more Christian magnanimity, and less petty selfishness and meanness than, I confess with sorrow and tears, are found among women to-day.

> ANNA DICKENSON, Illinois Woman's Rights Convention, 1869, *History of Woman Suffrage*, III, 1887

To me nothing seems so essential for a human being, whether man or woman, as knowing how justly and honorably to provide for the physical wants. Every woman should be able to turn her labor, either mental or manual, into money.

> VIRGINIA PENNY, *Think and Act*, 1869

Women of talent should not be content to occupy merely subordinate departments of labor, nor devote their time and talents to executing only mechanical drudgery. Let them qualify themselves for superior work, then take such a position as their abilities will command, and with dignity and firmness, maintain that position.

> Ibid.

It would be well for a woman to feel that she has the whole world to work in.

> Ibid.

Whoever controls work and wages, controls morals. Therefore, we must have women employers, superintendents, committees, legislators; wherever girls go to seek the means of subsistence, there must be some woman. Nay, more; we must have women preachers, lawyers, doctors—that wherever women go to seek counsel—spiritual, legal, physical—there, too, they will be sure to find the best and noblest of their own sex to minister to them.

> SUSAN B. ANTHONY, "Social Purity," 1875, in Ida Husted Harper, *Life and Work of Susan B. Anthony*, vol. II, 1898

The refusal of the Superior Court of Philadelphia to allow Carrie S. Burnham to practice law, because there was no precedent, was a weak evasion of common law and common sense. One hundred years ago there was no precedent for a man practicing law in the State of Pennsylvania, and yet we have not learned that there was any difficulty in establishing a precedent. I do not now remember any precedent for the Declaration of Independence of the United Colonies, and yet during a century it has not been overturned.

> BELVA A. LOCKWOOD, National Woman Suffrage Association Convention, 1876, *History of Woman Suffrage*, III, 1887

I have always held, with Florence Nightingale, that the woman who works beside men, must expect no favors on account of her sex, and accept none.

FANNY M. BAGBY, editor-in-chief, *St. Louis Chronicle*, letter to National Woman Suffrage Association Convention, *Report*, 1884

The moral qualities are more apt to grow when a human being is useful, and they increase in the woman who helps to support the family rather than in the one who gives herself to idleness and fashionable frivolities.

ELIZABETH CADY STANTON, to Senate Committee on Woman Suffrage, 1890, *History of Woman Suffrage*, IV, 1902

Work the object of which is merely to serve one's self is the lowest. Work the object of which is merely to serve one's family is the next lowest. Work the object of which is to serve more and more people, in widening range . . . is social service in the fullest sense, and the highest form of service that we can reach . . .

CHARLOTTE PERKINS GILMAN, *Women and Economics*, 1898

If married women could work some hours a day, or some days a week, or some months a year, or some years and not others, as circumstances indicated . . . it would seem advantageous, in more ways than one, for them not to drop out of industry at marriage. Both marriage and employment might become sufficiently universal to make it usual to train every girl for both . . .

EMILY GREENE BALCH, "The Education and Efficiency of Women," *Proceedings of the Academy of Political Science*, I, 1910

. . . for the present, we have no adequate scientific data from which to draw any conclusion, and any attempt to divide the occupations in which male and female intellects and wills should be employed, must be to attempt a purely artificial and arbitrary division: a division not more rational and scientific than an attempt to determine by the colour of his eyes and the shape and strength of his legs, whether a lad should be an astronomer or an engraver.

OLIVE SCHREINER, *Woman and Labour*, 1911

. . . *this* is our demand: We demand that, in that strange new world that is arising alike upon the man and the woman, where nothing is as it was, and all things are assuming new shapes and relations, that in this new world we also shall have our share of honoured and socially useful human toil, our full half of the labour of the Children of Woman. We demand nothing more than this, and we will take nothing less. *This is our* "WOMAN'S RIGHT!"

Ibid.

... when women demand "equality" with men, what they are asking is, that they shall have equal opportunities to do the things they feel able to do, and also that they should have for their peculiarly feminine work—the work which men cannot do—more help, more training, more expenditure of public money, and more scope altogether to do it in ways adapted to the modern world they live in.

H. M. SWANWICK, *The Future of the Women's Movement*, 1913

... it is the progressive working woman rather than the woman of the middle class who will in the future make the most important contribution to the thought of feminism and to a solution of our practical difficulties.

DORA RUSSELL, *Hypatia*, 1925

... real freedom is not a matter of the shifting of advantage from one sex to the other or from one class to another. Real freedom means the disappearance of advantage, and primarily of economic advantage.

SUZANNE LA FOLLETTE, *Concerning Women*, 1926

... economic freedom would set domesticity in competition with the interests of women rather than their needs ...

Ibid.

The woman labourer proves the *need* of women to earn; the business woman or professional woman who works because she wants to work, is establishing the *right* of women to earn.

Ibid.

In fact the opportunities that await the newly liberated and the soon to be liberated woman are as fascinating as they are numerous. She may go into preventive health work and hug to her consciousness the knowledge that the hours formerly spent in unnecessary and therefore meaningless drudgery, or in unhappy speculations as to why after all she was alive ... can now be spent in saving lives or in making them healthier and happier.

ALICE BEAL PARSONS, *Woman's Dilemma*, 1926

We must not for a moment think that unpaid housework is protected leisure, nor that a life of leisure is a reasonable aim for women. There is a given amount of labor to be done and women ought to shoulder their share.

HARRIOT STANTON BLATCH AND ALMA LUTZ, *Challenging Years*, 1940

If a job is to be the way out of the trap for a woman, it must be a job that she can take seriously as part of a life plan, work in which she can grow as part of society.

BETTY FRIEDAN, *The Feminine Mystique*, 1963

[A woman] must have a lot more drive to succeed. She must at a comparatively early age have encouragement, self-confidence, and commitment to a goal to go her own way against the full weight of society's opinion and expectations. That is asking much more of a young woman than we ask of a young man. Not many of us can do it at any age.

ELIZABETH DUNCAN KOONTZ, "Women as a Minority Group," *Voices of the New Feminism*, ed. Mary Lou Thompson, 1970

If all adults were required to work, and free to choose the kind of work they wanted, many women would leave their homes and thereby create more paying jobs. Baby-sitters and service workers, many of them now considered unemployable because of age or lack of education, would be drawn out of their isolation and into the labor force. But all of these newcomers would not necessarily find themselves doing what housewives used to do at home. Many would find jobs in services especially organized to do housework efficiently.

CAROLINE BIRD, *Born Female*, rev. ed., 1971

Housekeeping is the last unpaid customary job, and if most women worked, it would be professionalized, too. The errands, the repairs, the appointment-making, the bookkeeping, the snack-making, the chauffeuring and other odd jobs which make women feel disorganized and undervalued, could all be turned into professionally run services.

Ibid.

For a lot of middle-class women in this country, Women's Liberation is a matter of concern. For women on welfare it's a matter of *survival*.

JOHNNIE TILLMON, "Welfare Is a Women's Issue," *Ms.*, Spring 1972

When a woman breaks bread and serves wine, then cleans the vessels when all have been fed, we suddenly recognize that she has served a meal and done the dishes, just as women do at home. When a woman hears confession or gives absolution we recognize that women are the listeners and comforters at home, too.

EMILY C. HEWITT AND SUZANNE R. HIATT, *Women Priests: Yes Or No?* 1973

Our goal today should never be to open up the exclusive medical profession to women, but to open up medicine—to all women.

> BARBARA EHRENREICH AND DEIRDRE ENGLISH, *Witches, Midwives and Nurses*, 1973

Women have always been healers. They were the unlicensed doctors and anatomists of Western history. They were abortionists, nurses and counsellors. They were pharmacists, cultivating healing herbs and exchanging the secrets of their uses. They were midwives, travelling from home to home and village to village. . . . They were called "wise women" by the people, witches or charlatans by the authorities. Medicine is part of our heritage as women, our history, our birthright.

> Ibid.

War and Politics

I hope women will not copy the vices of men. I hope they will not go to war; I wish men would not. I hope they will not be contentious politicians; I am sorry that men are. I hope they will not regard their freedom as a license to do wrong! I am ashamed to acknowledge that men do.

> MRS. ELIZABETH JONES, Woman's Rights Convention, 1860, *History of Woman Suffrage*, I, 1881

They tell us that women are not fit for politics. This may be true; and as it is next to impossible to change the nature of a woman, why wouldn't it be a good idea to so change politics that it shall be fit for women.

> Arkansas *Ladies' Journal*, n.d., but after 1868, *History of Woman Suffrage*, III, 1887

Voting is a mere incident in the lives of men. It does not prevent the blacksmith from shoeing horses, or the farmer from planting fields, or the lawyer from attending courts; so I see no reason why it needs to prevent women from attending to their domestic duties. On certain subjects, such as intemperance, licentiousness and war, women would be almost universally sure to exert their influence in the right directions, for the simple reason that they peculiarly suffer from the continuance of these evils.

> LYDIA MARIA CHILD, letter to National Woman Suffrage Association Meeting, 1874, *History of Woman Suffrage*, III, 1887

... the majority of women would not declare war, would not enlist soldiers and would not vote supplies and equipments, because many of the most thoughtful believe there *is* a better way, and that women can bring a moral power to bear that shall make war needless.

> CATHERINE A. STEBBINS, to House Judiciary Committee, 1880, *History of Woman Suffrage*, III, 1887

It is better to have the power of self-protection than to depend on any man, whether he be the Governor in his chair of State, or the hunted outlaw wandering through the night, hungry and cold, and with murder in his heart.

> LILLIE DEVEREUX BLAKE, National Woman Suffrage Association Convention, 1884, *History of Woman Suffrage*, IV, 1902

Woman should not, even by inference, or for the sake of argument, seem to disparage what is weak. For woman's cause is the cause of the weak; and when all the weak shall have received their due consideration, then woman will have her "rights," and the Indian will have his rights, and the Negro will have his rights, and all the strong will have learned at last to deal justly, to love mercy, and to walk humbly . . .

> [ANNA JULIA COOPER] A Black Woman of the South, *A Voice from the South*, 1892

It is not the intelligent woman vs. the ignorant woman; nor the white woman vs. the black, the brown, and the red,—it is not even the cause of woman vs. man. Nay, 'tis woman's strongest vindication for speaking that *the world needs to hear her voice*.

> Ibid.

Unsanitary housing, poisonous sewage, contaminated water, infant mortality, the spread of contagion, adulterated food, impure milk, smoke-laden air, ill-ventilated factories, dangerous occupations, juvenile crime, unwholesome crowding, prostitution and drunkenness are the enemies which the modern cities must face and overcome, would they survive. Logically their electorate should be made up of those who can bear a valiant part in this arduous contest, those who in the past have at least attempted to care for children, to clean houses, to prepare foods, to isolate the family from moral dangers . . .

> JANE ADDAMS, "The Modern City and the Municipal Franchise for Women," National American Woman Suffrage Association Convention, 1906, *History of Woman Suffrage*, V, 1922

We are here, not because we are law-breakers; we are here in our efforts to become law-makers.

> EMMELINE PANKHURST, address to court at her trial in 1908, *My Own Story*, 1914

The real goddesses of Liberty in this country do not spend a large amount of time standing on pedestals in public places; they use their torches to startle the bats in political cellars.

> ELLA S. STEWART, in reference to Bartholdi's Statue of Liberty, National American Woman Suffrage Association Convention, 1909, *History of Woman Suffrage*, V, 1922

Women, though hating war, quite as frequently as men are deluded by the plea that peace can be ensured only by huge armaments. It is a question whether woman suffrage would greatly lessen the vote for these supposed preventives of war, but there is no question that more reliance on reason and less on force would exalt respect for woman and would remove the objection that woman's physical inferiority has anything to do with suffrage.

> MRS. LUCIA AMES MEAD, National American Woman Suffrage Association Convention, 1909, *History of Woman Suffrage*, V, 1922

The claim that women will purify politics may be advanced from many points of view. It is often based merely upon the old sickly sentiment that has survived from the days when men in search of self-approval promulgated the angel-idiot theory. . . . there is something to be said for the theory that if a sex has been kept cleaning and scrubbing and scouring and sweeping for a long series of generations, there will be a tendency for the habit to assert itself when that sex secures a wider sphere of existence.

> TERESA BILLINGTON-GREIG, *The Militant Suffrage Movement*, 1911

. . . women with political power would not brook that men should live upon the wages of captured victims, should openly hire youths to ruin and debase young girls, should be permitted to transmit poison to unborn children.

> JANE ADDAMS, *A New Conscience and an Ancient Evil*, 1912

I readily admit that the maintenance of order is one of the first duties of every Government. But another is to redress the grievances from which disorder has sprung.

> MILLICENT GARRETT FAWCETT, to Prime Minister Asquith, 1913, in Fawcett, *The Women's Victory—and After*, 1920

The world needs woman's restraining hand. Man's instinct has been militant since primitive times. . . . Woman's instinct has been to conserve and protect life. It is much easier to fight than to make peace.

> CARRIE CHAPMAN CATT, address, partly in response to Dudley Field Malone's "military preparedness" speech, National American Woman Suffrage Association Convention, 1915, *History of Woman Suffrage*, V, 1922

". . . why a women's peace movement?" . . . women stand a little outside . . . of politics and of commercialism, which are really the causes of war. . . . Now it is a very remarkable thing that while women have been really the great sufferers from war, there has never before in the history of the world been a women's protest against war. . . . but today women are beginning to see life in a different way and they have decided that they do not have to accept suffering of this sort.

> MRS. WILLIAM I. THOMAS, International Conference of Women Workers, 1915, *Women, World War and Permanent Peace*, ed. M. W. Sewall, 1915

As the thought of God slowly unfolded in the mind of woman, that great Power would have been apprehended as the Life-giver, the Teacher, the Provider, the Protector—not the proud, angry, jealous, vengeful deity men have imagined. She would have seen a God of Service, not a God of Battles.

> CHARLOTTE PERKINS GILMAN, *His Religion and Hers*, 1923

The emancipation of women within the political State will leave them subject, like the negro, to an exploitation enhanced by surviving prejudices against them. The most that can be expected of the removal of discriminations subjecting one class to another within the exploiting State, is that it will free the subject class from dual control—control by the favoured class and by the monopolist of economic opportunity.

> SUZANNE LA FOLLETTE, *Concerning Women*, 1926

Women, like Negroes, have managed, under whatever discrimination, to play a part in every progressive movement and war waged by the nation or by oppressed groups within the nation. Movement by movement, war by war, women have succeeded in loosening—if only by a little—the chains of tradition and prejudice that bind them. But the end is by no means yet.

> SUSAN B. ANTHONY II, *Out of the Kitchen—Into the War*, 1943

This world crisis came about without women having anything to do with it. If the women of the world had not been excluded from world affairs, things today might have been different. . . . What we want to do is to have some say in the movement of peace when it comes. Women had no voice in the making of

217

the treaty of Versailles, and if we had had, things would have been different today.

    ALICE PAUL, in *Current Biography*, 1947

[People] evidently fear there would be no trouble in the world if women were not at some point driven obviously, if only partially, insane. If there were no trouble in the world, what in the name of heaven would there be to do? For earning the family living and keeping house and having children no longer takes up the full time of the majority of the population. . . . So cleaning up trouble is an absolute necessity. Without a war or depression to cope with on a big scale, or individuals with disordered emotions to cope with on a small scale, where would you all be, since your insight is by rule insufficient to enjoy leisure.

    ELIZABETH HAWES, *Anything But Love*, 1948

If there were more women in politics, it would be possible to start cleaning it up. . . . A larger proportion of women in Congress and every other legislative body would serve as a reminder that the real purpose of politicians is to work for the people.

    SHIRLEY CHISHOLM, *Unbought and Unbossed*, 1970

I am led to the hypothesis that we will be unable to eradicate racism in the United States unless and until we simultaneously remove all sex barriers which inhibit the development of individual talents.

    PAULI MURRAY, to Rep. Edith Green's Special Subcommittee on Education, 1970, *Discrimination Against Women*, U.S. Government Printing Office, 1971

We are insisting that women who are outcast by society—fat, old, handicapped, homosexual, nonwhite—be accepted as worthwhile human beings and accept themselves as such. We are insisting that women who are beautiful and sexually appealing by society's standards also be accepted as human beings of personal worth and accept themselves as such.

    Unsigned editorial, *Women: A Journal of Liberation*, II, circa 1971

If women understand by emancipation the adoption of the masculine role then we are lost indeed. If women can supply no counterbalance to the blindness of male drive the aggressive society will run to its lunatic extremes at ever-escalating speed.

    GERMAINE GREER, *The Female Eunuch*, 1971

Women who adopt the attitudes of war in their search for liberation condemn themselves to acting out the last perversion of dehumanized manhood, which has only one foreseeable outcome, the specifically masculine end of suicide.
   Ibid.

It would be genuine revolution if women would suddenly stop loving the victors in violent encounters.
   Ibid.

Many women, I think, can take great comfort that in the now ended search for a Vice-President, Watergate passed women by. Briefly the media titillated themselves by offering the rumor that a woman was being considered as a token to add to other tokens of power being put together as a lightning rod to protect the Ford administration. . . . [Some of my sisters] believe the nomination of a woman by the Republicans would surely nudge the Democrats, with their base of solid male white power, to wake up and recognize the potential strength of women. I say let us wait. Rather than be used as a token to solidify the position of conservative men, let us wait until we can build a party of men and women together, neither sex the satellite of the other.
   MARY GAIL BLACK, editorial, *Central Democrat*, II, August 1974

. . . given the American world of athletics—based as it is on the most aggressive, dog-eat-dog patterns of male competitiveness— . . . we do not want to see women triumphing over women in ugly, masculine ways. Instead of turning talented people into superstars, we favor providing opportunity and encouragement for all.
   BOSTON WOMEN'S HEALTH BOOK COLLECTIVE, *Our Bodies, Ourselves*, 2d ed., 1975

Forced to retire on inadequate income, robbed of identity and devoid of purpose, her spirit under siege, the elderly woman "exhibiting senile behavior" does not need drugs to "cure" her—what she needs is to be responded to, and be allowed to respond, as a human being.
   RHONDA, "We Are All in This Together," *Runes*, II, December 1977

Let them not imagine that they know aught of the delights which intercourse with the other sex can give, until they have felt the sympathy of mind with mind, and heart with heart; until they bring into that intercourse every affection, every talent, every confidence, every refinement, every respect. Until power is annihilated on one side, fear and obedience on the other, and both restored to their birthright—equality.

FRANCES WRIGHT, *Course of Popular Lectures,* 1829

12   Liberation of the Body

Marriage

We would have man and woman what God intended they should be, companions for each other, always together, in counsel, government, and every department of industry. If they have homes and children, we would have them stay there, educate their children, provide well for their physical wants, and share in each other's daily trials and cares. Children need the watchful care and wise teachings of fathers as well as of mothers.

ELIZABETH CADY STANTON, letter, *Proceedings of the Woman's Rights Convention, Held at Worcester, October 23 & 24, 1850,* 1851

In presenting to you, therefore, my views of divorce, you will of course give them the weight only of the woman's intuitions. But inasmuch as that is all God saw fit to give us, it is evident we need nothing more. Hence, what we do perceive of truth must be as reliable as what man grinds out by the longer process of reason, authority, and speculation.

ELIZABETH CADY STANTON, Woman's Rights Convention, 1860, *History of Woman Suffrage,* I, 1881

Men complain that woman does not love home now; that she is not satisfied with her mission. I answer that this discontent arises out of the one fact, that you have attempted to mold seventeen millions of human souls in one shape,

220

and make them all do one thing. Take away your restrictions, open all doors, leave women at liberty to go where they will. The caged bird forgets how to build its nest.

> FRANCES D. GAGE, American Equal Rights Association Convention, 1867, *History of Woman Suffrage*, II, 1882

We are told that home is woman's sphere. So it is, and man's sphere, too . . .

> Ibid.

On the question whether it is desirable that women should marry more than they do, I will only say, that while men continue to preach the doctrine—implicitly believed by most of them—that in marriage lies the only possible salvation for women, and while the thoughts of women continue to be directed to it as the one aim of life, marriage is likely to become less and less desired by the nobler portion of the community . . .

> JOSEPHINE E. BUTLER, ed., Introduction, *Woman's Work and Woman's Culture*, 1869

Let women assist themselves as they have never assisted themselves before. . . . They have too long let their benevolent instincts work toward the church and men; let them now attend to themselves. . . . Make a social revolution. Carry the war if need be, into your own families; let the baby go without bibs, the husband's shirt without buttons, the home without care, until the men give in. . . . Women have too long petitioned and begged of men; let them now make siege and carry the war into their own homes.

> ELIZABETH CADY STANTON, circa 1873, in Alma Lutz, *Created Equal*, 1940

I often saw weary little women coming to the table after most exhausting labors and large, bumptious husbands spreading out their hands and thanking the Lord for the meals that the dear women had prepared, as if the whole came down like manna from Heaven. So I preached a sermon in the blessing I gave. You will notice that it has three heresies in it: "Heavenly Father and Mother, make us thankful for all the blessings of this life, and make us ever mindful of the patient hands that oft in weariness spread our tables and prepare our daily food. For humanity's sake, Amen."

> Ibid.

Co-operative labor and co-operative homes will remove many difficulties in the way of woman's success as artisan and housekeeper, when admitted to the governing power. . . . Each reform, at its inception, seems out of joint with all its surroundings: but the discusssion changes the conditions, and brings them in line with the new idea.

> E. C. Stanton, S. B. Anthony, and M. J. Gage, eds., *History of Woman Suffrage*, I, 1881

The married woman of the future will be set free by co-operative methods, half the families on a square, perhaps, enjoying one luxurious, well-appointed dining-room with expenses divided *pro rata*.

> Ruth C. D. Havens, "The Girl of the Future," National American Woman Suffrage Association Convention, 1893, *History of Woman Suffrage*, IV, 1902

The deliverance of woman must have as its corner-stone self-support. The first step in this direction must be to explode the fallacy that marriage is a state of being supported.

> Ellen Battelle Dietrick, "Best Methods of Interesting Women in Suffrage," National American Woman Suffrage Association Convention, 1893, *History of Woman Suffrage*, IV, 1902

Why should one hundred women in each of one hundred separate houses be compelled to do the work that could equally as well or better be done by less than one-fifth of that number by some reasonable and just system of coöperation? Why cannot the cooking and washing and sewing be all attended to in a coöperative establishment, and thus relieve women, and mothers particularly, of the heavy burdens their fourfold labors now impose upon them, and give them time for self-improvement and the care and culture of their children?

> Amelia Bloomer, "On Housekeeping—Woman's Burdens," undated essay, in D. C. Bloomer, *Life and Writings of Amelia Bloomer*, 1895

If divorce were made respectable, and recognized by society as a duty, as well as a right, reasonable men and women could arrange all the preliminaries, often, even, the division of property and guardianship of children, quite as satisfactorily as it could be done in the courts.

> Elizabeth Cady Stanton, *Eighty Years and More*, 1898

We may all have homes to love and grow in without the requirement that half of us shall never have anything else. We shall have homes of rest and peace for all, with no need for half of us to find them places of ceaseless work and care.

> Charlotte Perkins Gilman, *The Home*, 1903

222

... women or men who get themselves concerned about the universe at large, would do well not to plunge hastily into marriage, for they do not run smoothly in the double-harness of that honourable estate. *Sturm und Drang* should be faced alone, and the soul should go out alone into the wilderness to be tempted of the devil, and not bring his majesty and all his imps into the placid circle of the home.

ANNIE BESANT, *An Autobiography*, 1908

Any woman who is really a rebel longs to destroy the conventions which bind her in the home as much as those which bind her in the State. She wants a new home and a new motherhood and a great many more new things as well as a Parliamentary vote. The waters of purification she seeks must flow through the home as well as through the political world.

TERESA BILLINGTON-GREIG, *The Militant Suffrage Movement*, 1911

Such searching and sifting is taking place in the consciences of many women of this generation whose sufferings, although strikingly influencing conduct, are seldom expressed in words until they are told in the form of reminiscence after the edges have been long since dulled. Such sufferings are never so poignant as when women have been forced by their personal experiences to challenge the valuable conventions safeguarding family life.

JANE ADDAMS, *The Long Road of Woman's Memory*, 1916

Feminism led women away from the home that they might return armed and unsubdued to make marriage tolerable.

DORA RUSSELL, *Hypatia*, 1925

... sharing of the common task removes many former sources of irritation; it permits the free play of natural differentiation in choosing which part of the work the individual shall do, (sometimes the mother likes to mow the grass and the father to bathe the baby), and where the children are concerned it often has the happy consequence of giving them two parents instead of one.

ALICE BEAL PARSONS, *Woman's Dilemma*, 1926

... the mechanism for feeding a town from central kitchens, just as it is at present supplied with vegetables and fruits and meat and milk from central stores, is already in existence. All that is lacking is that this mechanism should be organized for specific service just as milk companies are organized to deliver the products of dairies to the home.

Ibid.

When all achievement is outside the home, women of enterprise and initiative hate to be told that they must confine themselves there, but when the home itself is undervalued, then also women will cease to enjoy being women, and men will neither envy nor value the female role.

MARGARET MEAD, *Male and Female*, 1949

... marriage should be a combining of two whole, independent existences, not a retreat, an annexation, a flight, a remedy.

SIMONE DE BEAUVOIR, *The Second Sex*, 1952

I saw no reason why I, as a woman, should give up my work for his [husband's]. I knew by now I could make more of a contribution to the labor movement than he could.

ELIZABETH GURLEY FLYNN, *I Speak My Own Piece—Autobiography of "The Rebel Girl,"* 1955

First, she must unequivocally say "no" to the housewife image. This does not mean, of course, that she must divorce her husband, abandon her children, give up her home. She does not have to choose between marriage and career; that was the mistaken choice of the feminine mystique.

BETTY FRIEDAN, *The Feminine Mystique*, 1963

There seems little evidence that the father of a family of ten respects his wife more than the father of a family of two or, indeed, that in the case of childless couples there is necessarily any lack of respect on the part of the husband for the wife.

CONSTANCE ROVER, *Love, Morals and the Feminists*, 1970

Now that the cloistering of wives is an impossibility, we might as well withdraw the guarantees [of paternity], and make the patriarchal family an impossibility by insisting on preserving the paternity of the whole group—all men are fathers to all children.

GERMAINE GREER, *The Female Eunuch*, 1971

... it isn't pathetic anymore to be single. As a friend of mine had the wit to reply when someone asked if she were married, "Good God, no, are *you*?" As much as anything, an unmarried person nowadays is the object of envy.

JANE HOWARD, *A Different Woman*, 1973

Motherhood

Society asks, What is to become of children that women are forced to bear? Society provides prisons for them and the death penalty now. Might it not be well to leave women the liberty to choose whether they will bear children to be hung or not?

> MARY S. GOVE NICHOLS, "The Murders of Marriage," *Marriage: Its History, Character and Results; Its Sanctities and Profanities; Its Science and Its Facts*, 1854

A mother economically free, a world servant instead of a house-servant; a mother knowing the world and living in it,—can be to her children far more than has ever been possible before. Motherhood in the world will make that world a different place for her child.

> CHARLOTTE PERKINS GILMAN, *Women and Economics*, 1898

Many parents are not fit to have control of children, hence the State should see that they are sheltered, fed, clothed, and educated. It is far better for the State to make good citizens of its children in the beginning, than, in the end, to be compelled to care for them as criminals.

> ELIZABETH CADY STANTON, *Eighty Years and More*, 1898

Does any one here believe that if the women had power to make themselves felt in the administration of school affairs we should have 80,000 children on half-time in New York City? Truly, if the mothers of these school children, as well as their fathers, spoke in the elections, the interest in the schools would be quite a different one.

> FLORENCE KELLEY, symposium on municipal suffrage, National American Woman Suffrage Association Convention, 1907, *History of Woman Suffrage*, V, 1922

Great beings come forth at the call of high desire. Fearless motherhood goes out in love and passion for justice to all mankind. It brings forth fruits after its own kind.

> MARGARET SANGER, *Woman and the New Race*, 1920

We object, however, to the State or the Church which appoints itself as arbiter and dictator in this sphere and attempts to force unwilling women into compulsory maternity.

> MARGARET SANGER, *The Pivot of Civilization*, 1922

It is from no mere feeling of brotherly love or sentimental philanthropy that we women must insist upon enhancing the value of child life. It is because we know that, if our children are to develop to their full capabilities, all children must be assured a similar opportunity.

Ibid.

And it is . . . [working mothers] who, when they sit in conference, demand of the State the right to stem the tide of children, to endow mothers, to pension widows, to teach and tend maternity and ensure rest for pregnant and nursing women; to see that houses and schools are built, and to control and purify the food-supply.

Dora Russell, *Hypatia*, 1925

A woman may, for instance, choose to devote herself to a study of the tubercle bacillus. She may not see her children from breakfast until dinner, and yet her work may conceivably be more important to them, actually closer to their health and happiness, than if she had been within call all day long.

Alice Beal Parsons, *Woman's Dilemma*, 1926

Motherhood must be revalued, not over-emphasized, not sentimentalized and surrounded with an aura of glory, but viewed in an intelligent, sensible light. To this end, I recommend motherhood endowment. Through motherhood endowment, the mother of tomorrow will escape from perpetual tutelage. . . . Setting her free will repay the world.

Harriot Stanton Blatch and Alma Lutz, *Challenging Years*, 1940

While only women can have babies, it must be remembered that they are not always having them.

Ruth Herschberger, *Adam's Rib*, 1948

. . . full-time motherhood is neither sufficiently absorbing to the woman nor beneficial to the child to justify a contemporary woman's devoting fifteen or more years to it as her exclusive occupation. Sooner or later—and I think it should be sooner—women have to face the question of who they are besides their children's mother.

Alice S. Rossi, "Equality Between the Sexes: An Immodest Proposal," *Daedalus*, Spring 1964

. . . in order to play out the roles shaped by . . . the male life style, the woman finds that she must either be childless or have someone else act as her "wife." . . . Women's liberation is therefore *impossible* within the present so-

226

cial system except for an elite few. Women simply cannot be persons within the present system of work and family, and they can only rise to liberated personhood by the most radical and fundamental reshaping of the entire human environment in a way that redefines the very nature of work, family and the institutional expressions of social relations.
ROSEMARY RADFORD RUETHER, *Liberation Theology*, 1972

To have a mother who loves you for being independent is to have a mother who fosters rebellion in your heart and revolution in your bones.
JUDY CHICAGO, *Through the Flower*, 1975

We could wish that there were more fathers—not one, but many—... fathers with the sensitivity and commitment to help them into a manhood in which they would not perceive women as the sole sources of nourishment and solace.
ADRIENNE RICH, *Of Woman Born*, 1976

The mother's battle for her child—with sickness, with poverty, with war, with all the forces of exploitation and callousness that cheapen human life—needs to become a common human battle, waged in love and in the passion for survival. But for this to happen, the institution of motherhood must be destroyed.
Ibid.

Sex

The conception that man's and woman's need of each other could be touched, or the emotions binding the sexes obliterated, by any mere change in the form of labour performed by the woman of the race, is as grotesque in its impossibility, as the suggestion that the placing of a shell on the seashore this way or that might destroy the action of the earth's great tidal wave.
OLIVE SCHREINER, *Woman and Labour*, 1911

The women of the future will have men on terms, or go without, and the terms must be the only honourable terms, of love and liberty and mutual service.
H. M. SWANWICK, *The Future of the Women's Movement*, 1913

Upon the shoulders of the woman conscious of her freedom rests the responsibility of creating a new sex morality. The vital difference between a morality thus created by women and the so-called morality of to-day, is that the new standard will be based upon knowledge and freedom while the old is founded upon ignorance and submission.

> MARGARET SANGER, *Woman and the New Race*, 1920

To me the important task of modern feminism is to accept and proclaim sex; to bury for ever the lie that has too long corrupted our society—the lie that the body is a hindrance to the mind, and sex a necessary evil to be endured for the perpetuation of our race.

> DORA RUSSELL, *Hypatia*, 1925

There is nothing in life to compare with this uniting of minds and bodies in men and women who have laid aside hostility and fear and seek in love the fullest understanding of themselves and of the universe.

> Ibid.

... the most potent emancipating influence [of the woman's movement] lay in the fact that new work brought in its train a quite new kind of companionship between women and women, and between women and men. ... Those who got to know each other in relation to common tasks found that ... there was a vast new area in existence, i.e. work, in which sex hardly counted, and into which it rarely entered.

> MARY AGNES HAMILTON, "Changes in Social Life," *Our Freedom and Its Results*, ed. Ray Strachey, 1936

On the day when it will be possible for woman to love not in her weakness but in her strength, not to escape herself but to find herself, not to abase herself but to assert herself—on that day love will become for her, as for man, a source of life and not of mortal danger.

> SIMONE DE BEAUVOIR, *The Second Sex*, 1952

A ... young man put the old question, "Do you really care about all this equal rights business? Wouldn't you rather be adored?"

My answer was firm. "No, I would rather *not* be adored. It's been tried, but it just makes me nervous."

> CAROLINE BIRD, *Born Female*, rev. ed., 1971

Maternal love was not only the first kind of love. For many millennia it was the only kind. When woman, after she had tamed man, extended her love for her children to include their father, then perhaps man began to learn for the first time what love was.

> ELIZABETH GOULD DAVIS, *The First Sex*, 1971

Sex must be rescued from the traffic between powerful and powerless, masterful and mastered, sexual and neutral, to become a form of communication between potent, gentle, tender people ...

GERMAINE GREER, *The Female Eunuch*, 1971

The one and only way to achieve equality and progress in human as well as love relationships lies in the expression of the whole bisexual nature of every man and woman.

CHARLOTTE WOLFF, M.D., *Love Between Women*, 1971

Liberated sex means an end to the double standard about who can enjoy sex and who can't, and how much, or who can initiate sex and who can't. It means an end also to the dehumanizing effect of the double standard, which detaches sex from a relationship of respect and caring. It means an end to "nice girls don't" and "real men must."

CHARLOTTE HOLT CLINEBELL, *Meet Me in the Middle*, 1973

To oppose the essential lovelessness of the sexually hierarchical society is the radically loving act. Seen for what it is, the struggle for justice opens the way to a situation in which more genuinely loving relationships are possible.

MARY DALY, *Beyond God the Father*, 1973

Reproduction

... how much cruel bondage of mind and suffering of body poor woman will escape when she takes the liberty of being her own physician of both body and soul!

ELIZABETH CADY STANTON, letter to Lucretia Mott, 1852, *Elizabeth Cady Stanton*, vol. II, ed. Theodore Stanton and Harriot Stanton Blatch, 1922

Call yourselves Christian women, you who sacrifice all that is great and good for an ignoble peace, who betray the best interests of the race for a temporary ease? It were nobler far to go and throw yourselves into the Ganges than to curse the earth with a miserable progeny, conceived in disgust and brought forth in agony. What means these asylums all over the land for the deaf and dumb, the maim and blind, the idiot and the raving maniac? ... Let us but use as much care and forethought in producing the highest order of intelligence, as we do in raising a cabbage or a calf, and in a few generations we shall reap an abundant harvest of giants, scholars, and Christians.

ELIZABETH CADY STANTON, letter to National Woman's Rights Convention, 1856, *History of Woman Suffrage*, I, 1881

I very much wish that a wife's right to her own body should be pushed at our next convention.

> Lucy Stone, letter to Elizabeth Cady Stanton, 1856, *Elizabeth Cady Stanton*, vol. II, ed. Theodore Stanton and Harriot Stanton Blatch, 1922

The first step toward getting life, liberty and the pursuit of happiness for any woman is her decision whether or not she shall become a mother. Enforced motherhood is the most complete denial of a woman's right to life and liberty.

> Margaret Sanger, "Suppression," *The Woman Rebel*, I, June 1914

Motherhood should not be the highest aim of a girl, for surely all animals may fulfill this function; rather let motherhood be one of the avenues through which the girl may pass in enriching her womanhood.

> Margaret Sanger, "Class and Character," *The Woman Rebel*, I, July 1914

The most far-reaching social development of modern times is the revolt of woman against sex servitude. The most important force in the re-making of the world is a free motherhood.

> Margaret Sanger, *Woman and the New Race*, 1920

War, famine, poverty and oppression of the workers will continue while woman makes life cheap. They will cease only when she limits her reproductivity and human life is no longer a thing to be wasted.

> Ibid.

No woman can call herself free who does not own and control her body. No woman can call herself free until she can choose consciously whether she will or will not be a mother.

> Ibid.

Birth Control, therefore, means not merely the limitation of births, but the application of intelligent guidance over the reproductive power. It means the substitution of reason and intelligence for the blind play of instinct.

> Margaret Sanger, *The Pivot of Civilization*, 1922

Birth Control concerns itself with the spirit no less than the body. It looks for the liberation of the spirit of woman and through woman of the child.

> Ibid.

When over-production ... is curtailed by voluntary restriction, when the birth rate among the working classes takes a sharp decline, the value of children will rise. Then only will the infant mortality rate decline, and child labor vanish.

Ibid.

Moral and sexual balance in civilization will only be established by the assertion and expression of power on the part of women. ... Woman's power can only be expressed and make itself felt when she refuses the task of bringing unwanted children into the world to be exploited in industry and slaughtered in wars.

Ibid.

For all Americans, and especially for the poor, we must put an end to compulsory pregnancy.

SHIRLEY CHISHOLM, *Unbought and Unbossed,* 1970

If women take their bodies seriously ... then its *full* expression, in terms of pleasure, maternity, and physical strength, seems to fare better when *women* control the means of production and reproduction. From this point of view, it is simply not in women's interest to support patriarchy or even a fabled "equality" with men.

PHYLLIS CHESLER, *Women and Madness,* 1972

Feminist ethics will see a different and more complex human meaning in the act of abortion. Rather than judging universally in fixed categories of "right and wrong" it will be inclined to make graded evaluations of choices. ... It will attempt to help women to orchestrate the various elements that come into play in the situation, including the needs of the woman as a person, the rights of women as an oppressed class, ... the negative aspects of her situation in a society which rewards the production of unwanted children with shame and poverty.

MARY DALY, *Beyond God the Father,* 1973

For if the phrase biology is destiny has any meaning for a woman right now it has to be the urgent project of woman reclaiming her self, her own biology in her own image, and this is why the lesbian is *the* revolutionary feminist ...

JILL JOHNSTON, *Lesbian Nation,* 1973

231

In order to live a fully human life we require not only *control* of our bodies (though control is a prerequisite); we must touch the unity and resonance of our physicality, our bond with the natural order, the corporial ground of our intelligence.

ADRIENNE RICH, *Of Woman Born,* 1976

> ... what we call the woman's movement is a re-
> volt from a pretense of being—it is at its best
> and worst a struggle for the liberation of per-
> sonality.
>
> ELLEN GLASGOW, "Feminism," *New York Times*,
> July 31, 1913

13 Independence of the Spirit

Independence I have long considered as the grand blessing of life, the basis of every virtue—and independence I will ever secure by contracting my wants, though I were to live on a barren heath.

MARY WOLLSTONECRAFT, A *Vindication of the Rights of Woman*, 1792

"Educate women like men," says Rousseau, "and the more they resemble our sex the less power will they have over us." This is the very point I aim at. I do not wish them to have power over men; but over themselves.

Ibid.

We never mention women's rights in our *lectures* except so far as is necessary to urge them to meet their responsibilities. We speak of their *responsibilities* and leave *them* to *infer* their *rights*.

ANGELINA GRIMKÉ, letter to Theodore Weld and John Greenleaf Whittier, 1837, *Letters of Theodore Weld, Angelina Grimké Weld, and Sarah Grimké, 1822–1844*, ed. Gilbert H. Barnes and Dwight L. Dumond, 1965

What Woman needs is not as a woman to act or rule, but as a nature to grow, as an intellect to discern, as a soul to live freely and unimpeded to unfold such powers as were given her when we left our common home.

MARGARET FULLER, *Woman in the Nineteenth Century*, 1845

... I would have Woman lay aside all thought ... of being taught and led by men. I would have her, like the Indian girl, dedicate herself to the Sun, the Sun of Truth, and go nowhere if his beams did not make clear the path. I would have her free from compromise, from complaisance, from helplessness, because I would have her good enough and strong enough to love one and all beings, from the fulness not the poverty of being.

Ibid.

. . . woman has her work to do, and no one can accomplish it for her. She is bound to rise, to try her strength, to break her bonds . . .

ELIZABETH BLACKWELL, letter to Emily Collins, 1848, *History of Woman Suffrage*, I, 1881

Let woman then go on, not asking favors, but claiming as right the removal of all hindrances to her elevation in the scale of being; let her receive encouragement for the proper cultivation of all her powers, so that she may enter profitably into the active business of life; employing her own hands in ministering to her necessities, strengthening her physical being by proper exercise and observance of the laws of health.

LUCRETIA MOTT, discourse, 1849, *History of Woman Suffrage*, I, 1881

Some men regard us as devils, and some as angels; hence, one class would shut us up in a certain sphere for fear of the evil we might do, and the other for fear of the evil that *might be done to us*; thus, except for the sentiment of the thing, for all the good that it does us, we might as well be thought the one as the other. But we ourselves have to do with what *we are* and what *we shall be*.

ELIZABETH CADY STANTON, letter to Woman's Rights Convention, 1850, *History of Woman Suffrage*, I, 1881

It is pitiable ignorance and arrogance for either man or woman now to prescribe and limit the sphere of woman. It remains for the greatest women whom appropriate culture, and happiest influences shall yet develop, to declare and to prove what are woman's capacities and relations in the world.

PAULINA WRIGHT DAVIS, address, *Proceedings of the Woman's Rights Convention, Held at Worcester, October 23 & 24, 1850*, 1851

. . . a love of liberty in woman, as well as in man, is inherent; it may be paralyzed, but not eradicated, and woman does love liberty as well as man.

ELIZABETH WILSON, letter, *Proceedings of the Woman's Rights Convention, Held at Worcester, October 23 & 24, 1850*, 1851

... there can be but one true method in the treatment of each human being, of either sex, of any color, and under any outward circumstances, to ascertain what are the powers of that being, to cultivate them to the utmost, and *then* to see what action they will find for themselves.

> HARRIET MARTINEAU, letter to Second National Convention, Friends of Woman Suffrage, 1851, *History of Woman Suffrage*, I, 1881

The girl must early be impressed with the idea that she is to be "a hand, not a mouth"; a worker, and not a drone, in the great hive of human activity.

> ELIZABETH CADY STANTON, letter to Woman's Rights Convention, 1851, *History of Woman Suffrage*, I, 1881

Self-reliance is one of the first lessons to be taught our daughters; they should be educated with our sons, and equally with them taught to look forward to some independent means of support ...

> MATILDA JOSLYN GAGE, Woman's Rights Convention, 1852, *History of Woman Suffrage*, I, 1881

The capacity to speak indicates the right to do so, and the noblest, highest, and best thing that any one can accomplish, is what that person ought to do, and what God holds him or her accountable for doing ...

> LUCY STONE, Woman's Rights Convention, 1855, *History of Woman Suffrage*, I, 1881

... ours only is the true revelation, based in nature and in life. That revelation is no less than the living, breathing, thinking, feeling, acting revelation manifested in the nature of woman. In her manifold powers, capacities, needs, hopes, and aspirations, lies her title-deed, and whether that revelation was written by nature or nature's God matters not, for here it is.

> ERNESTINE L. ROSE, Woman's Rights Convention, 1856, *History of Woman Suffrage*, I, 1881

... I assert that every woman, in the present state of society, is bound to maintain her own independence and her own integrity of character; to assert herself, earnestly and firmly, as the equal of man, who is only her peer. This is her first right, her first duty; and if she lives in a country where the law supposes that she is to be subjected to her husband, and she consents to this subjection, I do insist that she consents to degradation; that this is sin, and it is impossible to make it other than sin ...

> REV. ANTOINETTE BROWN BLACKWELL, Woman's Rights Convention, 1860, *History of Woman Suffrage*, I, 1881

The women who are called masculine, who are brave, courageous, self-reliant and independent, are they who in the face of adverse winds have kept one steady course upward and onward in the paths of virtue and peace—they who have taken their gauge of womanhood from their own native strength and dignity—they who have learned for themselves the will of God concerning them. This is our type of womanhood.

> ELIZABETH CADY STANTON, "Address to the Legislature of the State of New York," 1860, *History of Woman Suffrage*, I, 1881

If there is one feeling, above all others, I would implant in a girl, it is *self-reliance*, particularly if I had reason to think her path in life would be single and alone.

> VIRGINIA PENNY, *Think and Act*, 1869

Knowing, then, the qualities of woman and her courage and bravery under trials, I can never cease to demand that she shall have just as large a sphere as man has. All we want is, that you shall leave us free to act.

> MARY A. LIVERMORE, American Woman Suffrage Association Convention, 1870, *History of Woman Suffrage*, II, 1882

As the sphere of women enlarges, more and more is required of them; and they should therefore throw off all customs that tend to cramp them in any direction, and should endeavor to retain only such as liberate and enlarge their powers, and tend to invigorate both mind and body. In this way alone can they prepare themselves for greater usefulness.

> MERCY B. JACKSON, M.D., Lecture III, *Dress-Reform*, ed. Abba Goold Woolson, 1874

Independence is happiness.

> SUSAN B. ANTHONY, "Social Purity," 1875, in Ida Husted Harper, *Life and Work of Susan B. Anthony*, vol. II, 1898

Leave to my own perception what is proper for me as a lady, to my own discretion what is wise for me as a woman, to my own conscience what is my duty to my race and to my God.

> MARY CLEMMER, letter to Senator Bainbridge, 1878, *History of Woman Suffrage*, III, 1887

Women have always been in a state of half-concealed resistance to fathers and husbands and all self-constituted authorities as far as they dared, as far as good policy permitted them to manifest their real feelings. It has taken the whole power of the civil and canon law to hold woman in the subordinate position which it is said she willingly accepts. If woman naturally has no will, no self-assertion, no opinions of her own, what means the terrible persecution of the sex under all forms of religious fanaticism, culminating in witch-craft in which scarce one wizard to a thousand witches was sacrificed? So powerful and merciless has been the struggle to dominate the feminine element in humanity, that we may well wonder at the steady persistent resistance maintained by woman through the centuries.

> ELIZABETH CADY STANTON, "Self-Government the Best Means of Self-Development," National Woman Suffrage Association Convention, *Report*, 1884

Nothing strengthens the judgment and quickens the conscience like individual responsibility. Nothing adds such dignity to character as the recognition of one's self-sovereignty; the right to an equal place, everywhere conceded—a place earned by personal merit, not an artificial attainment by inheritance . . .

> ELIZABETH CADY STANTON, "Solitude of Self," speech 1892, *History of Woman Suffrage*, IV, 1902

Who, I ask you, can take, dare take, on himself, the rights, the duties, the responsibilities of another human soul?

> Ibid.

The advocates of equal rights believe that freedom and education and responsibility, which tend to develop a man into a noble man, will also tend to develop a woman into a noble woman, but will never in the least tend to turn a woman into a man. Nature has a way of looking out for herself.

> ALICE STONE BLACKWELL, "Making Women into Men," *The Woman's Journal*, January 14, 1893

No person is human who may not "will" to be anything he can be. When the woman says "I will," there is not anything this side of the throne of God to stop her, and the girls of the present day should learn this lesson. Now there is placed upon women the obligation of service without the responsibility of their actions. The man who leads feels the responsibility of his acts, and this urges him to make them noble. Women should have this same responsibility and be made to feel it. The most dangerous thing in the world is power without responsibility . . .

> ANNA HOWARD SHAW, sermon, National American Woman Suffrage Association Convention, 1894, *History of Woman Suffrage*, IV, 1902

Mrs. Nancy McKeen, of West Stoneham, Me., has the honor of having killed the largest bear ever captured in that region. The bear was chasing her sheep, when she attacked him with a club, and, after a hard-fought battle, succeeded in laying him out. Mrs. McKeen is eighty-three years of age, in good health, and says she is ready for another bear.

ALICE STONE BLACKWELL, ed., *The Woman's Column*, March 14, 1896

Strong, indeed, is the girl who can decide within herself where duty lies, and follow that decision against the combined forces which hold her back. She must claim the right of every individual soul to its own path in life, its own true line of work and growth. She must claim the duty of every individual soul to give to its all-providing society some definite service in return. She must recognise the needs of the world, of her country, her city, her place and time in human progress, as well as the needs of her personal relations and her personal home.

CHARLOTTE PERKINS GILMAN, *The Home*, 1903

I can well recall the years in which I felt myself averse to the participation of women in political life. . . . [But] at my first real contact with the suffragists of, say, forty years ago, I was made to feel that womanhood is not only static but also much more dynamic, a power to move as well as a power to stay. True womanliness must grow and not diminish, in its larger and freer exercise.

JULIA WARD HOWE, National American Woman Suffrage Association Convention, 1906, *History of Woman Suffrage*, V, 1922

The right to vote, or equal civil rights, may be good demands, but true emancipation begins neither at the polls nor in the courts. It begins in woman's soul.

EMMA GOLDMAN, "Woman Suffrage," *Anarchism and Other Essays*, 1911

It is this genius for living that must be altogether liberated, and with it we shall see an immense liberation of the organising and governing power of women.

H. M. SWANWICK, *The Future of the Women's Movement*, 1913

To allow no weakness to escape us, to challenge every falsehood as it passes, to brave every insinuation and sneer, is what duty demands.

CAROLINE WELLS DALL, *The College, The Market, and the Court*, 1914

No better education do I claim for woman than her entire *self-possession*, the ultimate endowment of all the promise she carries in her nature.

Ibid.

He'll find that there is but one thing in the world a little stronger than a woman's will, and that is—her won't.

ABIGAIL SCOTT DUNIWAY, *Pathbreaking*, 1914

. . . there is one emphatic caution to be given to the woman who would defy the conventions. If the working woman does this, let her do it without a rag of excuse, without reason or justification to anyone. Let her be herself and live for her ideal and her convictions not for the approval or the applause of fashionable feminism.

ELIZABETH KLEEN, "To Be a Woman Rebel," *The Woman Rebel*, I, March 1914

We are a race of women that of old knew no fear and feared no death, and lived great lives and hoped great hopes; and if today some of us have fallen on evil and degenerate times, there moves in us yet the throb of the old blood.

OLIVE SCHREINER, *The Woman Rebel*, I, May 1914

. . . feminism is the attempt of women to grow up, to accept the responsibilities of life, to outgrow those characteristics of childhood—selfishness and cowardliness—that we require our boys to outgrow, but that we permit and by our social system encourage our girls to retain.

HENRIETTA RODMAN, *New York Times*, January 24, 1915

The basic freedom of the world is woman's freedom.

MARGARET SANGER, *Woman and the New Race*, 1920

Woman must not accept; she must challenge. . . . When she chooses her new, free course of action, it must be in the light of her own opinion—of her own intuition. Only so can she give play to the feminine spirit.

Ibid.

She knows that regardless of what ought to be, the brutal, unavoidable fact is that she will never receive her freedom until she takes it for herself.

Ibid.

Courage calls to courage everywhere, and its voice cannot be denied.

MILLICENT GARRETT FAWCETT, *The Women's Victory—and After*, 1920

A woman today who has no goal, no purpose, no ambition patterning her days into the future, making her stretch and grow beyond that small score of years in which her body can fill its biological function, is committing a kind of suicide.

> BETTY FRIEDAN, *The Feminine Mystique*, 1963

In order to improve their condition, those individuals who are today defined as women must eradicate their own definition. Women must, in a sense, commit suicide, and the journey from womanhood to a society of individuals is hazardous.

> TI-GRACE ATKINSON, "Radical Feminism: Declaration of War," April 1969, *Amazon Odyssey*, 1974

Only when all people, each of us, refuse to submit, will oppression disappear. Each of us *is* the revolution.

> TI-GRACE ATKINSON, "Individual Responsibility and Human Oppression (Including Some Notes on Prostitution and Pornography)," May 1970, *Amazon Odyssey*, 1974

. . . women are seeking their own image of themselves nurtured from within rather than imposed from without.

> PAULI MURRAY, to Rep. Edith Green's Special Subcommittee on Education, 1970, *Discrimination Against Women*, U.S. Government Printing Office, 1971

Women are *instinctively* courageous. For courage involves a forgetfulness of self, a broad compassion, and a high evaluation of another's life—all of which are feminine attitudes, rare in men.

> ELIZABETH GOULD DAVIS, *The First Sex*, 1971

. . . women in American society are held to be the *passive* sex, but the majority of Black women have, perhaps, never fit this model, and have been liberated from many of the constraints the society has traditionally imposed on women.

> JOYCE A. LADNER, *Tomorrow's Tomorrow: The Black Woman*, 1971

Women must convert their "love" for and reliance on strength and skill in others to a love for all manner of strength and skill in themselves. Women must be able to go as directly to the "heart" of physical, technological, and intellectual reality as they presumably do to the "heart" of emotional reality.

This requires discipline, courage, confidence, anger, the ability to act, and an overwhelming sense of joy and urgency.

PHYLLIS CHESLER, *Women and Madness*, 1972

I have met brave women who are exploring the outer edge of human possibility, with no history to guide them, and with a courage to make themselves vulnerable that I find moving beyond the words to express it.

GLORIA STEINEM, "Sisterhood," *Ms.*, Spring 1972

Passivity is *the* dragon that every woman has to murder in her quest for independence.

JILL JOHNSTON, *Lesbian Nation*, 1973

Women . . . must reject any revival of the romantic trap. If white males need to recover their lost soul, women need to recover the rationality, autonomy, and self-definition which they have been denied as tools of male needs and negations.

ROSEMARY RADFORD RUETHER, *New Woman New Earth*, 1975

If I could have one wish for my own sons, it is that they should have the courage of women. I mean by this something very concrete and precise; the courage I have seen in women who, in their private and public lives, both in the interior world of their dreaming, thinking, and creating, and the outer world of patriarchy, are taking greater and greater risks, both psychic and physical, in the evolution of a new vision.

ADRIENNE RICH, *Of Woman Born*, 1976

As soon as I believe that you need protecting, as soon as you believe that my being threatens yours, then we have all become less human, not *"equal"* in the only meaningful sense of the word. I can't do anything to you. We may argue, cry, laugh, share, but you are still you and your feelings are yours, just as mine are mine. My being powerful does not give me any power over you, only you can do that. Just as your being powerful doesn't diminish me.

SHERRY THOMAS, "My Power Does Not Diminish Yours," *Country Women*, 24, April 1977

14   The Salvation of the World

It is time to effect a revolution in female manners—time to restore to them
their lost dignity—and make them, as a part of the human species, labour by
reforming themselves to reform the world.
    MARY WOLLSTONECRAFT, *A Vindication of the Rights of Woman*, 1792

. . . until women assume the place in society which good sense and good feeling alike assign to them, human improvement must advance but feebly. It is
in vain that we would circumscribe the power of one half of our race, and
that half by far the most important and influential. If they exert it not for
good, they will for evil: if they advance not knowledge, they will perpetuate
ignorance. Let women stand where they may in the scale of improvement,
their position decides that of the race.
    FRANCES WRIGHT, *Course of Popular Lectures*, 1829

My doctrine then is, that whatever it is morally right for man to do, it is morally right for woman to do. Our duties originate, not from difference of sex,
but from the diversity of our relations in life, the various gifts and talents
committed to our care, and the different eras in which we live.
    ANGELINA E. GRIMKÉ, Letter XII, *Letters to Catherine E. Beecher*, 1837

The reformation which we purpose, in its utmost scope, is radical and universal. It is not the mere perfecting of a progress already in motion, a detail of
some established plan, but it is an epochal movement—the emancipation of a
class, the redemption of half the world, and a conforming reorganization of

242

all social, political, and industrial interests and institutions. Moreover, it is a movement without example among the enterprises of associated reformations, for it has no purpose of arming the oppressed against the oppressor, or of separating the parties, or of setting up independence, or of severing the relations of either.

> PAULINA WRIGHT DAVIS, address, *Proceedings of the Woman's Rights Convention, Held at Worcester, October 23 & 24, 1850,* 1851

My friends, do we realize for what purpose we are convened? Do we fully understand that we aim at nothing less than an entire subversion of the present order of society, a dissolution of the whole existing social compact? Do we see that it is not an error of to-day, nor of yesterday, against which we are lifting up the voice of dissent, but that it is against the hoary-headed error of all times—error borne onward from the foot-prints of the first pair ejected from Paradise, down to our own time?

> ELIZABETH OAKES SMITH, *Woman's Rights Convention,* 1852, *History of Woman Suffrage,* I, 1881

The demand we to-day make, is not the idiosyncrasy of a few discontented minds, but a universal movement. Woman is everywhere throwing off the lethargy of ages, and is already close upon you in the whole realm of thought—in art, science, literature and government. Everything heralds the dawn of the new era when moral power is to govern nations.

> ELIZABETH CADY STANTON, "Address to the New York Constitutional Convention," 1867, *History of Woman Suffrage,* II, 1882

If the present arrangements of society will not admit of woman's free development, then society must be remodeled, and adapted to the great wants of all humanity.

> ELIZABETH BLACKWELL, letter, *History of Woman Suffrage,* I, 1881

. . . as man walked the earth desolate and forlorn until woman was formed, so now does the world wait for the coming of woman into an equal partnership with man in that joint dominion which was originally given, to redeem society and government, as of old Eve brought order and happiness even into Paradise.

> LILLIE DEVEREUX BLAKE, *Women's Place Today,* 1883

I think it can be demonstrated that woman has been always the unknown quantity in civilization, in progress and in politics, and that it has heretofore been impossible to calculate with certainty on the result of any great social reform or political revolution, because this mighty term, this "x" of the equation, has been overlooked or forgotten.

LILLIE DEVEREUX BLAKE, National Woman Suffrage Association Convention, *Report*, 1884

Women... have fought their own battles and in their rebellion against existing conditions have inaugurated the most fundamental revolution the world has ever witnessed. The magnitude and multiplicity of the changes involved make the obstacles in the way of success seem almost insurmountable...

ELIZABETH CADY STANTON, to Senate Committee on Woman Suffrage, 1888, *History of Woman Suffrage*, IV, 1902

... the light and the eager interest in the faces of American women show that they are going somewhere; and when women have started for somewhere, they are harder to head off than a comet...

JOSEPHINE K. HENRY, National American Woman Suffrage Association Convention, 1899, *History of Woman Suffrage*, IV, 1902

The Woman's Movement means a new religion, or rather a return of religion to its source...

EMMELINE PETHICK-LAWRENCE, editorial, *Votes for Women*, 1907

Whether we approve or not, the movement is here. The task nature has set herself through the subjection of women has been fulfilled; women's unconscious mission, operating by natural laws, has hitherto been to humanise the male. By the law of interlocked heredity the race has now sufficiently advanced for women to have a conscious mission: the perfecting of the human race.

LADY GROVE, *The Human Woman*, 1908

Attempted modifications of an essential evil always fail.

JOSEPHINE E. BUTLER, *Personal Reminiscences of a Great Crusade*, 1911

... emancipation is not wholly a matter of politics and votes...

TERESA BILLINGTON-GREIG, *The Militant Suffrage Movement*, 1911

... there has never been a franchise agitation which has attained any success in which the spirit of revolt has not been called forth by ultra-political wrongs. The vote has few of the characteristics or associations which stir the

mob to uprising; . . . alone the right to vote could not inspire more than a few to deeds of defiance and disorder.
Ibid.

We were suffragists as a matter of course, as all who believe in the greater sex-equality must be; but we knew that our revolt itself was of very much greater value than the vote we demanded. Women might have the one and still be slaves; to share in the other they would have to free themselves from at least some of their shackles and come nearer to personal emancipation.
Ibid.

From the judge's seat to the legislator's chair; from the statesman's closet to the merchant's office; from the chemist's laboratory to the astronomer's tower, there is no post or form of toil for which it is not our intention to attempt to fit ourselves; and there is no closed door we do not intend to force open . . .
OLIVE SCHREINER, *Woman and Labour*, 1911

We have called the Woman's Movement of our age an endeavour on the part of women among modern civilised races to find new fields of labour as the old slip from them, as an attempt to escape from parasitism and an inactive dependence upon sex function alone; but viewed from another side, the Woman's Movement might not less justly be called a part of a great movement of the sexes towards each other, a movement towards common occupations, common interests, common ideals, and towards an emotional sympathy between the sexes more deeply founded and more indestructible than any the world has yet seen.
Ibid.

The reforms of the future are going to be constructive, not punitive, and in all these women's gifts will be priceless.
H. M. SWANWICK, *The Future of the Women's Movement*, 1913

[The woman's movement] is everywhere surprisingly spontaneous and universal. It not only appears simultaneously in various nations in both hemispheres, but manifests itself in widely separated groups within the same nation, embracing the smart set and the hard driven working woman; sometimes the movement is sectarian and dogmatic, at others philosophic and grandiloquent; it may be amorphous and sporadic, or carefully organized and consciously directed; but it is always vital and is constantly becoming more wide-spread.

JANE ADDAMS, "The Larger Aspects of the Woman's Movement," *The Annals of the American Academy of Political and Social Science*, LVI, November 1914

Call on God, my dear, She will help you.

MRS. O. H. P. BELMONT, to a discouraged young suffragist, circa 1917–1918, in Doris Stevens, *Jailed for Freedom*, 1920

Women are too much inclined to follow in the footsteps of men, to try to think as men think, to try to solve the general problems of life as men solve them. If after attaining their freedom, women accept conditions in the spheres of government, industry, art, morals and religion as they find them, they will be but taking a leaf out of man's book.

MARGARET SANGER, *Woman and the New Race*, 1920

Her mission is not to enhance the masculine spirit, but to express the feminine; hers is not to preserve a man-made world, but to create a human world by the infusion of the feminine element into all of its activities.

Ibid.

Force, struggle, solidity, contact, may yield to gentleness, non-resistance, intermingling and uniting. . . . We shall no longer think of mind and matter as wronging or thwarting one another, because they are not different forces; and we shall no longer be able to separate physical from mental virtue or depravity.

DORA RUSSELL, *Hypatia*, 1925

What women had to do was to bring the feminine principle into an entirely masculinized world and thereby make the world human instead of only masculine.

ALISON NEILANS, "Changes in Sex Morality," *Our Freedom and Its Results*, ed. Ray Strachey, 1936

Woman's place is in the factory, in the office, in the professions, in the fields and at the council table—wherever human labor, human effort, is needed to produce and create.

SUSAN B. ANTHONY II, *Out of the Kitchen—Into the War*, 1943

Feminists have to question, not just all of *Western* culture, but the organization of culture itself, and further, even the very organization of nature.
SHULAMITH FIRESTONE, *The Dialectic of Sex*, 1970

Women are the real Left. We are rising powerful in our unclean bodies; bright glowing mad in our inferior brains; wild hair flying, wild eyes staring, wild voices keening; undaunted by blood we who hemorrhage every twenty-eight days; laughing at our own beauty, we who have lost our sense of humor; mourning for all each precious one of us might have been in this one living time-place had she not been born a woman; stuffing fingers into our mouths to stop the screams of fear and hate and pity for men we have loved and love still; tears in our eyes and bitterness in our mouths for children we couldn't have, or couldn't *not* have, or didn't want, or didn't want *yet*, or wanted and had in this place and this time of horror. We are rising with a fury older and potentially greater than any force in history, and this time we will be free or no one will survive. *Power to all the people or to none.* All the way down, this time.
ROBIN MORGAN, "Goodbye to All That," *RAT, Subterranean News*, February 6, 1970

Women's revolutions, unlike men's, are not apocalyptic. Women do not expect Armageddon. They are accustomed to a relatively slow pace.
JESSIE BERNARD, *Women and the Public Interest*, 1971

This revolution is the most universal, most humane, and most human revolution of all. Who can be opposed to a revolution that asks, "How do we live with others? How do we bring up our kids? How is family life and work shared? How can we all be human?"
Ibid.

A few people in our society have power. Our task is to build a movement which can change that fact. This means organizing around specific demands which can be won, and which in the process will alter power relations, thus building our power base as women.
DAY CREAMER AND HEATHER BOOTH, "Action Committee for Decent Childcare; Organizing for Power," *Women: A Journal of Liberation*, II, circa 1971

Women who do not rebel against the status of object have declared themselves defeated as persons in their own right.
CHARLOTTE WOLFF, *Love Between Women*, 1971

247

To seek the liberation of women without losing this sense of communal personhood is the great challenge and secret power of the women's revolution. Its only proper end must be the total abolition of the social pattern of domination and subjugation and the erection of a new communal social ethic.

ROSEMARY RADFORD RUETHER, *Liberation Theology*, 1972

Until the "feminine" values become human values, the world will not turn from its destructive course. A genuine respect for the traditionally feminine value of nurturing in men as well as in women will hasten the equality of women. Conversely, the valuing of women equally with men will hasten the valuing of nurturing and caring. We can't have one without the other.

CHARLOTTE HOLT CLINEBELL, *Meet Me in the Middle*, 1973

It can be easy to leap on the bandwagon of "human liberation" without paying the price in terms of polarization, tensions, risk, and pain that the ultimate objective of real human liberation demands.

MARY DALY, *Beyond God the Father*, 1973

... we have to learn to live *now* the future we are fighting for, rather than compromising in vain hope of a future that is always deferred, always unreal. This creative leap implies a kind of recklessness born out of the death of false hope.

Ibid.

This is the period when the women's movement, properly understood, encompasses all other liberation movements.

ROSEMARY RADFORD RUETHER, *New Woman New Earth*, 1975

Feminism is truly a venture into a *terra incognita*.

Ibid.

248

Acknowledgments

Grateful acknowledgment is made to the following for permission to reprint selections included in this book:

Aldine Publishing Company: quotations from *Women and the Public Interest* by Jessie Bernard.

Basic Books, Inc.: quotations from "Depression in Middle-Aged Women" by Pauline Bart, "Woman as Outsider" by Vivian Gornick, and "The Mask of Beauty" by Una Stannard, in *Woman in Sexist Society: Studies in Power and Powerlessness*, edited by Vivian Gornick and Barbara K. Moran, copyright © 1971 by Basic Books, Inc., Publishers, New York. Beacon Press: quotations from *Beyond God the Father* by Mary Daly, copyright © 1973 by Mary Daly, reprinted by permission of Beacon Press and the author. George Braziller, Inc.: quotations from *Ascent of Woman* by Elisabeth Mann Borgese.

Jonathan Cape Ltd.: quotations from *The Second Sex* by Simone de Beauvoir, translated by H. M. Parshley. Cassell & Co., Ltd.: quotations from *How to Make It in a Man's World* by Letty Cottin Pogrebin. Katharine S. Chamberlin: quotations from *His Religion and Hers* by Charlotte Perkins Gilman. Geoffrey Chapman: quotations from *The Church and the Second Sex* by Mary Daly. Phyllis Chesler: quotations from *Women and Madness*. Shirley Chisholm: quotations from "Women Must Rebel" in *Voices of the New Feminism* and from *Unbought and Unbossed*. Country Women: a quotation from "My Power Does Not Diminish Yours" by Sherry Thomas, in Country Women, 24, April 1977. Thomas Y. Crowell: a quotation from *Once Upon a Pedestal* by Emily Hahn, copyright © 1974 by Emily Hahn.

Mary Daly: quotations from *Beyond God the Father* by Mary Daly, copyright © 1973 by Mary Daly. J. M. Dent & Sons Ltd: quotations from *The First Sex* by Elizabeth Gould Davis. Doubleday & Company, Inc.: quotations from *Women and Madness* by Phyllis Chesler, copyright © 1972 by Phyllis Chesler; from *Tomorrow's Tomorrow* by Joyce A. Ladner, copyright © 1971 by Joyce A. Ladner; from *Words and Women* by Casey Miller and Kate Swift, copyright © 1976 by Casey Miller and Kate Swift; from *Sexual Politics* by Kate Millett, copyright © 1969, 1970 by Kate Millett; and from *How to Make It in a Man's World* by Letty Cottin Pogrebin, copyright © by Letty Cottin Pogrebin; all reprinted by permission of Doubleday & Company, Inc.

Faber and Faber Limited: quotations from *The Hard Way Up: The Autobiography of*

ACKNOWLEDGMENTS

Hanna Mitchell, Suffragette and Rebel, edited by Geoffrey Mitchell. Farrar, Straus & Giroux, Inc.: quotations from *Against Rape* by Andra Medea and Kathleen Thompson, copyright © 1974 by Andra Medea and Kathleen Thompson, excerpted with the permission of Farrar, Straus, & Giroux, Inc. The Feminist Press, Box 334, Old Westbury, N.Y. 11568: quotations from *Witches, Midwives and Nurses: A History of Women Healers* by Barbara Ehrenreich and Deirdre English, and from *Complaints and Disorders* by Barbara Ehrenreich and Deirdre English.

Glide Publications: quotations from *Lesbian/Woman* by Del Martin and Phyllis Lyon, 1972, all rights reserved, Glide Publications. Victor Gollancz Ltd.: quotations from *Words and Women* by Casey Miller and Kate Swift. Granada Publishing Limited: quotations from *Sexual Politics* by Kate Millet, and from *The Female Eunuch* by Germaine Greer, reprinted by permission of Rupert Hart-Davis Ltd./Granada Publishing Ltd. Susan Griffin: quotations from "Rape: The All-American Crime" in *Ramparts Magazine,* September, 1971.

Harcourt Brace Jovanovich, Inc.: quotations from *A Room of One's Own* by Virginia Woolf, copyright © 1929 by Harcourt Brace Jovanovich, Inc., copyright © 1957 by Leonard Woolf; reprinted by permission of the publisher. Harper & Row, Publishers, Inc.: quotations from *The Future of Marriage* by Jessie Bernard (The World Publishing Co.), copyright © 1972 by Jessie Bernard; from *Meet Me in the Middle* by Charlotte Holt Clinebell, copyright © 1973 by Charlotte Holt Clinebell; from *The Church and the Second Sex* by Mary Daly, copyright © 1968 by Mary Daly; from *Language and Woman's Place* by Robin Lakoff; and from "The Human Condition" by Betty Roszak, in *Masculine/Feminine,* edited by Betty and Theodore Roszak; all reprinted by permission of Harper & Row, Publishers, Inc. Ruth Herschberger: quotations from *Adam's Rib,* copyright © 1948 by Ruth Herschberger, copyright © renewed 1976; all rights reserved; reprinted by permission of the author. The Hogarth Press, Ltd: quotations from *Our Freedom and Its Results by Five Women,* edited by Ray Strachey, reprinted by permission of the Editor's Literary Estate and The Hogarth Press; and from *A Room of One's Own* by Virginia Woolf, reprinted by permission of the Author's Literary Estate and the Hogarth Press. Houghton Mifflin Company: quotations from *Unbought and Unbossed* by Shirley Chisholm, copyright © 1970 by Shirley Chisholm, reprinted by permission of the author and Houghton Mifflin Company.

Alfred A. Knopf, Inc.: quotations from *The Second Sex* by Simone de Beauvoir, translated by H. M. Parshley, copyright © 1952 by Alfred A. Knopf, Inc.; from *Crazy Salad: Some Things About Women* by Nora Ephron, copyright © 1975 by Nora Ephron; from *Shoulder to Shoulder: A Documentary* by Midge MacKenzie, copyright © 1975 by Midge MacKenzie; and from *Menstruation and Menopause, The Physiology and Psychology, the Myth and the Reality* by Paula Weideger, copyright © 1975 by Paula Weideger; all reprinted by permission of Alfred A. Knopf, Inc. Know, Inc.: quotations from *I'm Running Away from Home, But I'm Not Allowed to Cross the Street* by Gabrielle Burton.

McGraw-Hill Book Company: quotations from *The Female Eunuch* by Germaine Greer, copyright © 1971 by Germaine Greer, used with permission of McGraw-Hill Book Company. David McKay Company, Inc.: quotations from *The Politics of Women's Liberation: A Case Study of an Emerging Social Movement and Its Relation to the Policy Process* by Jo Freeman, copyright © 1975 by Jo Freeman; and from *Born*

Female by Caroline Bird, copyright © 1968 by Caroline Bird; both published by David McKay Company, Inc. Joyce [Cowley] Maupin: quotations from "Pioneers of Women's Liberation" in *Voices of the New Feminism*, edited by Mary Lou Thompson. Casey Miller and Kate Swift: quotations from *Words and Women*, copyright © 1976 by Casey Miller and Kate Swift. Monthly Review Press: quotations from "The Political Economy of Women's Liberation" by Margaret Benston, copyright © 1969 by Monthly Review Inc., reprinted by permission of Monthly Review Press. William Morrow & Co.: quotations from *The Dialectic of Sex: The Case for Feminist Revolution* by Shulamith Firestone, and from *Male and Female* by Margaret Mead. Ms. Magazine: quotations from "Sisterhood" by Gloria Steinem, in *Ms.*, Spring 1972; from "Welfare Is a Women's Issue" by Johnnie Tillmon, in *Ms.*, Spring 1972: from "If We're So Smart, Why Aren't We Rich?" by Gloria Steinem, in *Ms.*, June 1973; and from "How to Make Trouble: The Making of a Nonsexist Dictionary" by Alma Graham, in *Ms.*, December 1973.

National Council of Teachers of English: quotations from "Women Who Are Writers in Our Century: One Out of Twelve" by Tillie Olsen, in *College English*, October 1972, pp. 6–17. W. W. Norton & Company, Inc.: quotations reprinted from *Of Woman Born* by Adrienne Rich, copyright © 1976 by W. W. Norton & Company, Inc., and from *The Feminine Mystique* by Betty Friedan, copyright © 1963, 1974 by Betty Friedan; both with the permission of W. W. Norton & Company, Inc.

Peter Owen, London: quotations from *Against Rape* by Andra Medea and Kathleen Thompson.

Pantheon Books: quotations from *Woman's Estate* by Juliet Mitchell, copyright © 1971 by Juliet Mitchell, reprinted by permission of Pantheon Books, a division of Random House, Inc. Paulist Press: quotations from *Liberation Theology: Human Hope Confronts Christian History and American Power*, by Rosemary Radford Ruether, copyright © 1972 by The Missionary Society of St. Paul the Apostle in the State of New York. Laurence Pollinger Ltd.: quotations from *The Dialectic of Sex* by Shulamith Firestone and from *The Feminine Mystique* by Betty Friedan. G. P. Putnam's Sons: quotations from *Challenging Years: The Memoirs of Harriot Stanton Blatch* by Harriot Stanton Blatch and Alma Lutz, and from *The First Sex* by Elizabeth Gould Davis.

Quick Fox/Links Books: quotations from *Amazon Odyssey* by Ti-Grace Atkinson.

Random House, Inc.: a quotation from *From Parlor to Prison*, edited by Sherna Gluck, copyright © 1976 by Random House, Inc., reprinted by permission of the publisher. Debora Rogers Ltd: quotations from *Partriarchal Attitudes* by Eva Figes, copyright © 1970 by Eva Figes, edition by Virago Limited, London. Alice S. Rossi: quotations from "Women in Science: Why So Few" in *Science*, Vol. 148, 28 May 1965, pp. 1196–1202, and from "Equality Between the Sexes: An Immodest Proposal" in *Daedalus*, Spring 1964. Routledge & Kegan Paul: quotations from *Women at Work: A Brief Introduction to Trade Unionism for Women* by Mary Agnes Hamilton.

St. Martin's Press, Incorporated: quotations from *Love Between Women* by Charlotte Wolff, M.D. Grant Sanger: quotations by Margaret Sanger from *Woman and the New Race*, copyright © 1920, 1940; from *The Pivot of Civilization*, copyright © 1922, 1950;

ACKNOWLEDGMENTS

from "Marriage" in *The Woman Rebel*, April 1914; from "The New Feminists" in *The Woman Rebel*, March 1914; from "Suppression" in *The Woman Rebel*, June 1914; and from "Class and Character, Article No. 2" in *The Woman Rebel*, July 1914. Science: quotations from "Women in Science: Why So Few" by Alice S. Rossi, in *Science*, Vol. 148, pp. 1196–1202, 28 May 1965, copyright © 1965 by the American Association for the Advancement of Science. The Seabury Press: quotations from *Women Priests: Yes or No?* by Emily C. Hewitt & Suzanne R. Hiatt, copyright © 1973 by Emily C. Hewitt and Suzanne R. Hiatt; and from *New Woman New Earth: Sexist Ideologies and Human Liberation* by Rosemary Radford Ruether, copyright © 1975 The Seabury Press, Inc., used by permission. Laura Ellsworth Seiler: a quotation from *From Parlor to Prison*, edited by Sherna Gluck. Simon & Schuster: quotations from *Our Bodies, Ourselves* by The Boston Women's Health Book Collective, Inc.; from *Against Our Will* by Susan Brownmiller; from *Lesbian Nation* by Jill Johnston; and from *Religion and Sexism* by Rosemary Radford Ruether. Souvenir Press Ltd.: quotations from *The Descent of Woman* by Elaine Morgan. Stein and Day Publishers: quotations from *Patriarchal Attitudes* by Eva Figes, copyright © 1970 by Eva Figes; from *Descent of Woman* by Elaine Morgan, copyright © 1972 by Elaine Morgan; and from *Sappho Was a Right-On Woman* by Sidney Abbott and Barbara Love, copyright © 1972 by Sidney Abbott and Barbara Love; all reprinted with permission of Stein and Day Publishers.

Frederick Ungar Publishing Co., Inc.: quotations from *Out of the Kitchen—Into the War: Woman's Winning Role in the Nation's Drama* by Susan B. Anthony II. University of Washington Press: quotations from *The Troublesome Helpmate: A History of Misogyny in Literature* by Katharine M. Rogers.

Index of Authors
and Anonymous Sources

Index of Authors
and Anonymous Sources

Index of Subjects

Index of Subjects